MEDIA COMPOSER® 6:

PROFESSIONAL EFFECTS AND COMPOSITING

David East

Course Technology PTR
A part of Cengage Learning

COURSE TECHNOLOGY
CENGAGE Learning®

Australia, Brazil, Japan, Korea, Mexico, Singapore, Spain, United Kingdom, United States

COURSE TECHNOLOGY
CENGAGE Learning®

Media Composer® 6:
Professional Effects and Compositing
David East

Publisher and General Manager,
Course Technology PTR:
Stacy L. Hiquet

Associate Director of Marketing:
Sarah Panella

Manager of Editorial Services:
Heather Talbot

Senior Marketing Manager:
Mark Hughes

Acquisitions Editor:
Dan Gasparino

Development Editor:
Bryan Castle Jr.

Project Editor:
Kate Shoup

Technical Reviewers:
Trevor Boden, Phill Naylor

Copy Editor:
Kate Shoup

Interior Layout:
Shawn Morningstar

Cover Designer:
Mike Tanamachi

DVD-ROM Producer:
Brandon Penticuff

Indexer:
Larry Sweazy

Proofreaders:
Laura Gabler, Michael Beady

For product information and technology assistance, contact us at
Cengage Learning Customer & Sales Support, 1-800-354-9706

For permission to use material from this text or product,
submit all requests online at **cengage.com/permissions**
Further permissions questions can be emailed to
permissionrequest@cengage.com

Media Composer is a registered trademark of Avid Technology Inc.
All other trademarks are the property of their respective owners.

All images © Cengage Learning unless otherwise noted.

Library of Congress Control Number: 2011942193

ISBN-13: 978-1-133-59046-0

ISBN-10: 1-133-59046-2

Course Technology, a part of Cengage Learning
20 Channel Center Street
Boston, MA 02210
USA

Cengage Learning is a leading provider of customized learning solutions with office locations around the globe, including Singapore, the United Kingdom, Australia, Mexico, Brazil, and Japan. Locate your local office at:
international.cengage.com/region

Cengage Learning products are represented in Canada by Nelson Education, Ltd.

For your lifelong learning solutions, visit **courseptr.com**.

Visit our corporate Web site at **cengage.com**.

This book includes material that was developed in part by the Avid Technical Publications department and the Avid Training department.

Printed in the
United States of America
1 2 3 4 5 6 7 14 13 12

To Isabelle, who always brings a smile to my face.

Acknowledgments

My sincere thanks to Kate Shoup for her patience, her eagle eye for detail, and her amazing ability to transform my words into something approaching readable. Thanks also to Trevor Boden and Phill Naylor for wading through my exercises and reining me in when needed. Thanks, too, to the rest of the team at Cengage Learning for their efforts in making this possible. And of course, I don't want to forget all those at Avid who still passionately believe in this amazing software. Finally, thanks to Steven Black for providing me with some wonderful footage of Singapore, my adopted city, and to Brian Barnhart and Thomas Graham for their *Agent Zero* footage.

About the Author

David East graduated from London University with a degree in Astrophysics. After many years wandering the planet—driving trucks in Germany, working on oil rigs in China, and pulling dags out of sheep's wool in Australia—he ended up at the BBC, where he was introduced to the first PAL version of the Media Composer in 1991. From that moment he was hooked and has spent the remaining years wandering the planet evangelizing this software wherever anyone will listen. He edited the first program worldwide that went direct to air from Avid in 1994. (Before then, it was a strictly offline tool.) He now works as a Master Trainer and workflow consultant based in Singapore.

Contents

Exercise 1
Creating a Title and Video Wall
37

Lesson 2
Animating with Keyframes
43

Exercise 2
Creating a Simple Animation
85

Lesson 3
Using the 3D Warp Effect
91

Exercise 3
Creating Effects
121

Lesson 4
Importing Graphics and Mattes
131

Exercise 4
Importing Files   167

Lesson 5
Paint Effects   173

Exercise 5
Using Paint to Enhance Your Footage   219

Lesson 6
Keying   233

Exercise 6
Using Different Keying Techniques   271

Lesson 7
Tracking and Stabilizing   277

Exercise 7
Tracking   317

Lesson 8
Refining the Composite   323

Exercise 8
Compositing and Beyond!   347

Appendix A
Working with FluidMotion and Photoshop   353

Appendix B
Answers to Review/Discussion Questions 389

Index 397

Lessons on DVD

Lesson 9
Third-Party Plug-ins E-1

Exercise 9
Using Sapphire Plug-ins   E-33

Lesson 10
Introducing Avid FX   E-41

Exercise 10
Exploring Avid FX E-85

Lesson 11
Avid FX: Working with Multiple Tracks in Avid FX E-93

Exercise 11
Creating a Ring of Fire Effect E-139

Lesson 12
Avid FX: Titles and 3D   E-143

Exercise 12
Working with EPS and Particle Effects   E-211

Introduction

Welcome to *Media Composer 6: Professional Effects and Compositing* and the Avid Learning Series. Whether you are interested in self-study or would like to pursue formal certification through an Avid Learning Partner, this book is a key step toward developing your skills.

This book is all about the many effects that you can use in Avid Media Composer. You will learn how to enhance your sequence by applying effects to clips, transitions, and tracks. You will learn about animation and effect design, and how to import graphics and animated logos. You'll also learn about keying, tracking, and the various Avid Paint Effects. On the DVD that accompanies this book, you will learn about the multitude of third-party plug-ins that comes with Media Composer.

Using This Book

This book has been designed to familiarize you with the practices and processes you will use to complete a Media Composer project. Using real-world projects from Media Composer editors, the lessons provide information not only on how the features operate but also the concepts behind them. Media Composer projects and media are provided on the DVD, allowing you to follow step-by-step to perform each task. At the end of each lesson, review questions can help you retain the knowledge you've learned along the way. Additional exercises are also provided, giving you an extra opportunity to explore each feature and technique.

Using the DVD

The DVD-ROM included with this book contains projects and media files for the exercises in the book. These must be installed before you can use them. (See the upcoming section "Installation Instructions" for more information.)

If you purchased an ebook version of this book, you may download the contents from www.courseptr.com/downloads. Please note that you will be redirected to the Cengage Learning site.

Media

The media required for the project is in the folder called Avid MediaFiles. This is the standard folder for all Media Composer media.

Hands-On Project

The project you will use while reading the book is called MC205 Pro Effects. The project has several bins, which are divided into four folders:

- The first folder (Material for Lessons) contains the bins for each of the lessons. There are some demo sequences that have been prepared so that you can follow through the steps in the lessons.

- The second folder (Material for Exercises) contains the bins for the exercises that follow each of the lessons. You will be able to try these out to strengthen what you have learned in the lesson.

- The third folder (Completed Exercises) contains finished examples so that you can check that you got it right!

- The Footage folder contains some extra bins with the various footage used in the project for you to try your own effects. There are also some bins containing some saved effects.

Graphics

Some lessons require you to import some graphics files. The Graphics folder contains various examples of graphics—both still and animated—that you can use to learn the various techniques for importing. This folder can be copied to anywhere on your system drive, such as the desktop for easy capturing.

Settings

There is an optional settings folder called Pro FX User, which contains settings for bin layouts, keyboard buttons, and such used in the book.

Free Bonus Extras

A PDF file on the DVD contains four extra lessons. These are special bonus lessons that introduce the wonderful world of Avid AVX plug-ins. The lessons also have exercises for you to try the various plug-ins available. You will need to install a demo version of Sapphire plug-ins from GenArts and a demo version of Boris Continuum from Boris. You will also be shown how to use Avid FX, which is a free plug-in that comes with your Avid Media Composer.

Installation Instructions

Please follow these installation instructions exactly or you may not have access to all the project files and media associated with this course.

1. Make sure Media Composer 6 is installed and that you have opened the application at least once. Opening the application creates important folders that you will use during this installation.

2. Insert the accompanying DVD into your Windows or Macintosh computer's disc drive.

3. View the contents of the DVD. There are four folders on the DVD, and each folder must be copied to specific locations.

4. Drag the Graphics for Book folder to your desktop or a convenient place on your hard drive, such as your Documents folder.

5. The Avid MediaFiles folder on the DVD contains the individual media files you'll use for this book. This folder should be copied to the top level of your hard drive. If you've already used Media Composer on this system, it is possible that you have existing media folders, which you should not delete.

6. Navigate to the root level of the hard drive where you want to store the media files. This may be your internal drive, in which case navigate to C DRIVE:\ (Windows) or Macintosh HD (Mac). If you have a locally attached external hard drive you want to use, navigate to the root level of the external hard drive.

Note: **The root level of a hard drive is also called the top level. It is the highest level in the hierarchy of folders on your computer.**

7. Make sure at the top level of your hard drive that there is no existing Avid MediaFiles folder. If there is no existing Avid MediaFiles folder, drag the entire Avid MediaFiles folder from the DVD onto the top level of your hard drive. If an Avid MediaFiles folder does exist on the top level of your hard drive, double-click it to reveal the MXF folder.

8. On the DVD, double-click the Avid MediaFiles folder and then double-click the MXF folder.

9. Inside the DVD's MXF folder is a folder called 205. Drag this folder from the DVD into the MXF folder on your hard drive.

Caution: **Do not rename the folder named Avid MediaFiles located on the media drive. Media Composer uses the folder names to locate the media files.**

10. The project for the book is called MC205 Pro Effects. This should be dragged from the DVD to the place where you keep your projects. This is usually in a folder called Media Composer Projects in your Documents folder. However, you may also have an external location for your projects.

11. Finally, there is a folder called Pro FX user. This is a settings folder that can be used to replicate some of the settings that were used in the book. This is optional; you may have your own settings that you wish to use instead. These can be copied to your desktop and imported to the Media Composer from the Settings tab of the MC205 Pro Effects project.

Prerequisites

This book is aimed at students who have already completed the *Media Composer 6: Part 1–Editing Essentials* (MC101) and the *Media Composer 6: Part 2–Effects Essentials* (MC110) courses. You will be expected to have some previous experience using the Media Composer and you should be familiar with the basic editing functions.

System Requirements

This book is aimed at users working with Avid Media Composer version 6 and above. If you are running earlier versions of the Media Composer you will still be able to complete most of the lessons, although you may find some minor differences in the functionality of the application. Media Composer version 6 requires either Windows 7 64-bit or Mac OS Lion. To verify the most recent system requirements, visit www.avid.com/US/products/media-composer and click the System Requirements tab.

Becoming Avid Certified

Avid certification is a tangible, industry-recognized credential that can help you advance your career and provide measurable benefits to your employer. When you're Avid certified, you not only help to accelerate and validate your professional development, but you can also improve your productivity and project success. Avid offers programs supporting certification in dedicated focus areas including Media Composer, Sibelius, Pro Tools, Worksurface Operation, and Live Sound. To become certified in Media Composer, you must enroll in a program at an Avid Learning Partner, where you can complete additional Media Composer coursework if needed and take your certification exam. To locate an Avid Learning Partner, visit www.avid.com/training.

Media Composer Certification

Avid offers two levels of Media Composer certification:

- Avid Media Composer User Certification
- Avid Media Composer Professional Certification

User Certification

The Avid Media Composer Certified User Exam is the first of two certification exams that allow you to become Avid certified. The two combined certifications offer an established and recognized goal for both academic users and industry professionals. The Avid Media Composer User Certification requires that you display a firm grasp of the core skills, workflows, and concepts of non-linear editing on the Media Composer system.

Courses/books associated with User certification include the following:

- *Media Composer 6: Part 1–Editing Essentials* (MC101)
- *Media Composer 6: Part 2–Effects Essentials* (MC110)

These User courses can be complemented with *Color Grading with Media Composer 6 and Symphony 6.*

Professional Certification

The Avid Media Composer Professional Certification prepares editors to competently operate a Media Composer system in a professional production environment. Professional certification requires a more advanced understanding of Media Composer, including advanced tools and workflows involved in creating professional programs.

Courses/books associated with Professional certification include the following:

- *Media Composer 6: Professional Picture and Sound Editing* (MC201)
- *Media Composer 6: Professional Effects and Compositing* (MC205)

These Professional courses can be complemented with *Color Grading with Media Composer 6 and Symphony 6.*

For more information about Avid's certification program, please visit www.avid.com/US/support/training/certification.

Effect Design and Techniques

This lesson discusses effects in general. It goes beyond the basics to look at some of the more advanced effect techniques that will help you make your sequence really stand out.

Media Used: The media for this lesson is in the MC205 Pro Effects Project. Open the bin called Lesson 01 Effect Design.

Duration: 60 minutes

GOALS

- Identify different types of effects
- Grasp how the Effect Editor works
- Nest effects
- Prepare your system to work with effects
- Save and use templates
- Organize your templates
- Collapse and uncollapse tracks in the Timeline
- Design and deconstruct effects

Reviewing Effect Techniques

Suppose you have created a sequence and have all your shots in the right place. Now you need to take it to the next stage by adding effects so that your sequence will look polished and professional. A typical workflow would involve adding simple effects such as dissolves and wipes or more complex effects such as a Picture-in-Picture, a chroma key, or an imported matte. You might even need to hide parts of your images with some kind of Paint Effect such as a Blur, Mosaic, or Clone.

Effects can be applied to transitions, clips, or groups of clips, and can be built up in layers on different video tracks. You can stack effects on top of each other or nest effects inside each other, and you can even apply an effect to the entire sequence. You can save and organize custom-built effects for reuse and you can apply a saved effect to another part of the sequence—or just some of its parameters to a different effect.

Regardless of what kind of effect you plan to use, there are some fundamentals that apply to all Media Composer effects. Before diving in to specific features, you will begin by looking at some of the common elements that will help you with your workflow. If you would like to follow along as you read through this, you can open the sequence called Singapore Marina (a simple sequence that you can enhance by adding some effects) in the bin called 01 Effect Design. To find out what effects you can use, you will need to open the Effect Palette.

The Effect Palette

Media Composer has a palette of effects, called the Effect Palette, that you can access by clicking the Effect Palette button (the purple one) in the Project window (see Figure 1.1). If you prefer to open a separate window, as shown in Figure 1.2, open the Tools menu and choose Effect Palette or press the Command+8 (Mac) or Ctrl+8 (Windows) keyboard shortcut.

On the left side of the Effect Palette are many categories of effects listed alphabetically. Clicking a category opens a list of effects in that category on the right side, each with its own purple icon. The selection of possible effects includes both video and audio effects. Notice that most of the effects have a little green square on the left of the icon, which indicates that it is a real-time effect. That is, you do not need to render it in order to play it.

Note: The effects are grouped into categories, but it can still take some time to figure out where things are. Spend some time exploring the different categories of effects and familiarize yourself with where effects are located.

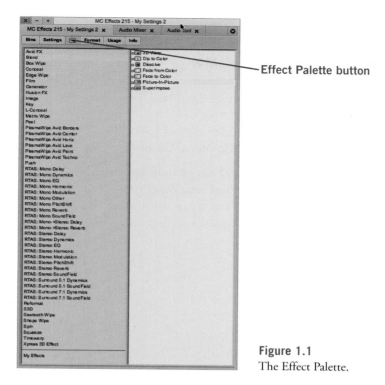

Effect Palette button

Figure 1.1
The Effect Palette.

Figure 1.2
The Effect Palette as a separate window.

Real-Time Effects

Over the years, as processors have become faster, the power of Media Composer has increased dramatically. In the early days, most effects were not real time. Significant time was spent rendering effects so they could play back. *Rendering* means creating a new media file that combines all the elements of your effect processed into a single video stream. Today, nearly all the effects—including processor-intensive ones like Blur, Mosaic, and most of the Illusion effects—are real time. That means not only can you apply and tweak effects without having to render each time, but you can also build up several layers of video, each with multiple effects, and in most cases Media Composer will happily play your sequence.

Applying Effects

There are two ways to add effects to your sequence:

- By dragging an effect icon from the Effect Palette to the Timeline
- By selecting a segment or transition and double-clicking an effect icon

Obviously, the easiest way to add an effect is the former—to simply drag the purple effect icon from the Effect Palette directly onto the Timeline. Note, however, that where you drag the icon will affect the way it works. That is, if you drag an effect to the dividing line between two clips, you will apply it as a transition effect. A *transition effect* is some kind of visual device to ease the viewer from one clip to another. Examples of transition effects include dissolves and all the various wipes.

If you drag the effect onto the clip segment itself, you will apply it as a *segment effect*. Segment effects apply to an entire clip. Examples of segment effects include color corrections and resizes. Figure 1.3 shows instances of both types of effects.

	V1	V1			Boat Quay	Bridge	Esplan	Marina	Sand	Marina	bour	Marina Bay Sands
	A1	A1			Boat Quay	Bridge	Esplanade	Marina Bay Sands		Marina Harbour		Marina Bay Sands
	A2	A2			Boat Quay	Bridge	Esplanade	Marina Bay Sands		Marina Harbour		Marina Bay Sands
		TC1			00:00		01:00:10:00			01:00:20:00		01:00

Figure 1.3
Transition and segment effects.

Note: Many effects can be used as either transition effects or segment effects. For example, a 3D Warp effect can be used to transition from one clip to another, and a wipe can be applied to a segment to give you a split screen.

You can also drag an effect from the Effect Palette to an empty area of the Timeline. In addition, you can drag an effect to an entire blank video track. This is especially useful because it allows you to apply an effect to the entire sequence. Any segment on a video track underneath the blank track will be affected by the effect. An example of this would be a film mask or the timecode burn-in effect (see Figure 1.4).

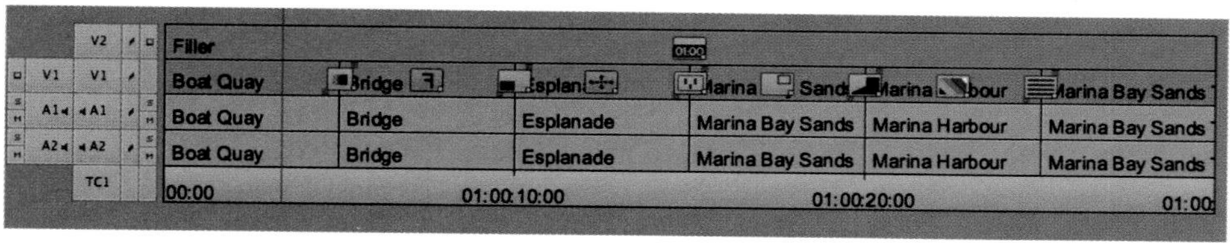

Figure 1.4
The timecode effect has been added to the empty V2 track.

In addition to dragging an effect from the Effect Palette, you can highlight a clip in the Timeline

There are two ways of doing this:

- When in Source/Record mode, you can use the Segment Mode selection tool to select clips or multiple clips.

- When in Effect mode, you can simply click on the segments.

Then apply the effect by double-clicking it in the Effect Palette. This is useful if you want to select multiple clips in the Timeline and apply the effect to all of them.

The great thing is that when you are in Effect mode, this method also works for transitions, as shown in Figure 1.5. Note that the clips do not have to be contiguous for this to work. You can select either the clips or transitions to which you wish to apply the effect.

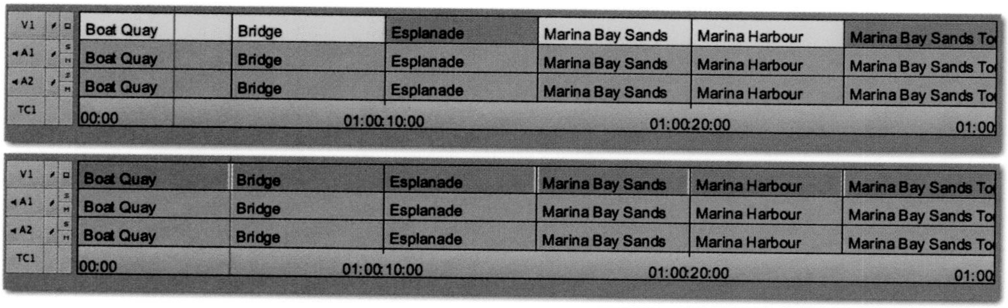

Figure 1.5
The Timeline with clips selected (top) and transitions selected (bottom).

Smart Tools

Since Smart Tools arrived in V5.0, the operation of the Segment Mode selection tool has changed slightly. In the old days, we referred to this tool as the red selection arrow and the yellow selection arrow. They were used to select clips in the Timeline to move them in some way. Now, they are grouped with the trimming tools and are collectively known as Smart Tools, as shown in Figure 1.6. The color of the tool will change depending on where you hover in the Timeline, but the tools can also be used just to select a clip. (In this case the color doesn't matter.) When I talk about selecting clips for the addition of effects, I will refer to both of these tools as the Segment Mode selection tool. I leave it to you to decide which color you want to use!

Figure 1.6
The Smart Tools.

To apply an effect to multiple clips, follow these steps:

1. Activate the Smart Tools. To do so, click on the gray bar that surrounds them.

2. Hover over the clip in the Timeline and you will see the Segment Mode selection tool.

3. Click a clip to select it; then Shift-click subsequent clips to select them, too.

Note: Version 5.0 introduced a **Link Selection** button (see Figure 1.7). When this button is toggled on, Media Composer links the video and audio of a clip when you select them so they are both highlighted. Normally, this is very useful, but when selecting clips for adding effects, you need to toggle it off so that only the video tracks are selected (unless you really want to try adding a **Color Effect** to an audio clip!).

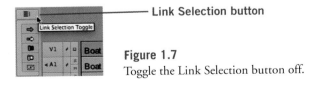

Link Selection button

Figure 1.7
Toggle the Link Selection button off.

4. Double-click the effect you want to apply in the Effect Palette.

To apply an effect to multiple transitions, follow these steps:

1. Click the **EFFECT MODE** button in the Timeline, as shown in Figure 1.8.

Figure 1.8
The Effect Mode button.

2. Click on a transition to select it; then Shift-click on subsequent transitions to select them, too.

3. Double-click the effect you want to apply in the Effect Palette.

Figure 1.9 shows the Timeline with multiple effects applied.

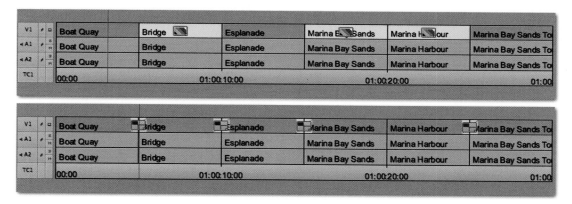

Figure 1.9
The Timeline with multiple segment (top) and transition (bottom) effects applied.

Note: While in Effect mode, you can select transitions or clips (but not both at the same time) without using the Segment Mode selection tool. Just point your mouse on the Timeline and Shift-click to add multiple clips or transitions.

Tip: A great way to delete multiple effects from clips or transitions is to Shift-click the effects you want to remove and press the Delete key on your keyboard. Again, you can select either transition or clip effects, but not both at the same time.

Exploring the Effect Editor

After you have applied an effect, you'll need to make various adjustments to it. For this, you will need to understand the Effect Editor. The Effect Editor, which is a separate window, has some features that are common to all effects and others that apply to specific effects only. You can open the Effect Editor in two ways:

- By positioning your cursor on a clip with an effect in the Timeline and clicking the Effect Mode button (refer to Figure 1.8)

- By positioning your cursor on a clip with an effect in the Timeline, opening the Tools menu, and choosing Effect Editor

Note: **You must have the appropriate video track selected in the Track panel of the Timeline. If you have no track selected, the Effect Editor will be empty. If you have effects on multiple active tracks, the Effect Editor will open for the highest track selected in the Track panel. Once you are in Effect mode, you can click any clip or transition in the Timeline that has an effect, and the Effect Editor will populate with controls appropriate for the selected effect.**

Add the Picture-in-Picture (PIP) effect, which is in the Effect Palette's Blend category, to one of the clips in your sequence. Then open the Effect Editor so we can take a look at some of its features. (See Figure 1.10.)

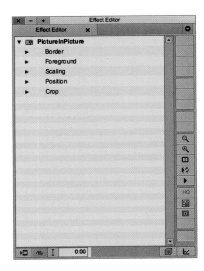

Figure 1.10
The Effect Editor.

Regardless of what effect is selected, the Effect Editor contains a column of buttons down the right side, some buttons and controls along the bottom, and various parameter controls in the main part of the window. Some effects have only a few or even no controls. The Flop effect, for example, is just a flop—you can't do anything with it other than flop the picture. Other effects have lots of controls. Some—especially third-party AVX plug-ins—can have hundreds of controls.

Some parameters are grouped. For example, a Position group of parameters might have X, Y, and even Z controls. Adjusting these controls will obviously change the way the effect looks. For example, adjusting X and Y scaling will change the size of a PIP. (This is covered in detail in Lesson 2, "Animating with Keyframes.") You reveal the parameters in a group by clicking the triangle to the left of the group name.

Tip: You can open and close *all* the parameter groups by Option-clicking (Mac) or Alt-clicking (Windows) any of the triangles.

Figure 1.11 shows the PIP effect with various parameter groups expanded, in addition to calling out several of the controls for the effect. (Many of these controls will be explored further in Lesson 2.)

■ **Reduce and Enlarge buttons.** These buttons enable you to take a closer look at what your effect is doing either inside the video frame or outside, in the case of a PIP.

■ **Dual Split button.** Clicking this button shows you a half screen—the right side with the effect applied and the left side without. The split screen can be adjusted by dragging the little white triangles on the edge of the split.

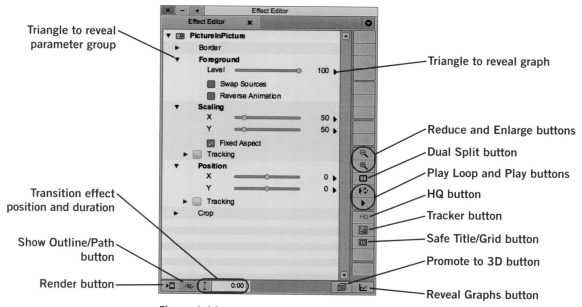

Figure 1.11
The PIP effect with some parameter groups expanded.

■ **Play Loop and Play buttons.** These buttons enable you to review the effect without leaving Effect mode.

■ **HQ.** Click this button to render in high quality. (This button is not available for all effects.)

■ **Tracker button.** Clicking this button opens the Tracker window, covered in Lesson 7, "Tracking and Stabilizing."

■ **Safe Title button.** Clicking this button displays the basic Safe Title and Safe Effect grids, but you can configure this to show much more with the Grid setting. For more information about how to configure the grid, see Appendix A, "Working with FluidMotion and Photoshop."

■ **Render button.** Click this button to render your effect.

■ **Show Outline/Path button.** Clicking this button toggles the wireframe display at the edge of some effects (such as the PIP) on and off. It also toggles the path of the image on and off if the position is animated.

■ **Transition Effect Alignment.** This setting adjusts the timing of a transition effect so that it starts, ends, or is centered on a transition. You can type in a new duration if required.

■ **Promote to 3D button.** If applicable, this button enables you to promote an effect (such as a PIP) to the 3D Warp effect, which has more controls.

■ **Reveal Graphs button.** Clicking this button reveals the keyframe graphs, which you can use to animate your effect with precision. When you reveal graphs, you will see additional controls along the bottom of the Effect Editor. These will be covered in the next lesson.

Here are a few other things you'll notice in the Composer window when you are in Effect mode:

■ The most important thing to notice when the Effect Editor is open is that instead of seeing the Timeline Position bar for the entire Timeline, you are now viewing the Effect Editor Position bar for just the duration of the segment (or transition). This is so you can more easily navigate your keyframes if you have any. Note that there is a small slider on the left side called the Keyframe Scale bar that enables you to zoom into the Position Bar if your keyframes are close together, as shown in Figure 1.12.

Figure 1.12
Slide the bar to zoom in and out of the Position Bar.

■ As shown in Figure 1.13, the timecode boxes in the Composer window will change to reflect that you are in Effect mode. Another important difference if you are working with *interlaced* material is that when you step along the clip with the Step Forward or Step Backward buttons, you are actually stepping one *field* at a time rather than one frame. The field on the far right will display the cursor's position in the effect in seconds, frames, and fields, with a .1 and .2 to show which field. The project for this course is using *progressive* material, so you won't see any field information.

Figure 1.13
Composer window info bar in Effect mode.

■ Below the Composer window, the top row of buttons will change. You will now see the same buttons that appear in the Effect Editor: Enlarge, Reduce, Play Loop, and so on.

When you are finished tweaking your controls, you can leave the Effect mode by clicking the Source/Record button to the left of the Timeline or by simply clicking anywhere in the timecode track on the Timeline.

Building Multilayer Effects

In many situations, you will want to build more complex effects than just applying a single effect to a clip in your sequence. You might, for example, want to create a PIP effect, but you also want to color-correct the picture in the foreground, the background, or both.

Nesting Effects

Applying multiple effects to a single clip is known as *nesting* effects. Suppose you start with a clip, and you add a Flop effect. Next, you want to add a color correction. Simply dragging the color correction onto the Flop effect will replace the Flop effect with the color correction. But if you Option-drag (Mac) or Alt-drag (Windows) the color-correction effect, you will *add* it to the existing Flop effect— one on top of the other. Although the Flop effect is now hidden, it is still applied to your clip underneath the color correction. You can keep adding more effects by Option-dragging (Mac) or Alt-dragging (Windows) each subsequent effect onto the last one. The result is a nested stack of effects, as shown in Figure 1.14. However, what you actually see in the Timeline is just the top-most effect. All the others are hidden behind it until you step in—which is discussed in the next section.

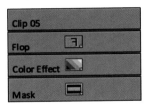

Figure 1.14
Nested effects.

Of course, the order you do this is important. If you have a color-corrected clip and you apply a mask on top of it, you will have a color-corrected clip with a mask. But, if you start with a mask and add a color correction on top, you will also color-correct the black mask, which may not be desirable. This is illustrated in Figure 1.15. The top picture shows the mask on top of the color correction, and the bottom picture shows the color correction on top of the mask.

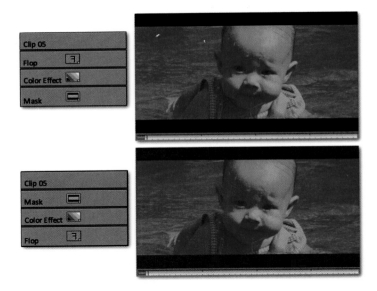

Figure 1.15
Effects applied in the correct order (top) and in the wrong order (bottom).

Stepping into the Nest

Stepping into the nest enables you to see the order in which your effects are applied. The simplest way to expand a nest is to double-click the top-most effect of your nest in the Timeline. This opens a new layer on the Timeline above the original clip. If you click this new layer, you will continue to expand your nest and you carry on clicking on each new layer until you reach your source clip. When you step into the nest in this way, the result of all the nested effects will be displayed in the Composer window. Note that for this to work, the Timeline Settings dialog box must be configured as shown in Figure 1.16, with the Double-Click to Show Nesting check box checked.

Figure 1.16
The Timeline Settings dialog box.

When you look at a nest, the order the effects are applied is in fact the reverse of the normal approach to viewing tracks in the Timeline. That is, the top-most effect is actually at the bottom of the stack. It sometimes helps to think of the nest in a 3D world, where the top-most effect—in this case, a mask—is in front of the next layer (the color correction, and so on). When you go back in 3D space, you are essentially going down the order of the effects, and the track at the very back is the original clip, as shown in Figure 1.17.

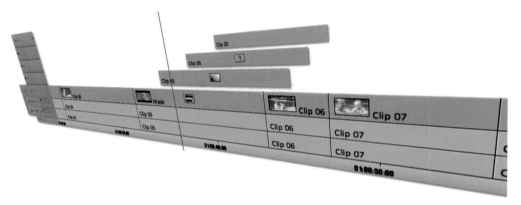

Figure 1.17
An imaginary 3D view of the Timeline with a nested stack of effects.

Using Step In and Step Out

Another way to see each of the nested effects is to use the Step In and Step Out buttons in the Timeline, shown in Figure 1.18. Stepping in reveals each successive effect in your nest in a single segment in the Timeline display. This is different in that you don't see all the effects stacked up in the Timeline, but just one effect at a time. In addition, what you see in the Composer window is the result of just that level of nest rather than the combined effect of each of the nested effects. This can be helpful if you just want to isolate what one effect is doing.

Figure 1.18
The Step In and Step Out buttons.

Note: When you step in, you no longer hear the audio tracks—although audio is
       still present. If the audio is important to the timing of an effect, expand the
       nest by double-clicking.

Changing the Order of Your Effects

In addition to displaying the effects nest expanded in the Timeline, Media Composer has a rather nifty feature in the Effect Editor that shows all the effects in the nest in the order they were applied. This time, however, they are ordered in the more logical way: with the upper-most effect at the top of the list, as shown in Figure 1.19.

Figure 1.19
The Effect Editor, with multiple effects applied.

To view your effects in this mode, while in Effect mode, click one of the segments in the expanded nest in the Timeline. You will see all the effects above (from a Timeline point of view) or behind (from the effect nest point of view) the one you have currently selected in the Effect Editor. Each effect can be expanded via the little triangle to reveal the controls.

The great thing about this view is that you can reorder the effects directly in the Effect Editor by simply dragging them up and down. There is one caveat, however: Some effects have a background track that is not actually functional but is reserved as a kind of key or alpha track for the effect to be composited. Such effects are mainly in the Blend category and include 3D Warp, PIP, and Superimpose, as well as the various key effects. When you step into these kinds of effects, you see a second, empty track under the source clip, as shown in Figure 1.20. Although you can put these types of effects in a stack, you can't change the order of tracks with a background track in the Effect Editor window if it involves moving it above or below an effect without a background track. You will get an error message saying you can't change the order of the stack. You can, however, reorder effects of the same type as long as they are together in the stack.

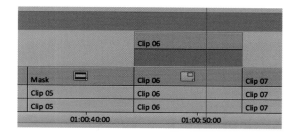

Figure 1.20
An effect with an alpha track.

If you really need to put a PIP above or below a mask, you can reorder effects directly in the Timeline:

1. Expand the nest.

2. Select the effect you want to reorder and press the **DELETE** key.

3. Drag the same effect from the Effect Palette to the desired location. You can drop it on the empty clip at the top of the stack, or Alt-drag it to an existing segment lower down. (You will need to step in again when you have done this.)

Creating a Container for Multiple Segments

Another useful feature of nesting is adding a single effect to multiple clips. In the last section, you applied an effect to multiple clips by selecting clips in the Timeline and double-clicking. This will apply the effect as an individually editable effect on each of the selected clips. In other words, if you have added a 50-percent PIP to many clips, you can change the size of the PIP in one of the clips without affecting the others. However, you may wish to apply a 50-percent PIP to a series of clips in the Timeline and affect all the clips together—for example, changing them all to 40 percent.

To affect all the clips at the same time, follow these steps:

1. Select a series of clips (this time, they must be contiguous or it won't work), as shown in Figure 1.21.

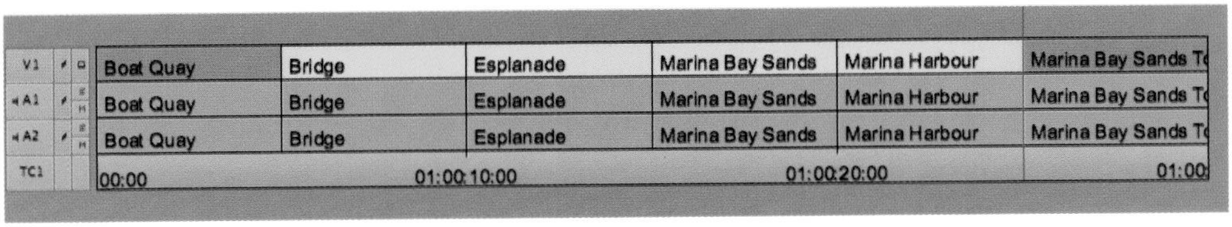

Figure 1.21
Selecting a series of adjacent clips.

2. Option-double-click (Mac) or Alt-double-click (Windows) the effect. This nests all your clips into one container, as shown in Figure 1.22. You can now adjust the top effect once to change the settings for all the clips inside the nest.

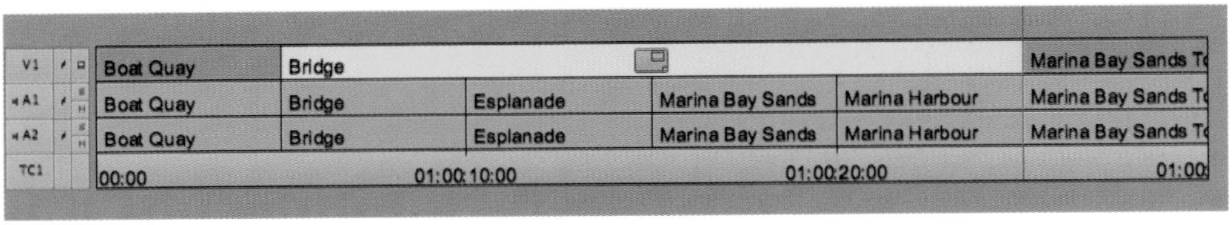

Figure 1.22
Option-double-click (Mac) or Alt-double-click (Windows) an effect—in this case the PIP—to place the selected clips in a container.

3. Step in to see what is going on inside the nest. This time, instead of seeing a stack of effects one on top of the other, you will see a series of clips inside the container, as shown in Figure 1.23. Inside this container, you can still trim and replace shots, as well as add effects to the transitions and clips, just as in the original Timeline (see Figure 1.24).

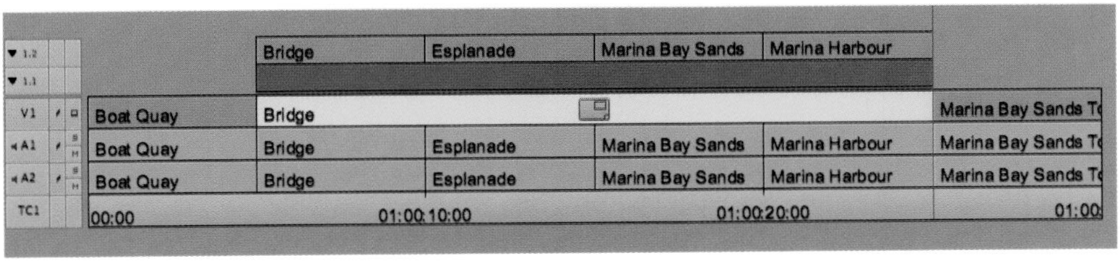

Figure 1.23
Expand the nest by double-clicking it.

▼ 1.0		Bridge		Esplana...		■Marina Bay Sands	■Marina [⌐]bour	
▼ 1.1								
V1	Boat Quay	Bridge				🖭		Marina Bay Sands T⌐
◄ A1	Boat Quay	Bridge		Esplanade		Marina Bay Sands	Marina Harbour	Marina Bay Sands T⌐
◄ A2	Boat Quay	Bridge		Esplanade		Marina Bay Sands	Marina Harbour	Marina Bay Sands T⌐
TC1	00:00		01:00:10:00			01:00:20:00		01:00:

Figure 1.24
Add more effects and transitions inside the nest.

Preparing Your System to Work with Effects

Many of the settings in Media Composer can be adjusted to optimize your work-flow when working with effects. In this section, you'll look at some of the things you can do to make your life easier.

Disabling Auto-Monitoring

When building effects, you usually work with more than one video track. That means you will be patching tracks to edit clips on different video tracks. You can configure how the patching works with the Timeline settings, which you can access by right-clicking anywhere in the Timeline and choosing Timeline Settings from the menu that appears or by clicking the Settings tab in your project window and choosing Timeline.

In previous versions of Media Composer, the Timeline setting for auto-monitoring was always on, which meant that when you patched a track, the monitor would follow the patch. For example, the monitor on V2 in Figure 1.25 would snap to V1. This was because older systems often took too long to refresh the video display on multiple track composites. With today's systems, however, the refresh is virtually instantaneous, making this feature annoying. In version 6 of Media Composer, it is off by default, but if you are on an older system, you can turn it off via to the Timeline Settings dialog box's Edit tab, as shown in Figure 1.26. When this feature is off, the monitor stays where it is until you assign it to a different track. (Generally, you will be monitoring the top-most video track to see the result of all your track effects.)

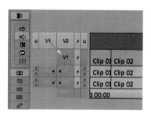

Figure 1.25
Patching V2 to V1.

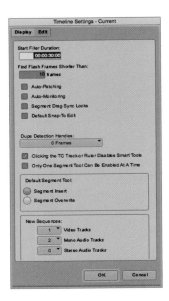

Figure 1.26
The Timeline Settings dialog box, with the Edit tab displayed. Uncheck the Auto-Monitoring checkbox to disable this feature, if necessary.

Tip: To quickly open the Timeline Settings dialog box, click anywhere in the Timeline window to make it active and press the Command+= (Mac) or Ctrl+= (Windows) keyboard shortcut. This applies to any window that has associated settings, so activating the Composer window and pressing the Command+= (Mac) or Ctrl+= (Windows) keyboard shortcut will bring up the Composer Settings dialog box.

Note: Notice the Auto-Patching check box in the Timeline Settings dialog box's Edit tab. This makes the source video track snap to the highlighted sequence video track. Some people find this useful, but the most intuitive way to patch tracks is to use the drag-and-snap method, so you may wish to leave this unchecked as well.

Soloing Video Tracks

Occasionally, you will need to see the result of an effect on just one video track. For example, you might have multiple PIP tracks and want to isolate one of them against a black background. That's where soloing comes in. Soloing is also very useful when working with multiple layers or non–real-time AVX plug-in effects, which might cause older systems to slow down.

To solo a video track, simply Command-click (Mac) or Ctrl-click (Windows) on the monitor icon for the desired track. The icon will turn green (see Figure 1.27), and you will see the result of the effect on that track only against a black background (if appropriate). To turn off the solo, Command-click (Mac) or Ctrl-click (Windows) again on the monitor icon.

Figure 1.27
The soloed video track is highlighted in green.

Configuring the Effect Editor

You can modify the appearance and behavior of the Effect Editor with the Effect Editor settings (see Figure 1.28), found with all the other settings in the Settings tab or by activating the Effect Editor and pressing the Command+= (Mac) or Ctrl+= (Window) keyboard shortcut. Some of the options are cosmetic, while others affect the functionality:

Figure 1.28
Effect Editor settings.

- **Indent Rows.** Select this check box to indent the parameter groups in the Effect Editor. This makes it easier to distinguish one group of parameters from another, but it does take up a bit more space.

- **Large Text.** Unless you have very sharp eyes, this check box should be selected. These days, most monitors are quite high resolution, and smaller text can be hard to read.

- **Thumbwheels.** This check box enables you to choose what tool to use to adjust parameters. The default is sliders. Thumbwheels, however, take up slightly less space.

- **Real Time Update.** This setting is inherited from the days of slower processing, and is now always on by default. It ensures that you see the effect update as you change a parameter setting. It is difficult to think of a reason why you would not want to do this.

- **Set Position to Keyframe.** When this setting is enabled, the position indicator will snap to a keyframe when you click on it. This can be annoying. Sometimes, you just want to select a keyframe to move it or align it with another one, and you may wish to have the position indicator stay where it is. In that case, you can disable this setting.

Note: This only applies when you are using the keyframe graph. If your graphs are not displayed, the position indicator will always snap to the keyframe regardless of the setting.

- **Update Position While Playing.** When this check box is checked, Media Composer lets you see the position indicator move in the Effect Editor as you play the effect. With today's fast systems, there is no reason to turn this off.

- **Show Add Keyframe Mode Menu.** This setting affects what happens when you click the keyframe button in the Effect Editor. When you click, you either add a keyframe or display a menu of options that affect the way the effect is applied. (See Lesson 2 for more information.)

Tip: You can view all these settings by right clicking in the parameter controls region of the Effect Editor.

Zooming and Panning

When applying an effect, it is often necessary to zoom in (or out) to see how the effect is working. Media Composer can cycle through various screen sizes in the Composer window. Sizes include 25 percent, 50 percent, 75 percent, fit to window, 100 percent (1×), 200 percent (2×), 400 percent (4×), and 800 percent (8×). (You might think that fit to window and 100 percent would be the same thing, but 100 percent is a fixed enlargement whereas fit to window will make the picture fill your composer monitor as you resize it.)

To enlarge or reduce the picture in the Composer window, you can use the enlarge and reduce buttons (see Figure 1.29). Alternatively, click in the window (this works in the Source monitor too) and press Command+K (Mac) or Ctrl+K (Windows) to reduce, or Command+L (Mac) or Ctrl+L (Windows) to enlarge. If you have enlarged your image, you may also want to pan around. You do this by pressing Command+Option (Mac) or Ctrl+Alt (Windows). A little hand will appear that lets you pan the image; click and drag to move it around. When you let go of the keys, the hand will go too.

Figure 1.29
The Enlarge and Reduce buttons.

Tip: You can cycle through the various increased sizes by Command-clicking (Mac) or Ctrl-clicking (Windows) on the screen directly. This lets you zoom into a particular area because it zooms in on the pixel you click rather than zooming in from the center.

Adding Video Tracks

If you are planning to create some PIPs, or perhaps you want to key in some fore-ground tracks against a background, then you will need to add video tracks. Normally, you can add a video track by pressing Command+Y (Mac) or Ctrl+Y (Windows). This adds tracks numbered from V1 up to V24. However, you may sometimes wish to *insert* a video track. For example, you may have a top video track for titles or captions, but you later decide you want to add a new video track underneath this for some kind of effect. If you simply added a video track, you would get a new track above the title track—meaning would have to shift all the titles up one, which could be quite tedious. A much quicker approach is to insert a track wherever you want!

To insert a new track somewhere underneath an existing track, follow these steps:

1. Press **OPTION+COMMAND+Y** (Mac) or **ALT+CTRL+Y** (Windows). This opens the Add Track dialog box, shown in Figure 1.30.

Figure 1.30
The Add Track dialog box.

2. By default, the new video track number is the next one up on the list. So, for example, if your top track is V3, the next track will be V4. Suppose you want to insert a track underneath the existing V3 track. In that case, simply open the **TRACK NUMBER** menu and choose **V3** instead of V4.

3. Click the **OK** button. Media Composer displays an alert saying that the track you selected already exists, as shown in Figure 1.31.

Figure 1.31
Media Composer alerts you that the track you selected already exists.

4. Click the **INSERT** button and voilà! You now have a new empty track 3, and all the tracks above are bumped up by one.

Using Workspaces to Change Layouts

A *workspace* is a way of saving the layout of your desktop. You will naturally wish to rearrange windows, and it is nice to have everything where you want. But you also need to have different layouts for different tasks. Workspaces let you do that. The workspace concept has been much improved in Media Composer version 6. Previously, there were both toolsets and workspaces. Although they were very similar, there were subtle differences. Toolsets could be changed, but you couldn't add new ones or rename them. In contrast, you could have as many workspaces as you wanted, and you could call them what you liked. Now, there are no more toolsets, just workspaces. They are managed in a single menu: the Workspaces menu, accessible from the Windows menu, as shown in Figure 1.32.

Figure 1.32
The Workspaces menu.

You can create as many workspaces as you want and name them as you wish. And with workspaces, you can do more than just change layouts. If you have a Timeline view that you would like to see when you are in Effect mode, you can link the workspace to the Timeline view.

To create a new workspace for working with effects and link it to a Timeline view, follow these steps:

1. Choose **Windows > Workspaces > New Workspace** and type a name for your workspace in the dialog box that appears. I called mine "Big Effects."

2. Rearrange all your windows until they are where you would like them. For example, your Composer window doesn't really need to show both the Source and Record monitors. Just the Record monitor will do, so you can shrink the Composer window down to show the Record monitor only. You may wish to create more space for your Effect Editor—particularly if you open the graphs—so you can make this bigger. You may wish to put your bins neatly out of the way in one corner. Of course, all this depends on whether you are working on one screen or two, but this is where you have control over where everything should go!

Note: You can resize any window from all edges or corners on both Mac and Windows. This makes rearranging your windows easy and intuitive.

3. Choose WINDOWS > WORKSPACES > SAVE CURRENT to save your work-space layout. (You can update this at any time if you need to make further changes.)

4. Now let's work on a Timeline view. You may wish to shrink your audio tracks, as you won't be needing them in Effect mode. Remember, pressing Command+K (Mac) or Ctrl+K (Windows) will reduce the size of selected tracks, and pressing Command+L (Mac) or Ctrl+L (Windows) will enlarge them. It is a good idea to turn on Dupe Detection in the Timeline Fast menu; this will not only highlight dupes, but also freeze frames if you have any. When you are happy with a Timeline view, you can save it. To do so, click the TIMELINE VIEW menu and choose SAVE AS. In this case, let's call the saved Timeline view "Effects." Your normal editing view could be called "Edit," and so on.

5. Now it's time to link your workspace to the Timeline view. That way, when you switch workspaces, you'll switch Timeline views, too.

6. Choose WINDOWS > WORKSPACES > PROPERTIES to open the Workspace View Setting dialog box, where you can manage your selected workspace. In the example shown in Figure 1.33, the Timeline view (with the reduced audio tracks) is called "Effects," so type EFFECTS in the dialog box as shown and click OK.

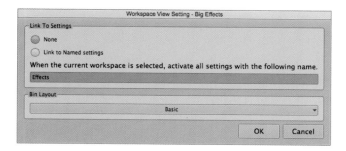

Figure 1.33
The Workspace View Setting dialog box.

You can also save a bin layout. That is, if you want to save the position of your bins, you can link it to a workspace. Thus, you have total control of your desktop, with all the windows and bins in the correct place.

To save your bin layout, follow these steps:

1. Arrange your bins where you want them. With tabbed bins you can put all your bins in one place and keep them there.

2. Choose **WINDOWS > BIN LAYOUT > NEW BIN LAYOUT**. This opens a dialog box where you can name your bin layout.

3. Name your layout. In this example, I named my bin Basic.

4. Choose **WINDOWS > WORKSPACES > PROPERTIES** to open the Workspace View Setting dialog box. Then open the **BIN LAYOUT** drop-down list and choose **BASIC** to add the bin layout you just saved.

Note: Bin layouts do not auto update. So if you open a different bin and put it in your tabbed bin, that bin will be closed if you change your workspace. Remember to manually save a bin layout if you make any changes.

But there's more! As you've seen, you can use your workspace to open the Effect Editor or you can click the Effect Mode button. But by default, clicking the Effect Mode button does not call up your workspace; it simply opens up the Effect Editor.

There is a third function that gives you the best of both worlds: You can link the Effect Mode button to the workspace. That means when you click the Effect Mode button, you don't just open the Effect Editor, but you also load your Effects workspace (in this case, Big Effects) and change your Timeline view at the same time. This is all done with a new setting, called Workspace Linking. All the settings are found in the Media Composer settings window. To access these settings, click the Settings tab in the Project window. Click on the Workspace Linking settings to open the dialog box shown in Figure 1.34.

Figure 1.34
The Workspace Linking Settings dialog box.

By default, the Effect Mode button is not linked to your workspace, so the Effect Mode drop-down list will show None selected. To link the Effect Mode button to your workspace, click the Effect Mode drop-down list and choose your workspace from the list that appears. Then click the OK button. Now, you have two ways to switch to the workspace: by clicking the Effect Mode button or assigning a keyboard shortcut to the saved workspace.

What's more, the Command Palette, which you access by pressing Command+3 (Mac) or Ctrl+3 (Windows), has a new Workspace tab, as shown in Figure 1.35. Here, you can see the default saved workspaces, and you can add your own. You can then drag a button to your keyboard so you can swap workspaces with just one keystroke! This is a great timesaver, as you can use it to instantly snap from one layout to another, and your Timeline view will follow.

Figure 1.35
The Command Palette.

Saving and Using Templates

When you use one of the effects in the Effect Palette, you are applying a default effect with parameters at the default settings. You might wish to change certain parameters—such as a crop or a border—and then reuse them on a different clip. You can save a customized effect by simply dragging the effect icon into a bin.

Organizing Your Effects in a Bin

Suppose you have applied a PIP effect, resized to 45 percent, applied a pink border with a width of 12 and a softness of 4, and positioned it in the top-right corner, as shown in Figure 1.36.

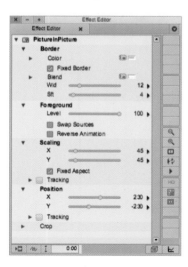

Figure 1.36
A customized PIP.

Now let's say you want to save this PIP so you can use it again. Here's how:

1. First, create a bin specifically for customized effects. This makes them easier to find and organize.

2. Drag the icon in the top-left corner of the Effect Palette into this bin.

3. Rename the effect to reflect how you have customized it. (See Figure 1.37.)

Figure 1.37
The Effect Palette with a bin for custom effects.

Tip: If your effect bin is open, you will see it in the Effect Palette at the bottom of the category list. Click the bin name to see a list of the effects you have created in the bin. You have just created your own new category of effects!

You can now apply this effect rather than the original (default) effect to any other clip in the Timeline.

Applying Individual Effect Parameters

You can go one further. Suppose you have a customized effect and you want to apply just one particular parameter. To use the example, suppose you want to apply the 45 percent size to a new clip, but not the position. Dragging the custom effect icon onto your clip in the Timeline will apply all the parameters you have changed.

To apply just the 45 percent size, follow these steps:

1. Load a default effect. (In this case, apply a new PIP effect.)

2. Open the Effect Editor.

3. Open the group you want to modify (in this example, the Scaling group). (Note that the graphs don't need to be open, just the parameter tracks.)

4. Drag the custom effect icon onto the appropriate parameter tracks in the Effect Editor. In this example, you would drag the custom effect icon to the scaling parameter tracks.

Note: You don't have to apply your custom parameter to the same type of effect. For example, if you create a colored border in a wipe, you can use that same color in a PIP effect to create a colored border for the PIP.

Custom Transitions

By default, the Quick Transition dialog box enables you do add effects from a pre-determined list—dissolves, film fades, and so on. You can, however, add your own effects to this list.

To add your own effects to this list, follow these steps:

1. Create a new bin and name it QUICK TRANSITIONS. (Note that it must be exactly this name.)

2. Add any customized transitions you want to this bin. You can use any effects—shape wipes, matrix wipes, plasma wipes, and even AVX plug-in effects such as BCC Continuum Complete. You can add as many as 30 effects to the bin (actually, you can add as many as you like, but only 30 will appear in the Quick Transition dialog box), but you mustn't save an effect with source. (See the next section for more information about saving effects with source.)

3. Close the bin, making sure it is at the top level of your project and not in a folder.

Tip: You can copy this bin from your project in the Finder (Mac) or Windows Explorer (Windows) and paste it into any other project to get the same selection of transitions.

Once you've created the bin and added your effects to it, you can use the Quick Transition dialog box to access the effects. Here's how:

1. Place the blue position indicator on or near a transition in the Timeline.

2. Click the QUICK TRANSITION button, shown in Figure 1.38, or press the \ (BACKSLASH) keyboard shortcut. The Quick Transition dialog box opens.

Figure 1.38
The Quick Transition button.

3. Click the **ADD** drop-down list. You will see all your effects at the bottom of the list, as shown in Figure 1.39. You can add the transition from here and adjust the duration in the normal way.

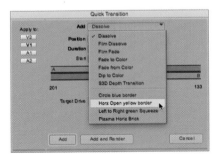

Figure 1.39
The effects stored in the Quick Transitions bin appear at the bottom of the Add menu in the Quick Transition dialog box.

Saving Templates with Source

In addition to saving a customized effect template, you can save the effect and the source clip together. This is a way of saving a source clip that you have modified with an effect—for example, you might have a clip that you wish to use again, but to which you have applied a flop or a zoom. To save the effect with source, Option-drag (Mac) or Alt-drag (Windows) the effect icon from the Effect Editor to the bin. Your effect will now have the suffix "with src," as shown in Figure 1.40. Although it looks like an effect, it actually behaves like a clip—you can load it into the Source monitor, edit it in the Timeline, and even trim it as if it were any other clip. In Lesson 8, "Refining the Composite," you will see that this can be taken one step further to save a whole stack of effect tracks as one multilayer effect template. In that scenario, all you have to do is replace the source footage for each of the tracks.

Note: **This works only with segment effects, not with transition effects.**

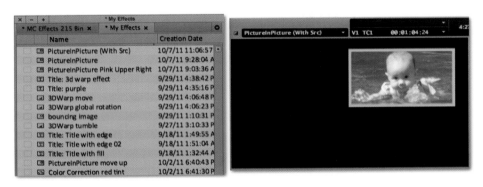

Figure 1.40
Effect template saved with source and loaded into the Source monitor.

Collapsing Tracks in the Timeline

When you have started to build your effects on multiple tracks, you might find that your Timeline gets rather cluttered. Collapsing a series of tracks not only simplifies your Timeline, but it gives you a whole bunch more tracks to play with. Remember, by default you get only 24 video tracks. But if you collapse 24 PIPs into just one track, you still have another 23 tracks to add yet more PIPs!

We have discussed nesting your effects so that they are stacked up on one clip. You may, however, have an effect that uses several different clips, such as a video wall or split screen (see Figure 1.41). While building your effect, it is convenient to have the different video tracks with clips on top of each other, but it can cause problems with long sequences when you trim. For example, suppose you have a stack of clips at one place in your Timeline, but later you decide to trim or insert a clip on V1 that is before your stack. If you forget to turn on your sync locks, you may end up offsetting the clips on the higher tracks, as shown in Figure 1.42.

Figure 1.41
A video wall with four PIPs.

> **Note:** Some people like to have clips spread over multiple video tracks—for example, stacking different choices for a shot on top of each other. That is perfectly okay as long as you remember to use the sync locks. Otherwise, you can end up with clips being offset every time you trim something!

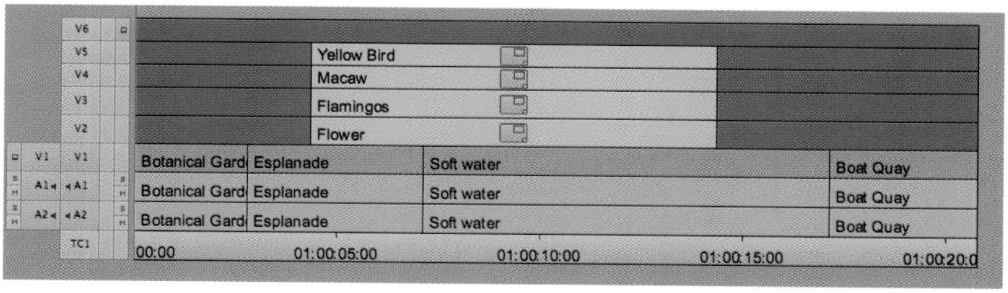

Figure 1.42
A new clip is inserted, and the stack is now offset.

If you find yourself with a cluttered Timeline, it is a good idea to collapse your tracks into one level, which is rather like creating a container for all of your clips that just looks like one clip on V1. Now, when you trim anywhere else in the Timeline, your stack won't be affected; it will just shift along as one unit. Another good reason to collapse is if you wish to apply a fade to a whole collection of tracks (again, using the example of the video wall, if you want to fade four PIPs together). Rather than fade each individual layer, you can collapse all of them into one container (known as a *submaster*) and apply just one fade to that. To try this out, load the sequence called "Video Wall" in the Lesson 01 Effect Design bin.

To collapse a series of tracks, follow these steps:

1. As shown in Figure 1.43, select the clips you want to collapse either using the Segment Mode selection tool or lassoing them. The tracks must have a common start point and end point. If you have staggered clips in the Timeline, simply create an add edit on the black track at the start and end of where you want to collapse.

V6							
V5			Yellow Bird				
V4			Macaw				
V3			Flamingos				
V2			Flower				
V1 V1	Botanical Gard	Esplanade	Soft water			Boat Quay	
A1◀ ◀A1	Botanical Gard	Esplanade	Soft water			Boat Quay	
A2◀ ◀A2	Botanical Gard	Esplanade	Soft water			Boat Quay	
TC1	00:00	01:00:05:00		01:00:10:00		01:00:15:00	01:00:20:0

Figure 1.43
Select all the segments in your effect.

Tip: Normally, if you click the Add Edit button, you will add an edit on all the tracks that are highlighted in the Timeline Track panel. But if you Option-click (Mac) or Alt-click (Windows) the Add Edit button, it will add an edit on all black tracks regardless of what tracks are selected. A very useful feature!

2. Click the **COLLAPSE** button, shown in Figure 1.44. Your tracks will collapse down into one, and the different effects will be replaced by one submaster effect, as shown in Figure 1.45.

Figure 1.44
The Collapse button.

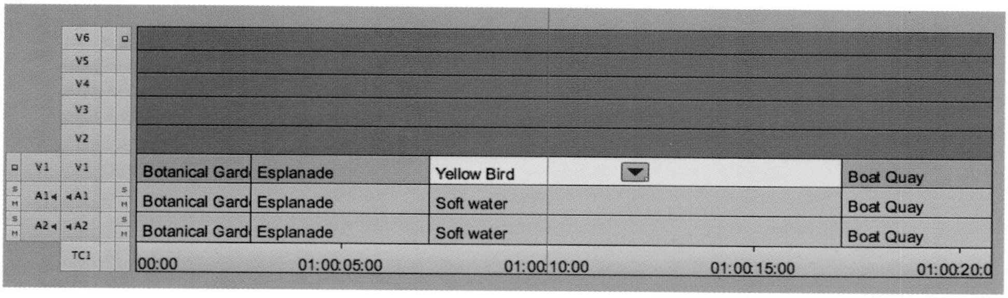

Figure 1.45
Collapsed segments are replaced by one submaster effect.

You can step into the collapsed tracks in the usual way: by double-clicking or using the Step In and Step Out buttons (see Figure 1.46). Any clip inside the collapsed tracks can be edited, trimmed, and even replaced without affecting your overall composition.

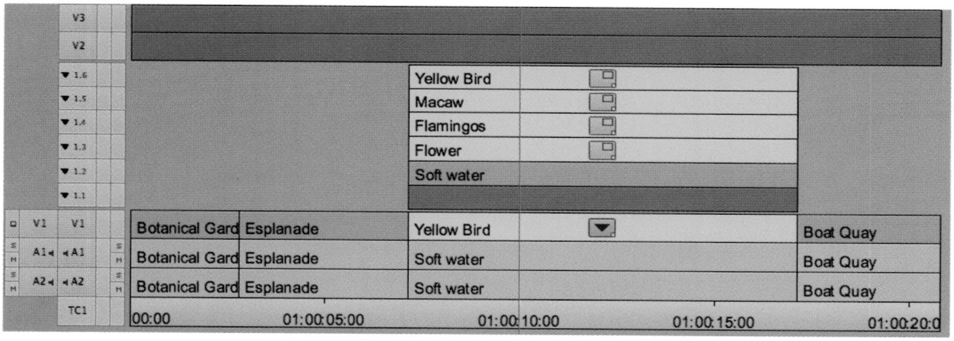

Figure 1.46
Double-click to reveal the clips inside the collapsed tracks.

Media Composer does not have an Uncollapse button, but it is quite easy to uncollapse tracks. Here's how:

1. Step into the collapsed nest to see how many video layers you have. Let's say for the sake of example that there are four PIPs.

2. Step back out and make sure you have at least four empty video tracks above the collapsed tracks.

3. Double-click the nest to expand it and drag each segment up out of the expanded nest and onto the Timeline track above, in the same order as they appeared in the collapsed track. (See Figure 1.47.)

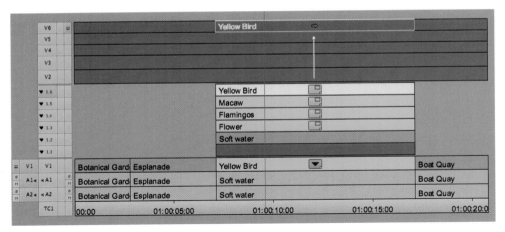

Figure 1.47
Dragging the segments from inside the collapsed track to the Timeline above.

Tip: To ensure that your segments go to the new video track without slipping
      horizontally, press Shift+Command (Mac) or Shift+Ctrl (Windows) when you
      drag your segments. This forces the clip to move only in the vertical plane.

Creating a Video Mixdown

Sometimes, it is necessary to render (flatten out) a section of complex effects in
the Timeline. You can achieve this by creating a mixdown.

The advantage of creating a mixdown is that you make just one video clip out of all
your effects tracks, so the system is no longer working hard to play it. You actually
create a new source clip and a new media file that behaves like any other clip.

For example, you might want to put a Motion effect on the mixdown, which
would not be possible on a series of video tracks with different effects. Also, once
you've created a video mixdown, you can never accidentally move one of the video
layers, change the effect, or un-render it. It is as if you have recorded it to tape.
The disadvantage is that once you have made a mixdown, you can't make any more
changes. The new video clip is not linked in any way to the original effects. You
are committed to what you have mixed down.

Tip: When you perform a mixdown, it is a good idea to save the pre-mixed
      sequence somewhere just in case you need to go in and tweak something.

To perform a video mixdown, follow these steps:

1. Mark an IN point and an OUT point in the area of the Timeline that you wish to mix down.

2. Make sure you are monitoring the highest track that you wish to mix down. Then, open the **SPECIAL** menu and choose **VIDEO MIXDOWN**. The Video Mixdown dialog box opens, as shown in Figure 1.48.

Figure 1.48
The Video Mixdown dialog box.

3. Click the **TARGET BIN** drop-down list and choose the bin in which you want to save the mixdown clip.

4. Click the **TARGET DRIVE** drop-down list and choose the media drive in which you want to save the mixdown clip.

5. Click the **RESOLUTION** drop-down list and choose the resolution for the new media file.

6. Click the **OK** button. A new mixdown clip appears in the bin; this can be loaded in the Source monitor and edited into your sequence, replacing the original effects.

Designing and Deconstructing Effects

When designing an effect, it is always a good idea to plan and perhaps sketch out your effect before you begin working on it. Think about how many layers you will need, about what video elements you want, and about timing—that is, what happens to your elements over time.

Watch TV for ideas and think about how the effects you see might have been achieved. Start by breaking down the effect into the various components and think about how one element is composited on another. Is there a background? Will you need to perform tracking? If so, what is tracked and what is the reference for the track? How do things appear and disappear? Will you need graphic elements— titles, shapes, and so on?

In the course of this book, you will look at different types of effects and how to combine them to create interesting compositions. Once you know how to use the tools, the rest is up to your imagination!

In the bin there is a sequence called "Exercise 3 Completed." In the exercise at the end of this lesson you will attempt to re-create this effect. Let's look at this effect and see how it might have been done. First, how many video layers do you think were used to achieve this effect? You have a background layer and some extra layers. Next, think of timing. At what point does the effect start to animate? Your clips all fade up at the same time, but are you going to apply your fade effect to each clip independently or all together? Is there an easy way of doing this?

When you have learned more about the various effects in the Avid Media Composer, you will return to this subject.

Review/Discussion Questions

1. What is auto-monitoring?
   a. When your client monitor always follows the track you are on
   b. When the track monitor always follows how you patch the source track to the sequence track
   c. When your monitor turns on and off automatically when you take a break

2. How do you solo a video track?

3. How do you create a set of custom transitions to appear in the Quick Transition dialog box?

4. You have magnified a clip in your Source monitor. How do you pan around to see different parts of the image?

5. How can you insert a new video track under an existing track?
   a. Press Command+Y (Mac) or Ctrl+Y (Windows)
   b. Press Option+Y (Mac) or Alt+Y (Windows)
   c. Press Option+Command+Y (Mac) or Ctrl+Alt+Y (Windows)

6. What are two ways to step into a nest, and how are they different?

7. How do you collapse a series of segments on different video layers?

8. What is a video mixdown and why is it useful?

9. True or false: You can step into a video mixdown and re-edit the effects.

10. Following is the procedure for uncollapsing a nested stack of effects. Fill in the gaps.

    1. _____ the collapsed nest to see how many video layers you have.

    2. Step back out and make sure you have the same number of empty video tracks above the collapsed tracks.

    3. Expand the nest by _____ and drag each segment up out of the expanded nest and onto_____, in the same order as they appeared in the collapsed track.

Lesson 1 Keyboard Shortcuts

Key	Shortcut
Command+= (Mac)/Ctrl+= (Windows)	Open the settings for the selected window
Command+Y (Mac)/Ctrl+Y (Windows)	Add new video track
Option+Command+Y (Mac)/Alt+Ctrl+Y (Windows)	Insert new video track
Command+3 (Mac)/Ctrl+3 (Windows)	Open the Command Palette

Creating a Title and Video Wall

A colleague, Betty, has asked you to help out at the Mad Dogs Post House facility while their day editor is on leave. They have a simple task for you: to create a few shots with a title for the Singapore Tourist Board. After that, they want you to create a video wall.

Media Used:

The media for this lesson is in the MC205 Pro Effects Project.
Open the bin called Lesson 01 Effect Design.

Duration:

45 minutes

GOALS

- Apply and save custom effects
- Create more complex effects by nesting

Creating a Nest with Different Effects

As mentioned, you've been asked to create a few shots with a title for the Singapore Tourist Board. The idea is that the shot is cropped and shifted to the left so that a title can be put on the right (see Figure 1.49).

Figure 1.49
How it should look.

To begin, load up the sequence Exercise 1; these are the three shots they want to use. Then follow these steps:

1. Add a **RESIZE** effect (Image category) to the first clip, the flamingos. Use the sliders to adjust the size (using a fixed aspect) and position. (Don't move the image in the Composer window or you'll add keyframes.) Also, crop the right side. Finally, add the title **BIRD PARK** to track 2. It has been created for you already.

2. Save the effect so you can use it again. Then drag it into a bin.

3. Apply the custom **RESIZE** effect to the next shot, the macaw. You need to keep the size of the image the same because it must match the first clip, but the bird's head is being cut off! Betty is worried about this. She also wants the macaw to be facing the other way so it is looking at the title.

4. The answer is to use a Flop effect as well as the Resize effect. If you Option-drag (Mac) or Alt-drag (Windows) the Flop effect on top of the existing Resize effect you will see another problem. The bird is facing the right way, but the Flop effect has flopped everything including the Resize effect. What can you do to fix this?

5. Yes, your effects have been applied the wrong way round. You need to reverse the order. The simplest way to do this is to open the Effect Editor and switch the order of the effects by dragging the **FLOP** icon *below* the Resize effect. Now the bird is facing the right way and is correctly centered in the effect.

6. Look at the last clip. This time you have a similar problem, but you know how to deal with that. You apply your **FLOP** effect *underneath* the Resize effect.

7. Betty is still not happy. She wants the bird to be slightly bigger in the frame and ever so slightly to the left. So what can you do now? Add another Resize effect—only this time, behind the first one.

Note: Since you have already added the Flop effect, does it matter if the second Resize effect goes above or below it? Try adding it above by double-clicking on the Flop effect to reveal the clip beneath. (Okay, you are really adding it *below* the shot. Remember, it is just the Timeline display that expands *upward* to reveal a shot below!)

8. Open the Effect Editor again and make sure you are adjusting the correct Resize effect—the one at the top of the stack. Experiment with the Resize effect (again, remember to click on Fixed Aspect) and position. You'll notice that moving the Y position (up and down) is okay, but moving the X position moves the bird in the opposite direction to what you'd expect. That is because you are flopping the *result* of your move, so a move to the left is flopped to the right. (Just like the *Rocky Horror Picture Show!*)

9. Betty is still not quite happy. She wants you to apply a little color correction to make the bird really stand out. Again think about where you apply the color correction. If you add it on top of all the other effects, you will color-correct the black background as well. You need to step in again and color-correct the back layer. Just keep expanding upward until you find the original bird clip. If you are not familiar with color correction, you should complete the color-correction course! Until then, there is a custom color correction provided for you in the bin. Your final effect should look something like Figure 1.50.

Figure 1.50
Nested bird.

Working with Titles: Replacing Fill with Video

When you create a title in Media Composer, whether using Marquee or the traditional Avid Title tool, you are in fact creating a nested effect. If you add a title in the Timeline and step into it or expand it, you will see there are three layers, as shown in Figure 1.51. One is an empty background track, which is not used; the second is a graphic fill track; and the third is the alpha matte track. The Avid Title tool will generate the title in the fill track and key it onto your sequence with the alpha matte. Generally speaking, the alpha matte is not editable. In fact there is a little lock icon on the V3 track button that shows this track can't be changed. The graphic fill, however, can be replaced with any clip you like. That means instead of having letters with a graphic fill, you can have a video layer cut onto your Timeline with the shape of the letters (or any other object you create in the Avid Title tool). The title is still real-time with the new video fill.

Figure 1.51
The title applied to the Timeline and stepped in to reveal the nested layers.

Betty now wants you to create a title for the bird park piece that will have some flamingos inside the letters. Figure 1.52 shows what she wants it to look like.

Figure 1.52
Betty's plan for the title.

Your title has already been created for you in Marquee. (For more information on how to use Marquee see the 101 course.) To begin, load up the sequence Exercise 2. This is just a background clip. Then follow these steps:

1. Create a new video track and edit the title **Bird_Park Solid** into track **V2**.

2. Step into the title and replace the **Graphic Fill** track with the flamingos shot.

3. If you want, fine-tune the effect to make the flamingos fill to the edge of the letters. You could use the Resize effect for this. Think about where you would place the effect.

4. Betty is impressed, but she thinks you can do better. She wants to see the edge more clearly defined. Place the **Bird Park Edge** title on video track 3. Betty is truly impressed and wants you to do another job!

Think about how you might add a soft edge shadow to this title effect. Which layer would you put it? Can you remember how to insert a video layer into your existing layers? The shadow has been created for you, in case you might like to try…. To add a soft shadow, you need three layers:

- The bottom layer is simply the title with the shadow.

- The second layer is the title with the replaced fill.

- The top layer is the title with just the edge.

You can also add even more effects to an expanded title background fill. You might want to add a Color Effect to change the color.

Creating a Video Wall

Finally, Betty would like you to create a video wall for her bird park. Again, a simple affair: just four pictures on the same background as the title. (See Figure 1.53.) Can you do this for her?

To begin, load sequence Exercise 3—the background clip again.

1. Add four extra video tracks. Then place the three bird shots and one flower shot on each of the four tracks.

2. Apply a **PIP** to the top clip and open the editor.

3. Adjust the sliders until you are happy. You'll need the grid to make sure the pictures remain video safe. A size of **40** percent works well. The positions should be around **250** for X and **250** for Y. It is quicker just to type these in. Add a border if you like. Choose some nice colors.

4. A quick way to reuse an effect you have customized is to simply drag the icon in the top-left corner of the Effect Editor onto each clip in the Timeline.

5. Change the position for each of the four effects. Click on each layer in turn and type all combinations of **+** and **−250** for the **X** and **Y** positions.

6. Change the colors of the borders if you like.

Figure 1.53
Betty's plan for the video wall.

As a final flourish, Betty wants you to fade all the pictures up at the start and down at the end. How can you do this in one go? Hint: Remember the Collapse Tracks button? If you use that, you can apply a head fade and a tail fade to all the shots at once. These buttons are on your Timeline button bar. Experiment with them to get the right effect.

Betty is beside herself with joy and nominates you for an Oscar!

Animating with Keyframes

This lesson looks at adding and managing keyframes, using keyframe graphs and customizing keyframe graphs' behavior. It contains some practical examples to guide you through the philosophy of animation and keyframing.

Media Used: The media for this lesson is in the MC205 Pro Effects Project. Open the bin called Lesson 02 Animation.

Duration: 60 minutes

GOALS

- Add, move, and adjust keyframes
- Use the keyframe graphs
- Understand the options in the Add Keyframe Mode menu
- Copy and paste keyframes
- Use different keyframe interpolation methods
- Use Bézier curves

Understanding Keyframes

Most of the effects you will use in Media Composer have parameters that can be animated using keyframes. Think of a keyframe as a snapshot of an effect's parameters at a point in time. You adjust keyframe parameters in the Effect Editor, which features a series of controls that can be changed using either sliders or thumbwheels or by entering a number on your keypad. For more precise control over how your effect is animated there are keyframe graphs, which you can use to create and manipulate animation curves. In addition, you have control over the type of animation curve and exactly how it is applied to your effect.

The secret to animation is understanding how keyframes work. In the first part of this lesson, you will use the Picture-In-Picture effect to demonstrate the concepts of animation using keyframes. If you load sequence PIP in the Lesson 02 Animation bin you will see that there are two tracks: Video 1 and Video 2. Drop a Picture-In-Picture onto the first clip on V2 and click the Effect Mode button to open the Effect Editor.

By default, when you add an effect, it has no keyframes, as shown in Figure 2.1 (which shows the Effect Editor expanded to show the keyframe tracks). That means if you make an adjustment—for example, to the scaling of a PIP—the clip will be scaled the same amount throughout the duration of the clip. No keyframes are necessary. However, if you want the scaling to *change* throughout the duration of the clip, you will need at least two keyframes: one for the scaling at the start of the animation and one for the scaling at the end of the animation. Note that the animation may not necessarily start at the beginning of the clip; you may wish to have the PIP hold its size for a few seconds before it starts to animate.

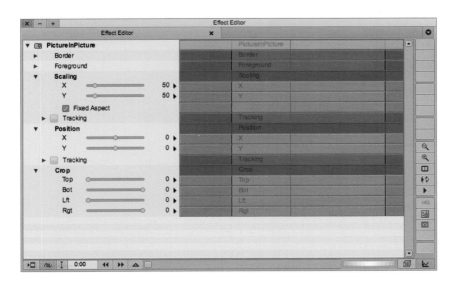

Figure 2.1
The PIP effect with no keyframes and no parameter animation.

Note: If you want to work with a start and end keyframe, there is a command in the Effect Editor context menu that enables you to add them automatically. To view this, right-click any of the keyframe tracks on the right side of the Effect Editor and you'll get the menu shown in Figure 2.2, which you'll use throughout this lesson.

Figure 2.2
The Effect Editor context menu.

Adding Keyframes

When you want to add a keyframe, there are various methods:

■ Press the Add Keyframe key on your keyboard. (This is the apostrophe key by default.)

■ Click the Add Keyframe button underneath the Composer window, as shown in Figure 2.3.

Figure 2.3
The Add Keyframe button.

■ Click the add keyframe icon at the bottom of the Effect Editor window.

■ Right-click a keyframe track and choose Add Keyframe from the menu that appears.

■ Right-click the keyframe graph and choose Add Keyframe from the menu.

Note: There are three types of keyframe tracks. The yellow bar at the top is the Effect Keyframe track and shows all the keyframes in the effect. Below are the Parameter Group Keyframe tracks, which are dark green and show all the keyframes for a group such as the Position group. Finally, the lighter green tracks are the Parameter Keyframe tracks, which show keyframes for individual parameters. Expanding these will reveal the graphs for each parameter. Depending on which type of track you select, you'll add a keyframe to all parameters, all the parameters within a group, or just an individual parameter.

Depending on how you have configured the Effect Editor, the results of these methods will vary. (You will explore this in more detail in the next section.) If you are still looking at the Effect Editor with your PIP, you will see the various controls for the PIP. You can also see that some of the buttons under the Composer window have changed. When you drag the cursor along the position bar, you can see the clip and its effect updates in the Composer window.

When you add keyframes, they will show up in different places. Figure 2.4 shows the Effect Editor window with keyframes added in the following locations:

- The position bar in the Composer window
- The Effect Keyframe track
- The Parameter Group Keyframe track

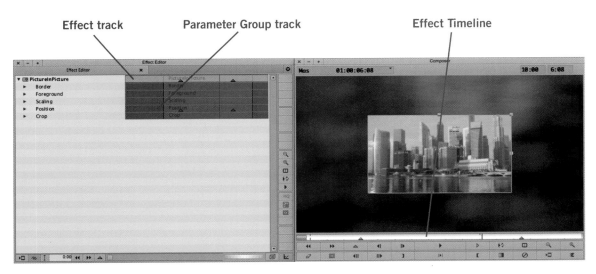

Figure 2.4
The Effect Editor window with keyframes added.

If you expand the Parameter Group Keyframe track, you will also see keyframes on the individual Parameter Keyframe tracks. Expanding further will reveal keyframes on the graphs for each parameter.

Let's add two keyframes, the first about one second into the effect and the next about a second from the end. There are many ways to add keyframes; for now, let's use the easiest method.

Note: The other methods of adding keyframes may not work right now depending on how the Effect Editor is configured. This is covered later.

To add keyframes:

1. Right-click the parameter group track (in this case, the **POSITION** track) in the Effect Editor window. A context menu appears.

2. Choose **ADD KEYFRAME**, as shown in Figure 2.5, to add a keyframe where your blue position indicator is parked.

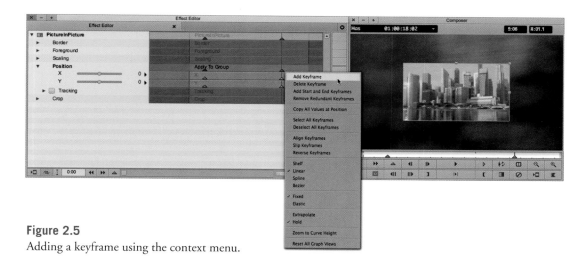

Figure 2.5
Adding a keyframe using the context menu.

Here are some things to keep in mind about keyframes:

- As shown in Figure 2.6, when keyframes are added, you will see two purple triangles in the Parameter Group Keyframe track, in the Effect Keyframe track at the top and in the Effect Editor position bar.

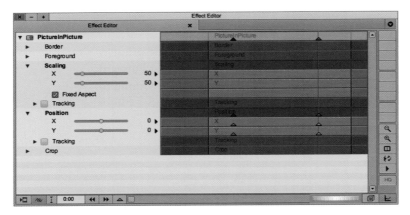

Figure 2.6
Two keyframes are added to each of the X and Y position tracks.

Tip: The yellow Effect Keyframe track at the top is useful. This is where all the keyframes in an effect appear, regardless of which parameter they are applied to. It allows you to select all the keyframes at a particular point in time and move them together. (For more information, see the section "Moving and Nudging Keyframes.")

- You can expand out the various parameters by clicking the triangle on the left to reveal that the keyframes have been added to specific parameters. In this case, the Position parameters have been expanded to reveal keyframes on the X and Y position bars.

- Keyframes can be selected, in which case they are purple, or deselected, in which case they are gray. When you select a keyframe, you can adjust its parameters using the slider or thumbwheel controls in the Effect Editor. If it is not selected (gray), then adjusting a keyframe's controls will have no effect.

- To select more than one keyframe, Shift-click individual keyframes. To select *all* the keyframes in an effect, press Command+A (Mac) or Ctrl+A (Windows).

Tip: If you have keyframes selected, you can *deselect* all keyframes by pressing Shift+Command+A (Mac) or Shift+Ctrl+A (Windows).

Jumping from Keyframe to Keyframe and Segment to Segment

After you add keyframes, you may need to change various parameter values to animate your effect. To adjust these parameters on different keyframes, you'll need to navigate in the position bar or the keyframe graphs.

If you press the Left Arrow and Right Arrow keys on your keyboard, you will shift the blue position indicator one field (or one frame if you are working in progressive, as in this project) back or forward, respectively. But if you click the Fast Forward or Rewind buttons, shown in Figure 2.7, you will jump from one keyframe to another along the Effect Editor position bar and in the various keyframe tracks in the Effect Editor.

Figure 2.7
The Fast Forward and Rewind buttons.

When you are in Effect mode, and you have effects on different clips in the Timeline, you can jump from one segment to the next by clicking the Go to Previous Edit and Go to Next Edit buttons, shown in Figure 2.8. (The shortcut keys for these buttons are the A and S keys by default.) Using these buttons takes you from segment to segment without leaving Effect mode. This is very useful when you have many effects of the same type to tweak (such as the Reformat effect), and you want to quickly skip down the Timeline to make adjustments.

Figure 2.8
The Next and Previous buttons.

Moving and Nudging Keyframes

In addition to moving your position indicator along the position bar, you may want to actually move a *keyframe* along the position bar. This can be done in two ways:

- By Option-dragging (Mac) or Alt–dragging (Windows) the keyframe directly in the Keyframe position bar, or any of the keyframe tracks. Note that when you Option-drag (Mac) or Alt-drag (Windows) the keyframe in the Effect Keyframe track, you move *all* the keyframes at that particular position regardless of which parameter they are added to. This is very handy for moving a number of keyframes together.

- By nudging with the same buttons you use for trimming (see Figure 2.9). (This works in the Composer window's position bar only. In the keyframe tracks, the trim buttons adjust the *amount* of the parameter, not the position of the keyframe.) When you nudge a keyframe, the position indicator stays where it is. You may see your effect change because the keyframe will have moved further along the Keyframe position bar, but you are seeing the result of that shift at a different point in time.

Figure 2.9
Trim buttons

Tip: **The trim buttons are assigned on the keyboard as follows: Press the M key to nudge 10 fields or frames backward, the comma key to move one field or frame back, the period key to move one field or frame forward, and the forward slash key to move 10 fields or frames forward.**

Deleting Keyframes

You can delete keyframes from either the Keyframe position bar or the various keyframe tracks. There are a few methods for deleting keyframes:

- Select a keyframe in any of the aforementioned places and press the Delete key.

- Select a keyframe or Shift-select multiple keyframes in the individual keyframe track, right-click, and choose Delete Keyframe to delete all selected keyframes in just that track.

- Select a keyframe or Shift-select multiple keyframes in the Group Keyframe tracks, right-click, and choose Delete Keyframe to delete all selected keyframes in that group.

- Select a keyframe or Shift-select multiple keyframes in the Effect Keyframe track, right-click, and choose Delete Keyframe to delete the selected keyframes for all tracks.

Adjusting Parameters

To change the value of a parameter, you can use the controls in the Effect Editor window. You can use sliders or, if you prefer, you can use thumbwheels. You can quickly toggle between the two by right-clicking anywhere in the Effect Editor window and choosing Thumbwheels from the menu that appears, as shown in Figure 2.10. This menu is also where you access various appearance settings—font size, whether sliders are indented, and so on—covered in the section "Configuring the Effect Editor" in Lesson 1, "Effect Design and Techniques."

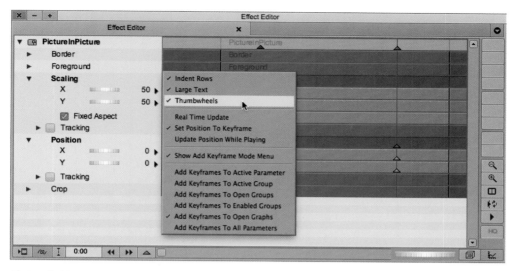

Figure 2.10
Swapping between thumbwheels and sliders.

Here are a few more tips for adjusting parameters:

■ While you can drag sliders to adjust a parameter value, you can achieve a more precise control by holding down the Shift key as you drag. This gives you a fine-tune mode, in which you can drag the sliders for a much smaller adjustment.

■ You can make adjustments one unit at a time by pressing the Left Arrow and Right Arrow keys. Alternatively, you can hold down the Shift key as you press the arrow keys to adjust by 10 units at a time.

■ You can use the same buttons you use to trim (refer to Figure 2.9) to move the sliders 10 units up, one unit up, and one unit down, and 10 units down, respectively.

■ You can enter a value directly by using the number keys and pressing enter.

Zooming in the Keyframe Position Bar

As mentioned, the Keyframe position bar changes when you are in Effect mode. Instead of enabling you to scroll the entire Timeline, it lets you scroll the duration of your effect. Sometimes you may find that your keyframes are too close together to make navigation possible. The slider on the left side enables you to zoom in so that your keyframes are clearly separated and you can easily select keyframes, even if they are just one frame apart, as shown in Figure 2.11.

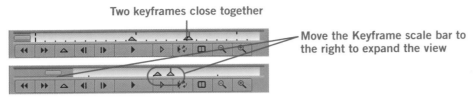

Figure 2.11
In this case, by sliding the Keyframe scale bar to the right, you make two keyframes visible.

You can also zoom into the keyframe parameter tracks using the slider at the bottom of the Effect Editor window. The scroll wheel on the right lets you scroll along the track to view your keyframes at a particular place in time. At the bottom right of the Effect Editor is the Show Keyframe Graphs button, which you can click to reveal the keyframe tracks and graphs. See Figure 2.12.

Figure 2.12
Tools for resizing and scrolling the keyframe tracks horizontally, and for revealing keyframe tracks and graphs.

Resetting an Effect

Sometimes, when you're playing around adding keyframes and changing parameters, you just want to reset everything. There is no Reset button in the Effect Editor, but you can easily reset all parameters to their defaults by simply dragging a new effect (for example, a new PIP effect) from the Effect Palette on top of the old one. Everything will be reset to the default values for that effect. The 3D Warp effect also has an enable button for each parameter, which can be used to reset individual values. This is covered in the next lesson.

Advanced Keyframe Techniques: Exploring the Graphs

Keyframe graphs show a visual representation of how keyframe values change over time and give you much more control over your keyframes. Using these graphs, you can add keyframes to individual parameters and precisely control how one keyframe transitions to another. To display a keyframe graph, you expand the individual keyframe tracks by clicking the triangle on the right of the slider, as shown in Figure 2.13.

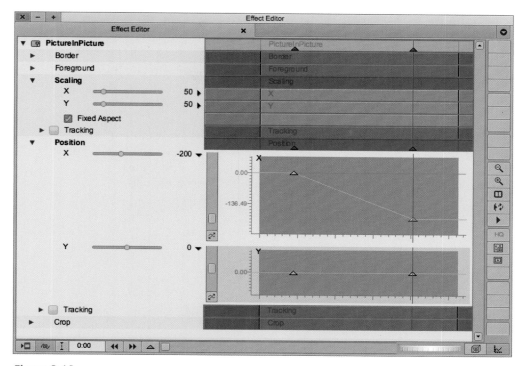

Figure 2.13
The graphs for Position (X and Y) are opened.

Note: Not all effects have graphs (although these days, most of them do). The main exceptions are the Intraframe (Paint) effects, which include Mosaic, Blur, and AniMatte, and the Plasma effects. Also, the Timewarps have their own type of animation graphs; these are covered in *Media Composer 6: Part 2–Effects Essentials.*

Resizing the Graph

You can use the same scrollbar at the bottom of the Effect Editor window to zoom and scroll along your keyframe graph that you used with the keyframe tracks (refer to Figure 2.12). The slider on the left enables you to zoom into the graph for more detail, and the scroll wheel on the right lets you scroll along the Timeline to view your animation graph at a particular place in time.

If you wish to expand your graphs vertically, you can hover your mouse pointer at the bottom of the graph until an up/down arrow appears, as shown in Figure 2.14. Use this to drag the bottom of your graph up to shrink the graph, or down to expand the graph. The mouse pointer will revert back to normal as soon as you move away from the bottom of the graph.

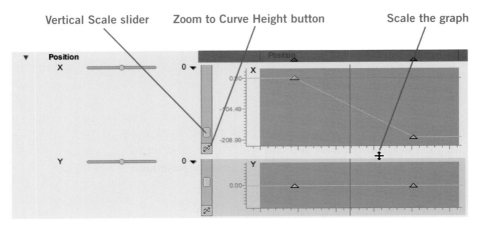

Figure 2.14
Graph scaling tools.

You can also change the vertical scaling in your graph with the Vertical Scale slider on the left of the graph. Below this is the nifty Zoom to Curve Height button, which will instantly zoom your graph so that the keyframes with the highest and lowest values will snap to fill the entire graph view. Finally, to pan around your graph, press the Command+Option (Mac) or Ctrl+Alt (Windows); your pointer will change to a hand, which lets you move your graph in the X and Y axes to view keyframes in more detail.

Tip: You can also scroll in the vertical scale with your mouse wheel.

Moving Keyframes in the Graph

In addition to moving keyframes in the parameter tracks, you can also move them directly in the graph using your mouse. By default, keyframes can be moved up and down only, but if you press the Option key (Mac) or Alt key (Windows), you can move them in time as well as by amount. If you wish to constrain to just the horizontal (time) axis, press Shift+Option (Mac) or Shift+Alt (Windows) instead.

When you select a keyframe, you will also select the slider (or thumbwheel) to the left. Thus, the same keys for adjusting the sliders also work when you select a keyframe as discussed earlier in the section "Adjusting Parameters."

Adding Keyframes to Selected Parameters

The trick to keyframing is knowing which parameters to apply them to. In other words, you must know when to use keyframes, and when *not* to use them. In the case of PIP, for example, you might wish to animate the position of your PIP but not the crop or the border. Or, you might want to animate the size of the PIP but to keep the position constant throughout the effect.

To achieve this in early versions of Media Composer, the only option was to add keyframes to all the existing parameters. This made animation somewhat difficult. For example, suppose you had a PIP in the center of the screen, and you wanted to add a one-second fade-in and fade-out by animating the foreground. In the old days, this would require a keyframe at the start and end with foreground set to zero, and a keyframe one second in and one second before the end with foreground set to 100 percent.

Then, suppose you wanted to animate the position so that the PIP moved across the screen at a steady speed. You might choose to set the first keyframe so that the position was on the left side and the last keyframe so that the PIP was on the right side. But the two inner keyframes, which you set for the fade-in and fade-out, would be set to center screen, so the animation would not be correct. You would have to delete the fade-in and fade-out and start again. With more recent versions of Media Composer, you can add keyframes to just the parameters you want. In this example, the fade-in and fade-out would use completely different keyframes to the position keyframes.

You saw in the last section that you could add a keyframe by right-clicking the parameter track of the desired parameter. This adds a keyframe to just that param-eter at the position of the cursor. Alternatively, you can add a keyframe to all parameters by right-clicking the Effect Keyframe track at the top of the window.

However, you also have the Add Keyframe button; its keyboard shortcut is the single quote (') key by default. Clicking the button in the Effect Editor will pro-duce a menu that gives you various choices (see Figure 2.15). Using the keyboard shortcut will add a keyframe too, but the way it does this is user configurable in the Keyframe Mode menu.

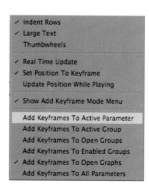

Figure 2.15
The Add Keyframe Mode menu.

To configure how keyframes are added, right-click the button (or any part of the gray area in the Effect Editor window). You have six choices for adding keyframes:

■ **Add Keyframes to Active Parameter.** Choose this option to add a keyframe to a single parameter. In Figure 2.16, the keyframe is added to the X scale parameter, which is active because the slider is selected. In addition, the keyframe appears on the Scaling track and the Effect Keyframe track. The Position group is not affected.

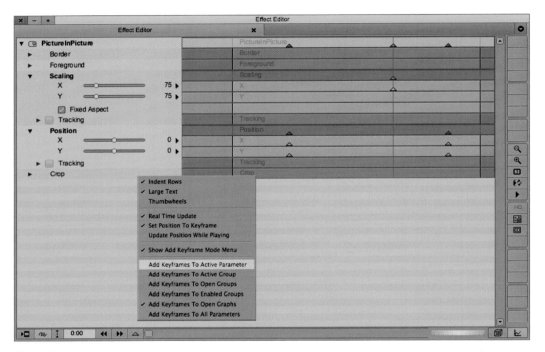

Figure 2.16
Choosing Add to Active Parameter from the Add Keyframe Mode menu.

■ **Add Keyframes to Active Group.** Choose Add Keyframes to Active Group to add a keyframe to all the members of the active group. In Figure 2.17, the keyframe is added to the X and Y parameters in the Scaling group because the X slider in that group is selected. Selecting the X slider makes that group active.

■ **Add Keyframes to Open Groups.** Choose this option to add a keyframe to all open groups. In Figure 2.18, both the Scaling and the Position group are open—that is, the right-pointing triangle to the left of the group name has been clicked to display the group's parameters—meaning keyframes are added to all the parameters in both groups regardless of whether they are active.

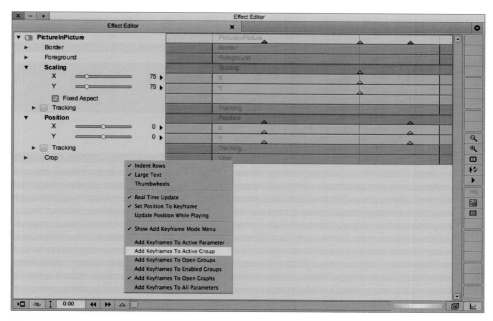

Figure 2.17
Choosing Add Keyframes to Active Group from the Add Keyframe Mode menu.

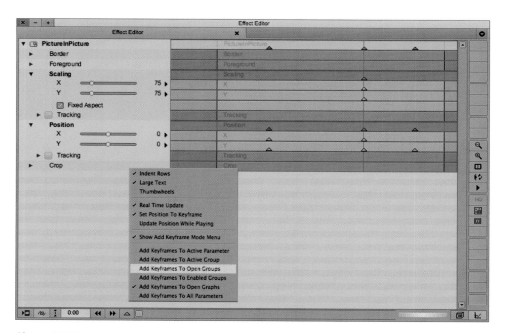

Figure 2.18
Choosing Add Keyframes to Open Groups from the Add Keyframe Mode menu.

■ **Add Keyframes to Enabled Groups.** Enabled groups are a special case, for when you promote an effect to 3D (see Lesson 3, "Using the 3D Warp Effect"). 3D effects have additional boxes for each group, which enable them. (Enabled groups are indicated by a highlighted box.) You can make changes to parameters in a group, but you can also turn off the enable button so that changes are not applied to parameters in those groups. In Figure 2.19 the Scaling, Position, and Foreground groups are enabled, and keyframes are applied. (Note that the Scaling group is not open, so the keyframe is visible only on the Scaling group track.)

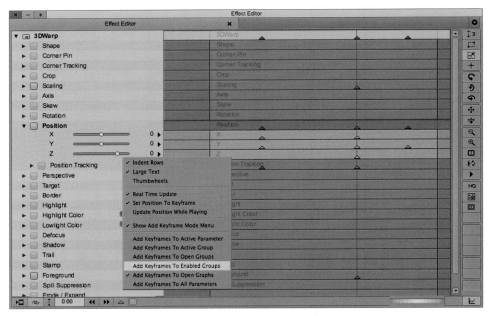

Figure 2.19
Choosing Add to Enabled Groups from the Add Keyframe Mode menu.

■ **Add Keyframes to Open Graphs.** Select this menu option to apply keyframes to open graphs. In Figure 2.20, the Scaling X and the Position Y graphs are open, so keyframes are added to those parameters only.

■ **Add Keyframes to All Parameters.** Choose this option to add keyframes to all parameters, as shown in Figure 2.21.

Note: Your selection in the Add Keyframe Mode menu is mirrored in Delete Keyframe mode. For example, when you change your selection to Add Keyframes to Open Groups in the Add Keyframe Mode menu, the Delete Keyframe mode changes to Delete Keyframes from Open Groups.

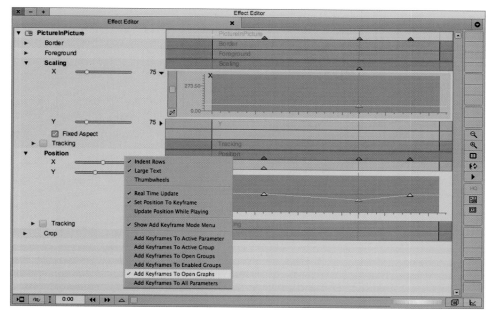

Figure 2.20
Choosing Add Keyframes to Open Graphs from the Add Keyframe Mode menu.

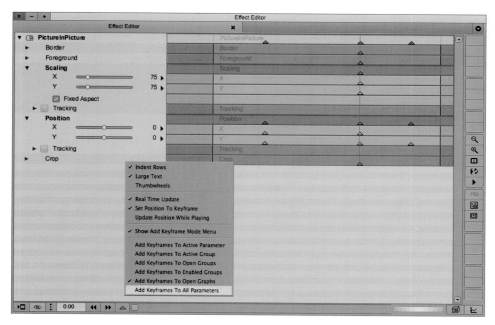

Figure 2.21
Choosing Add Keyframes to All Parameters from the Add Keyframe Mode menu.

There is one more important option in the Add Keyframe Mode menu: Show Add Keyframe Mode Menu, as shown in Figure 2.22, which is on by default. With this selected, Media Composer will display a menu each time you click the Add Keyframe button (see Figure 2.23). That way, you can quickly select which mode to use each time. Some of the options will be grayed out depending on whether your parameter is active or open, etc.

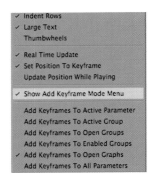

Figure 2.22
Choosing Show Add Keyframe Mode Menu from the Add Keyframe Mode menu.

Figure 2.23
Clicking the Add Keyframe button now gives you a choice of add options.

Note: If you use the keyboard shortcut for adding a keyframe, it will just add the keyframe according to how you have set it in the right-click menu. No options are given.

Other Ways to Add Keyframes

So far, you have seen that you can add a keyframe by clicking the Add Keyframe button in all its various modes. You have also used the menu that appears when you right-click a keyframe track. Remember that the different keyframe tracks will let you add keyframes in different ways.

Right-clicking a Parameter Keyframe track and choosing Add Keyframe from the menu that appears will add a keyframe for just that parameter. Adding a keyframe to a Parameter Group Keyframe track will add the keyframe to all parameters in the group, and adding a keyframe to the Effect Keyframe track at the top of the window will add the keyframe to all parameters. (See Figure 2.24.) Additionally, if you open a graph, you will see that you can also add a keyframe by right-clicking the graph itself.

Note: Most actions—adding, aligning, slipping, copying (which will be covered
       in a minute), and deleting keyframes—have different results depending on
       which track you right-click. To let you see exactly what you are affecting, the
       text in the track will change. So, for example, if you right-click the group
       track, you will see the text Apply to Group; if you right-click the Effect
       Keyframe track, the text will change to Apply to All. (Refer to Figure 2.24.)

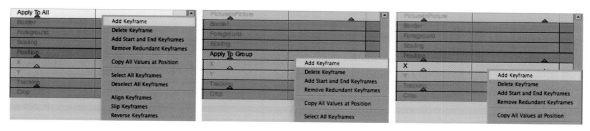

Figure 2.24
The track you select affects how keyframes are added.

Another way to add keyframes is to use the direct manipulation controls in the
Effect Editor Composer window. If you reposition the PIP by dragging it around
or resize it by using the handle in the top-right corner, you will add keyframes on
either the Position (X and Y) parameters or the Scaling (X and Y) parameters.

Note: If you use direct manipulation of your PIP or any other effect, you will add
       keyframes even if you start with none. This can be undesirable; sometimes
       you might simply want to move a PIP without animating it. This is better
       done using the parameter sliders, which won't add keyframes if you start
       with none in the first place.

Adjusting the Timing of Your Animation

After you have added keyframes to your effect, you might want to adjust the timing so that various elements move or scale at a particular point. Or you might want
several elements to start to move at the same time. Whatever is required, you will
often need to move the keyframes in some way.

Previously, you saw that you can move keyframes by Option-dragging (Mac) or
Alt-dragging (Windows) them along parameter tracks and by nudging them.
Other methods that are well suited for particular situations also exist. You can find
these in the Effect Editor's context menu (see Figure 2.25), which you can access by
right-clicking a keyframe track. Let's look at some of these options more closely
using an example. To begin, load the Keyframe Animation sequence in the Lesson
02 Animation bin. This has various PIP effects already applied on Video 2.

Figure 2.25
The Effect Editor context menu.

Aligning Keyframes

Sometimes, not all keyframes appear exactly at the same point in time. Look at the first PIP effect in this sequence. In this example, there is a move in X direction, but it does not coincide with the move in the Y direction. To align them so the X and Y movements start at the same moment, you can align the keyframes.

To align a group of keyframes in different parameters so they all appear at the same point in time:

1. Make sure the Position graph is open and click the first Y keyframe. This is the keyframe you are going to align.

Note: Do not select more than one keyframe per parameter. If you do, the *last* keyframe you selected will be used for the alignment, and the other keyframes will *slip* in time relative to that one.

2. Move the position indicator to the desired new position for the selected keyframe. In this case it is at the first X keyframe.

Tip: If you click the X keyframe, you will deselect the Y keyframe, so the easiest way to move the position indicator is to Shift-click the X keyframe. Now both keyframes are selected and the position indicator is aligned with the first X keyframe.

3. Right-click the **PARAMETER GROUP KEYFRAME** track and choose **ALIGN KEYFRAMES**. Figure 2.26 shows a before and after view with multiple parameters.

Figure 2.26
Aligning keyframes, before and after.

You can align multiple keyframes by Shift-clicking keyframes in different parameter groups. As with adding keyframes, where you right-click is critical to how the keyframes will be aligned:

■ If you right-click the keyframe track for a single parameter, you will align a single active keyframe.

■ If you right-click the keyframe track for a group, you will align *all* the active keyframes in that group.

■ If you right-click the Effect Keyframe track, you will align *all* the active keyframes in the entire effect.

Slipping Keyframes

Now move to the second PIP in the sequence (remember you can use the S key to jump to the next segment when you are in Effect mode). Here, you can see there are also movements in the X and Y directions, but in this case the start and end keyframes are out of alignment.

Slipping keyframes will move them so that *all* the keyframes in a parameter are slipped together, aligning the active keyframe with the position indicator. This is useful when you want to maintain the relative keyframe timing of a parameter, but wish to begin or end the animation at a different point in time. The difference between slipping and aligning is that when you align, you are adjusting the position of just the selected keyframe. When you slip, you will adjust *all* the keyframes in the same parameter using the selected keyframe as a reference. If you had tried to slip the keyframes in the first PIP in this sequence, the start keyframes would be aligned, but the end keyframes would now be at a separate point in time.

Note: When slipping, all the keyframes in a parameter are slipped. You can't just slip certain keyframes.

To slip keyframes:

1. Select the first Y keyframe from the **Position** parameter.

Note: Again, be careful to select just one keyframe in a parameter. If you select more than one, the last keyframe that you selected will be aligned with the position indicator.

2. Move the blue position indicator to the same position as the X keyframe. Again you can either Shift-click the X keyframe or you can simply move the position indicator along the Y graph so that it lines up with the X keyframe.

3. Right-click the keyframe track and choose **Slip Keyframes**. You can see that both the Y keyframes have moved. Figure 2.27 shows a before and after view for multiple keyframes.

Figure 2.27
Slipping keyframes, before and after.

Again, where you right-click is critical to how the keyframes will be slipped:

■ If you right-click the keyframe track for a single parameter, you will slip all the keyframes in that parameter by the same amount to align the active keyframe with the position indicator.

■ If you right-click the keyframe track for the group, you will slip *all* the keyframes together in that group so the active ones line up with the position indicator.

■ If you right-click the Effect Keyframe track, you will slip *all* the keyframes in the *entire* effect so that the active ones line up with the position indicator.

Tip: Sometimes, you may create keyframes that are so close together they appear to be just one keyframe. If you select the keyframe in the Effect Keyframe track for the effect, you may notice that one or two keyframes are not selected in the tracks below even though they appear to be in the same location. If you use the Horizontal scale bar at the bottom-left to take a closer look, however, you may see that you actually have multiple keyframes that are not at the same point in time. When zoomed in, it is much easier to align or slip misplaced keyframes.

Reversing the Order of Keyframes

You can reverse the order of the keyframes in an effect, for a single parameter, a group, or the entire effect. When you reverse keyframes, *all* the keyframes in the parameter, group, or effect are reversed in relation to the effect's duration. (Note that you can't reverse a subset of keyframes.) You can use the same PIP effect as the previous example to try this.

To reverse keyframes:

1. Move your mouse to the **GROUP KEYFRAME** track. (You don't need to select any keyframes.)

2. Right-click the keyframe track and choose **REVERSE KEYFRAMES**. You can see that both the X and the Y keyframe graphs have been reversed.

Again, right-clicking the different tracks produces different results.

■ To reverse the keyframes in a single parameter, right-click the parameter track and choose Reverse Keyframes.

■ To reverse the keyframes in a parameter group, right-click the group track and choose Reverse Keyframes.

■ To reverse all the keyframes in an effect, right-click the Effect Keyframe track and choose Reverse Keyframes.

It makes no difference whether the keyframes are selected or not. They will be reversed regardless. Figure 2.28 shows a before and after view for multiple keyframes.

Figure 2.28
Reversing keyframes, before and after.

Copying and Pasting Keyframes

Keyframes can be copied and pasted in the Effect Editor, enabling you to repeat an animation or part of an animation. There are various options:

■ Copying and pasting selected keyframes in a single parameter

■ Copying and pasting selected keyframes in multiple parameters

■ Copying and pasting all values at a point in time

You can use any segment in the sequence to try this.

To copy and paste selected keyframes:

1. Click on a keyframe to select it.

2. Press **COMMAND+C** (Mac) or **CTRL+C** (Windows) to copy the selected keyframe. You can copy from the parameter track or the expanded graph.

3. Move your position indicator to the location where you want to paste. Alternatively, select a keyframe to which you want to apply the copied parameter. Then, press **COMMAND+V** (Mac) or **CTRL+V** (Windows) to paste. The keyframe you copied is now pasted to the new location, as shown in Figure 2.29.

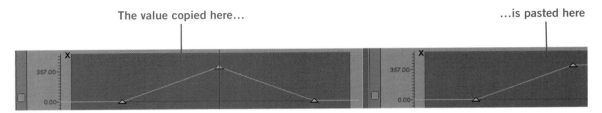

Figure 2.29
Copying and pasting keyframes.

Note that you don't need to have a keyframe to copy the value at that point. If you have graphs open, you can place your position indicator at any point regardless of whether there is a keyframe or not. If the graphs are closed, you can also park your position indicator between two keyframes. Right-click at that point and choose Copy All Values at Position (see Figure 2.30); then move the position indicator where you want to paste the values or click a keyframe that you want to update and press Command+V (Mac) or Ctrl+V (Windows) to paste.

Figure 2.30
Copy a value at a position and paste to a new keyframe.

Note: **This will add keyframes at all the parameters in your effect. They were all copied, and now they are all pasted. However, the extra keyframes can be easily removed. (See the next section, "Deleting Redundant Keyframes," for more information.)**

Deleting Redundant Keyframes

When building complex effects, you can often end up with many more keyframes than you really need. This is particularly true if you accidentally add keyframes to all parameters when you really only needed to add them to just one parameter. Redundant keyframes are keyframes on a graph that have a value just the same as if they were not there. If a straight line between two different keyframes has multiple keyframes that don't change the direction of the line, then these keyframes are *redundant* and can be deleted without affecting the animation. Redundant keyframes can cause problems when you try to animate an effect, so it is a good idea to remove them.

If you select the third segment in the sequence you'll see there are many redundant keyframes.

To remove redundant keyframes:

1. Position your mouse on a **Parameter Keyframe** track, a **Group Keyframe** track, or the **Effect Keyframe** track.

2. Right-click the keyframe track and choose **Remove Redundant Keyframes**. You can see that all the redundant keyframes have been removed on the track.

As before, if you right-click the parameter track and choose Remove Redundant Keyframes, you'll remove just the redundant keyframes on that track. If you right-click the group track, then all the redundant keyframes in the group will go. Finally, if you right-click the Effect Keyframe track, you will remove all redundant keyframes in the effect. The effect of removing redundant keyframes is shown in Figure 2.31 and Figure 2.32.

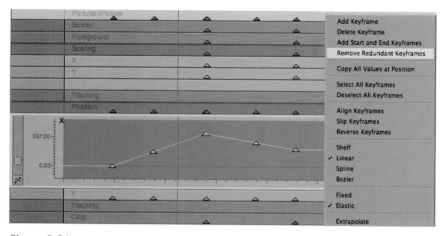

Figure 2.31
Removing redundant keyframes, before.

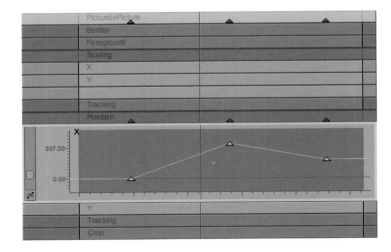

Figure 2.32
Removing redundant keyframes, after.

Tip: Another way to globally remove redundant keyframes is to right-click the sequence in a bin and choose Remove Redundant Keyframes from the menu. This will create a duplicate of your sequence with all the unwanted keyframes removed.

Trimming a Clip with an Effect

When you trim a clip with an applied effect that uses keyframing, the animation is retimed by default. That is, if you make the clip longer, the animation will be longer. You might, however, want to keep the animation timing the same because other clips might be affected. You have two options for how keyframes behave when an effect is trimmed. Right-click either the keyframe track or the graph in the Effect Editor, as shown in Figure 2.33:

- **Fixed.** If you choose Fixed, when you trim, the animation does not change. The keyframes remain fixed at the same place in the sequence Timeline.

- **Elastic.** This is the default keyframe mode. This mode stretches the keyframes with the trim. If you make the clip longer, the animation retimes so that the keyframes are moved accordingly along the Timeline.

There is a very subtle difference between how fixed keyframes appear in the Effect Editor compared to how elastic keyframes appear. Fixed keyframes, which are anchored to a particular frame of video, have a small bump at the bottom, like a hovering spaceship (see Figure 2.34). Elastic keyframes are basic triangles. You only see this distinction in the graph itself, not in the Keyframe scale bars.

Figure 2.33
Choosing fixed or elastic keyframes.

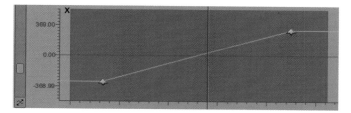

Figure 2.34
Fixed keyframes.

Within a parameter group, all keyframes must be of the same type. Within the effect as a whole, however, some groups can be elastic and some can be fixed. For example, you might want the position of the effect to animate in time with music, so you would make those keyframes fixed. But if you wanted the fade up and down to be a percentage of the clip's duration, you would make those keyframes elastic. As usual, you can toggle all the parameter groups by right-clicking the Effect Keyframe track or you can toggle individual groups on the parameter track or graph for that group.

Note: The Timewarp effect also has graphs that can be adjusted with keyframes, but the default keyframe setting is fixed rather than elastic. When you trim a clip with a Timewarp effect, you need not change the animation timing by default.

Working with Animation Curves

Graphs provide more than just a visual representation of how a parameter's value changes over time. You can also use graphs to change the transition between keyframes in a number of ways. Display your keyframe graph by clicking the small triangle on the left of the keyframe track. Figure 2.35 shows the main features of the keyframe graph display.

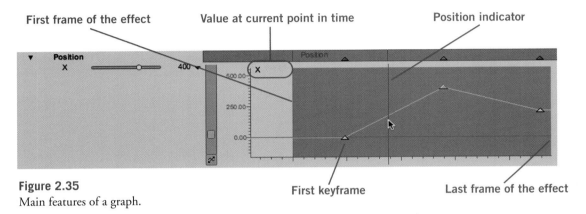

Figure 2.35
Main features of a graph.

The graph shows the calculated value of a parameter at any given point. In fact, when you scroll along the graph with the position indicator, you will see the value at the current point displayed in green in the top-left corner. This value is affected by both the position of the keyframes and the shape of the curve—also known as the interpolation. You can choose which kind of interpolation by right-clicking on the graph and choosing the desired curve option from the menu that appears. When it comes to the shape of the curve, there are four options:

■ **Shelf.** This type of curve simply holds the value of a keyframe until the next one, as shown in Figure 2.36. The animation jumps from one value to another with no motion in between. Shelf curves are useful for creating strobe effects.

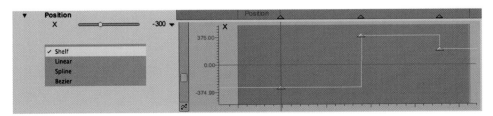

Figure 2.36
A shelf curve.

■ **Linear.** This type of curve, which is the default, creates a straight line path between two keyframes, for a constant animation motion (see Figure 2.37). Use this if you don't want to ease in and ease out.

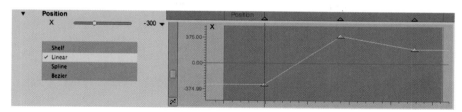

Figure 2.37
A linear curve.

■ **Spline.** This creates a smooth curve with a natural ease-in and ease-out at every keyframe (see Figure 2.38). The amount of ease-in and ease-out is calculated automatically and can't be adjusted.

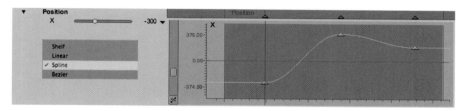

Figure 2.38
A spline curve.

■ **Bézier.** Bézier curves give you the most control of an object's animation. With this type of curve, each keyframe has two handles, called Bézier handles (see Figure 2.39). These enable you to affect the direction of the curve at all points between keyframes. In the case of position parameters, this means you can adjust the actual path of the object, as shown in Figure 2.40. (This is covered in more detail in the next section.)

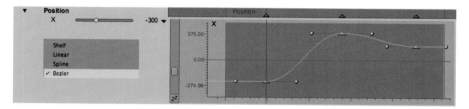

Figure 2.39
A Bézier curve.

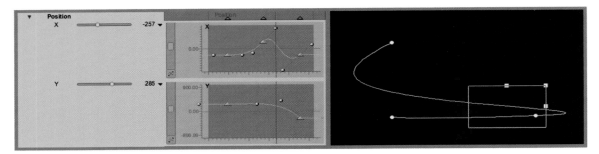

Figure 2.40
Adjusting the path with Bézier keyframes.

You can change the interpolation method in exactly the same way you change other keyframe options: by right-clicking the parameter track to affect just that parameter, right-clicking the group track to affect the whole group, or right-clicking the Effect Keyframe track to make the entire effect interpolate in the same way, and choosing the desired curve option from the menu that appears.

Note: Only one interpolation method is allowed within a single track. For example, if you start with a linear interpolation between the first and second keyframes, then you can't switch to spline between the second and third. If you want a variety of curves between keyframes however, then choose Bézier as the interpolation method for the greatest flexibility, as you will see momentarily.

Using Spline Mode

In spline mode, you affect how the effect starts and stops. An animation will start gradually, accelerate to the midpoint between keyframes, and then slow down gradually to the end. But if you use spline mode on the position parameters (X and Y in a PIP, for example) you also affect the *path* of the PIP. This is done in a very natural way.

Consider the case of just two keyframes on both the X and the Y parameters—one at the beginning and one at the end of an animation. In this case, the path is a straight line, but the PIP will start moving slowly, speed up, and then slow down again, as shown in Figure 2.41. The case for three keyframes is different, however. Now you can make the path of the PIP move in a natural curve so that the *direction* of the movement is affected, as shown in Figure 2.42.

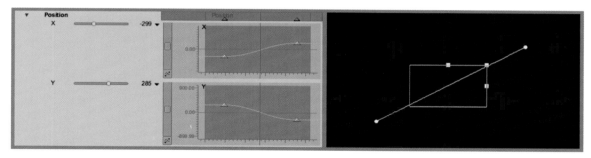

Figure 2.41
Spline path with two keyframes.

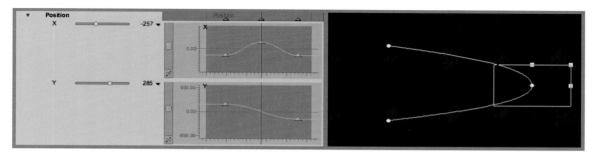

Figure 2.42
Spline path with three keyframes.

The good news is that in this case, the easing in and out of the *motion* of the PIP is calculated from just the first and last keyframes, which is exactly what you want. There is no ease-in or ease-out at the middle keyframes. Furthermore, if you want to hold a position so that there are two keyframes with identical values, you get the ease-in or ease-out of the motion and the path does not bounce at the hold point.

Keyframe Interpolation

In the old days, before keyframe graphs, the only way you could adjust the interpolation between keyframes was with a control called *acceleration*. This affected every keyframe in an effect. And although you had a curved path, the PIP would ease in and ease out at every keyframe, which caused a very unnatural motion. There were some spline controls in the 3D Warp effect that gave you slightly more control, but holding a position was even more of a problem because you would get a bounce at the hold keyframes, which had to be manually removed. Now everything is much easier!

Using Bézier Keyframes

Bézier keyframes enable you to adjust the amount of ease-in and ease-out on each side of the keyframe, whereas with spline keyframes, the ease-in and ease-out are automatically configured. This extra control allows you to create some interesting effects. For example, suppose you want a PIP (or any other object) to "bounce" into your frame. With spline, your PIP will slow down as it approaches the bottom of its path, but with Bézier you can make it accelerate all the way down and bounce back in a more natural way, as shown in Figure 2.43.

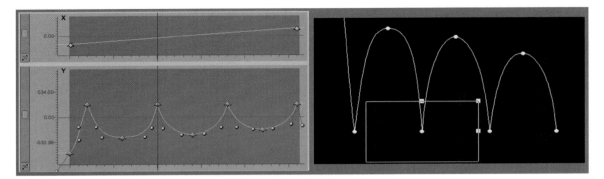

Figure 2.43
Using Bézier to make a bounce.

Bézier Curves

Bézier curves were first used by a French designer, Pierre Bézier, who used them to design automobile bodies. To control the shape of the curve, he used two handles at each point for making adjustments. Bézier handles crop up in many different places—particularly when drawing objects. You will also come across them when drawing shapes using the Paint tools (see Lesson 5, "Paint Effects"). The basic idea is that you have a point (in this case, a keyframe) that can be moved, and a path, the direction of which can be adjusted with the two handles. By default, the handles will be attached to each other so if you pull one up, the other goes down. If you pull the handle away from the point, the path will tend to veer off toward the handle rather than toward the next (or previous) keyframe. As a general rule, the curve will be smoother if you do not extend your Bézier handles more than one third of the distance between two keyframes in the direction you wish the path to go. (See Figure 2.44.)

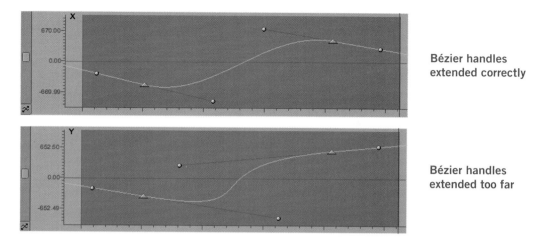

Bézier handles
extended correctly

Bézier handles
extended too far

Figure 2.44
An example of Bézier handles used correctly, and an example of these handles extended too far.

If you apply Bézier handles, you will see that the curve will ease in and ease out at a keyframe, as shown in Figure 2.45. You can increase the amount of ease-in and ease-out by pulling the handle horizontally away from the keyframe (see Figure 2.46). This will tend to reduce the acceleration of an object so that it starts to move very slowly, but increases more quickly. If you pull the handle toward the keyframe, you will reduce the ease-in or ease-out. If the handle is directly on top of the keyframe, there is no ease-in or ease-out, and your path will be similar to a linear interpolation, so there will be more or less no acceleration.

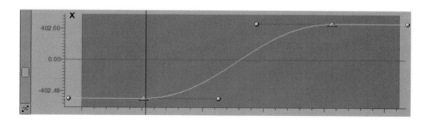

Figure 2.45
Bézier handles in the
default position.

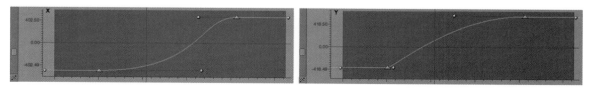

Figure 2.46
Bézier handles in the default position and extended and reduced horizontally.

If you drag the handle vertically, you can change the acceleration of your PIP in a different way. Now, instead of easing in, the PIP will continue to accelerate as it approaches the keyframe and then suddenly stop. If you drag the handle in the exact direction of the curve, you will remove all ease-in or acceleration. (See Figure 2.47.)

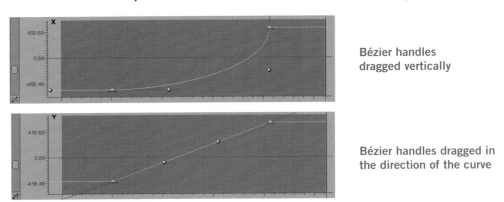

Bézier handles dragged vertically

Bézier handles dragged in the direction of the curve

Figure 2.47
Different ways of adjusting Bézier handles.

Locking and Unlocking Bézier Handles

Although the handles are locked together by default, so that moving one will move the other in the opposite direction, you can easily unlock them by Option-clicking (Mac) or Alt-clicking (Windows) the handle and dragging it to toggle between three possible configurations:

- **Asymmetrical.** In this configuration, the handles are unlocked in length, but locked in angle. (See Figure 2.48.) This is the default configuration.

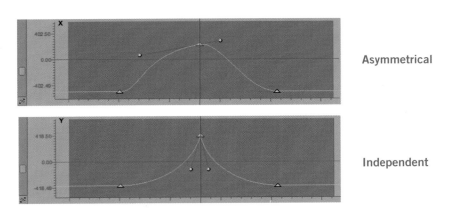

Asymmetrical

Independent

Figure 2.48
Unlocking Bézier handles.

- **Independent.** In this configuration, the handles are unlocked in both length and angle. This is used to create a bounce and any abrupt change in direction or acceleration.

- **Symmetrical.** In this configuration, the handles are locked in both length and angle. This makes the interpolation on each side of the keyframe the same. (See Figure 2.49.)

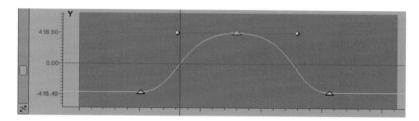

Figure 2.49
The Symmetrical configuration.

Understanding How Bézier Keyframes Affect the Motion Path

For many parameters, such as a resize or a fade-in, adjusting the shape of the graph simply changes how the parameter eases in or out. But when you adjust the position parameters, you are actually *moving* an object such as a PIP in X and Y space. The Bézier keyframes will change the *path* of an object as well as the acceleration. Changing the shape of the graph with Bézier handles will actually change the parameter's value at the points prior to and after the keyframe. You can see the path on the composer preview screen as long as the Outline/Path button is turned on. When you are using a single parameter and just two keyframes, the way it works is quite straightforward. When you combine motion in X and Y and you have more than two keyframes, however, it can get more complicated. Following are some examples.

Example 1: Changing the Path by Adjusting the Bézier Handle on a Single Keyframe

Suppose you have a PIP that animates across the screen, bouncing up and down as it does so. As shown in Figure 2.50, there are two keyframes for the X position (across the screen) and three for the Y: the start and end position at the bottom and the middle position at the top of the screen.

If you move the Bézier handle horizontally away from the first X keyframe, the trajectory will change: The X position will start to change more slowly, so because the Y position has not changed at a given point in time, the overall trajectory will appear to shift as shown in Figure 2.51. Moving the X handle vertically, however, will shift the trajectory in the other direction, as shown in Figure 2.52.

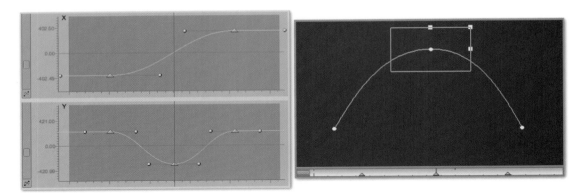

Figure 2.50
Bézier curves in the default positions.

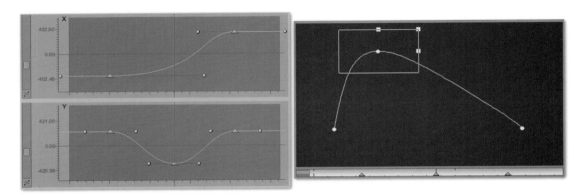

Figure 2.51
Shifting trajectory.

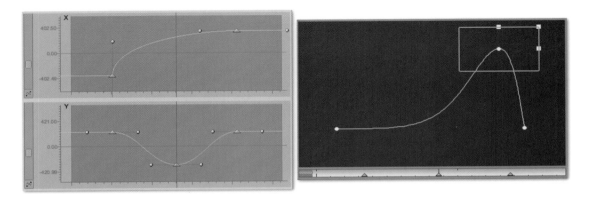

Figure 2.52
X handle, shifted vertically.

Another way to change the trajectory is to adjust the handles of the Y start and end frames so they move in the direction of the curve. Now you will get a bounce as shown in Figure 2.53.

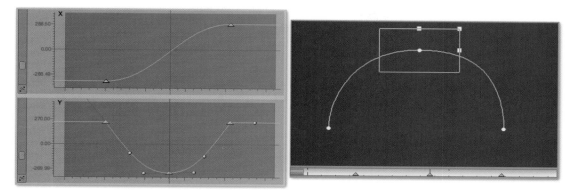

Figure 2.53
Hard bounce.

Example 2: Creating a Circular Path

Creating a circular path is done by making two sine curves for the X and Y positions. The key to making this work is to make all the Bézier handles symmetrical and adjust them so they all move in the direction of the path. The default is to add a slight kink at each keyframe, which means that the default path is not truly circular. Figure 2.54 shows a circular path with spline curves, while Figure 2.55 shows a circular path with Bézier curves.

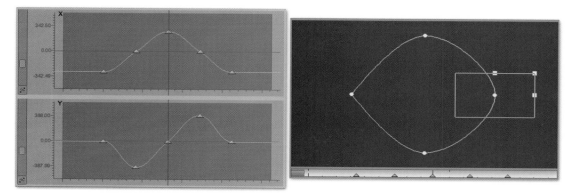

Figure 2.54
A circular path with spline curves.

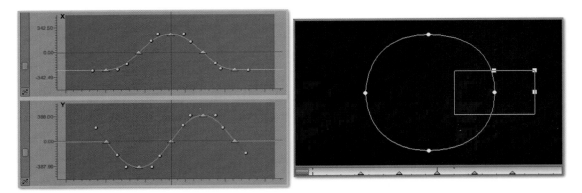

Figure 2.55
A circular path with Bézier curves.

Animating Beyond the Keyframes: Hold and Extrapolate

You can place the first keyframe anywhere you wish within an effect. However, you still have to consider the value of a parameter before the first (or after the last) keyframe. There are two options:

- **Hold.** This extends the value of the first keyframe to all frames prior to that keyframe and the value of the last keyframe to all subsequent frames. This is the default setting. Thus, an object will hold its position before and after the first and last keyframes. (See Figure 2.56 and Figure 2.57.)

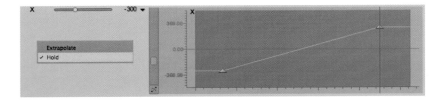

Figure 2.56
Hold for a linear graph.

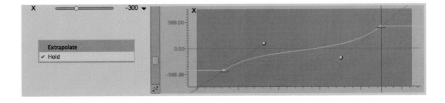

Figure 2.57
Hold for a Bézier graph.

■ **Extrapolate.** This calculates the value beyond the keyframes based on the path inside the keyframes. Note that you can't extrapolate when you are in spline mode because spline always eases the movement so that the graph trajectory is horizontal at the start and end keyframes. In Bézier mode, however, the trajectory is calculated based on the direction of the Bézier handle. (See Figure 2.58 and Figure 2.59.)

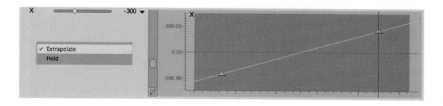

Figure 2.58
Extrapolate for a linear graph.

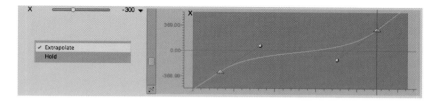

Figure 2.59
Extrapolate for a Bézier graph.

The Extrapolate function enables you to animate a parameter beyond its normal limits. For example, by default, a rotation goes to plus or minus 720 degrees, which only gives you four rotations. (See the next lesson.) By turning on Extrapolate, however, you can have as many rotations as you wish!

Note: As usual, you can turn on Extrapolate for just the individual parameter by right-clicking the parameter track, the group by right-clicking in the group track, or all parameters in the effect by right-clicking the Effect Keyframe track.

Review/Discussion Questions

1. How can you control where keyframes are added when you click the Add Keyframe button?

2. Which of the following statements is true?

    a. Aligning keyframes moves selected keyframes in multiple tracks to the same point in time without affecting other keyframes in the track, whereas slipping keyframes will move all the keyframes in a track so that the first keyframes are all aligned.

    b. Aligning keyframes moves all the keyframes in a track so that the first keyframes are all aligned, whereas slipping keyframes will move a group of keyframes to the same point in time without affecting other keyframes in the track.

    c. Aligning keyframes moves selected keyframes in the same track to the same point in time, whereas slipping keyframes will move all selected keyframes so they align with the first one.

3. How do you reverse keyframes for a single parameter group? Fill in the blanks:

    1. Right-click the _____ _____.

    2. Choose _____ _____ from the menu.

4. What kind of keyframes are these and what is the difference between these and normal keyframes?

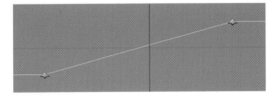

5. What are the four different keyframe interpolation modes and what does each one do?

6. How do you remove all the ease-in or ease-out at a Bézier keyframe?

    a. Switch to Hold mode.

    b. Move the handle so it coincides with the keyframe.

    c. Option-click (Mac) or Alt-click (PC) to break the handles and move it to the vertical position.

7. What would you do if you wanted to have more rotations for an object than the usual four?

8. How do you jump from keyframe to keyframe in the Keyframe scrollbar?

    a. Use the A and S keys.

    b. Use the 3 and 4 keys.

    c. Use the Fast Forward and Rewind buttons.

9. How do you nudge the position of a keyframe?

10. What is a redundant keyframe and how do you remove it?

Lesson 2 Keyboard Shortcuts

Key	Shortcut
M	Nudge keyframe 10 frames left
, (comma)	Nudge keyframe one frame left
. (period)	Nudge keyframe one frame right
/ (forward slash)	Nudge keyframe 10 frames right
← (left arrow)	Move position indicator one frame left
→ (right arrow)	Move position indicator one frame right
A (when in Effect mode)	Jump to the previous segment
S (when in Effect mode)	Jump to the next segment
Command+A (Mac)/Ctrl+A (Windows)	Select all (for example, all keyframes)
Shift+Command+A (Mac)/Shift+Ctrl+A (Windows)	Deselect all

Creating a Simple Animation

Mad Dogs Post House facility is back for more! Betty was pleased with the video wall you created in Lesson 1, but she wants it to animate. That is, she wants to create a transition between the various clips in the original sequence.

Media Used:

Open the Bin 02 Exercises to find your material.

Duration:

45 minutes

GOAL

- Create a simple animation and experiment with different interpolation methods

Animating the Video Wall

You will start with the macaw and transition into the yellow bird. The transition needs to be 2 seconds. In the first second, the picture will reduce from full screen into the top-left corner, revealing the other three pictures underneath. Then, the top-right picture will animate out to fit the full screen. (See Figure 2.60.) If you would like to see this animation play through, you will find a clip in the 02 Exercises bin called Exercise 1 transition mixdown.

Figure 2.60
Video wall animation.

Again, think about how you will create this effect. You'll need the original PIPs as a starting point, but you'll need to apply some animation. You'll need a background picture as well. You'll also need to change the order of the layers so that the macaw is on top during the first part of the transition, but the yellow bird is on top during the second. Let's see how this might work.

1. Load the **EXERCISE 01** sequence from the 02 Exercises bin. It has the macaw shot and the background shot ready for you.

2. You'll need some more video tracks. Press **COMMAND+Y** (Mac) or **CTRL+Y** (Windows) a few times until you have five tracks in total.

3. Add two seconds of each of the clips on top of the soft water background clip. Put the macaw clip on the top track (V5). Except for the macaw clip, all these should start from the beginning of the clip. The macaw clip, however, needs to be match framed so that it carries on from the clip on track 1.

4. To match frame correctly, go to the *last* frame of the macaw on track V1, just before the soft water shot. Then, with **V1** highlighted, open the Timeline **FAST** menu and choose **MATCH FRAME**.

5. The shot will load into the source monitor. In the source monitor advance *one* frame and mark a new IN point.

6. Edit two seconds of this clip onto track V5. It should now play without jumping when you get to the transition.

7. Apply the PIP effect. To save you time, these have been copied from the previous lesson. Put the top-left PIP on the macaw, the top-right PIP on the yellow bird, and so on.

8. Now for the animation. Let's start with the macaw. He needs to start full frame and shrink to 40 percent after 1 second. He also needs to move to the top left. But you also need to make the border vanish when the clip is full frame. You can adjust the static PIP quite easily by adding some keyframes. To start, switch to Effect mode and make sure the top track is highlighted.

9. You need to animate three things: the position, the scaling, and the border width. The last part of the shot has the frame in the correct position, so we just need to adjust the start. Open the **BORDER WIDTH** (note the border width is in the **BLEND** subcategory of the **BORDER** parameter group), **SCALING**, and **POSITION** parameters and expand their graphs. Your Effect Editor should look something like Figure 2.61.

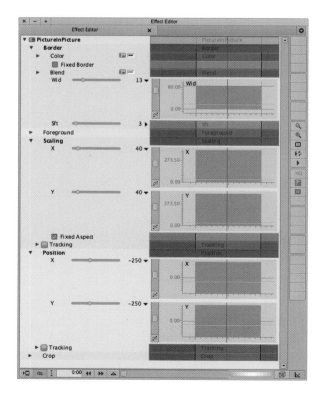

Figure 2.61
Effect Editor.

10. Move your blue position indicator until you are halfway through the effect, at 1 second.

11. Click the **ADD KEYFRAME** button at the bottom of the Effect Editor to add a keyframe to the open graphs.

12. Move to the first frame and repeat. You should have two keyframes on all the open graphs.

13. Adjust the first keyframes so that the border width is 0, the scaling is 100 (remember to enable the **FIXED ASPECT** setting), and the position is 0 for X and Y.

Tip: **You can easily jump from one selected slider to the next by pressing the Tab key. Pressing Shift+Tab will jump you backward to the previous slider.**

14. Scroll through the effect. The macaw will animate to the top-left corner.

Using Bézier Curves

Betty thinks you can do better. She thinks the animation is a bit linear. She wants the path to start heading toward the center and then veer off to the corner. You can impress her by using Bézier curves to do this.

1. In the Position parameters, click the **ZOOM TO CURVE HEIGHT** button to expand the curve a little and set the interpolation type to Bézier if it is not already.

2. Adjust the curve handles so the positions of both X and Y start horizontally and then dip down to the final keyframe. Your curves should look a bit like Figure 2.62. You may need to experiment a bit to get an animation that you are happy with.

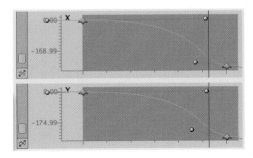

Figure 2.62
Position graphs.

Tip: Older systems might struggle to play five layers of HD in real time, so you can solo the V5 track to view just your animation.

3. Next, you need to do the same for the yellow bird clip, only the other way round. To start, click the yellow bird clip on V4.

4. Add keyframes at all the open graphs at both the midpoint and the *last* keyframe.

5. Set the parameters on the last keyframe to default, just as you did before.

6. Adjust the Bézier handles of the Position parameters so the bird does a similar type of move from the top right to center frame.

7. Play back the effect by soloing V4. Make sure you are happy with your work.

Changing the Clip Order

There is only one more thing to fix. When you turn on V5 again, you will see that although the animation is fine, the yellow bird is behind the macaw. This is because the bird video track is underneath the macaw track. You can fix this with an add edit.

1. Park your blue position indicator halfway along the effect.

2. Select the top two tracks and click the Add Edit button.

Using an Add Edit to Split an Effect

The Add Edit button is great for splitting a clip, but it is also very useful for splitting an effect. What it does is to slice the animation into two sections. The keyframes will exactly match at the cut so that the animation is seamless, even though you may put the resulting clips on to a different track.

3. You've split your effect in two on the top two tracks. You need to shuffle them around a bit, but you'll temporarily need a new video track to do this. Create a new video track.

4. Swap the clips so the second half of the effect has the bird on top, like in Figure 2.63.

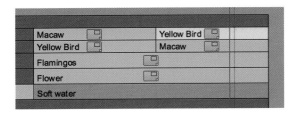

Figure 2.63
The bird is on the top track at the end of the effect.

5. Of course, you don't want the sequence to finish at the last frame of the expanding bird effect. You need this to be a transition effect, so the bird shot must continue after the transition. Click the **MATCH FRAME** button to load the last frame of the bird shot.

6. Step forward one frame in the source monitor and edit in the rest of the bird shot.

7. As a final touch, you might wish to add the Color Correction effect for the bird (provided in the bin) both to the full frame shot on track 1 and by stepping in to the PIP effect on *both* halves of the clip in the effect.

Congratulations! You have designed a nice transition. Betty is very happy. If you have time, you could try to do the same again at the next transition. After five seconds of the full frame bird clip, you can try to animate the bird clip down and the flamingo clip up.

Using the 3D Warp Effect

The 3D Warp effect is the Swiss Army knife of Media Composer. It is found in the Blend category. There is also a 3D lite version in the Xpress 3D group, which has some of the parameters removed. Both can be applied as a segment or transition effect. This lesson introduces you to the features of this tool, which allows you to manipulate clips in 3D space and much more besides.

Media Used: The media for this lesson is in the MC205 Pro Effects project. Open the bin called Lesson 03 3D Warp.

Duration: 45 minutes

GOALS

- Apply the 3D Warp effect as a segment and transition effect
- Use the direct manipulation tools
- Understand the order of processing
- Understand 3D space
- Use borders and highlights
- Apply defocus, shadows, and shapes
- Understand the foreground options

Applying the 3D Warp Effect

As you saw in Lesson 1, "Effect Design and Techniques," many effects can be used as both segment effects and transition effects. For example you may wish to make a PIP with additional features such as rotation, or perhaps you want to animate a clip off the screen to reveal another, or animate a new clip onto the screen. You can do all of this and much more with 3D Warp.

Applying the 3D Warp as a Segment Effect

When you drop the effect onto a segment, by default nothing happens. It is up to you to use the various parameters to create the many different types of effects. For example, you might wish to reduce the size of the image either by cropping or scaling, to apply a rotation, perhaps to blur the picture, and even to apply a highlight. You can apply 3D Warp to multiple layers to quickly make video walls and animations that involve multiple pictures animating around the screen.

Applying the 3D Warp as a Transition Effect

If you drop a 3D Warp effect onto the transition between two clips, it is applied as a transition effect, which means you can use it to somehow move one of the images on or off the screen, revealing the other. By default, the 3D Warp effect is applied to the *incoming* shot—the one that is further down the Timeline. Thus, when you open the Effect Editor, you will see the new shot in the Effect Editor Composer window; if you apply some kind of position change, you'll see the outgoing shot underneath. You can change this so that you are manipulating the *outgoing* shot to reveal the new one by clicking the Swap Sources button in the Foreground parameter group. (I'll discuss this more later.)

Basic Concepts

When referring to 3D space, the terms X, Y, and Z refer to the three axes or dimensions of the image that you can manipulate in the 3D effect's coordinate space (see Figure 3.1):

- X refers to the left/right direction (with values increasing from left to right)

- Y refers to the up/down direction (with values increasing from bottom to top)

- Z refers to the front/back direction (with values increasing from back to front)

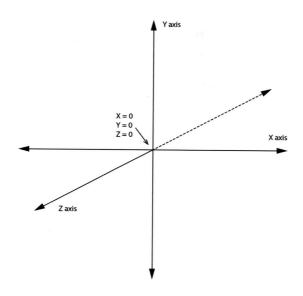

Figure 3.1
The coordinates of 3D space,
with Z coming out of the page.

The Rotation parameters in the 3D Warp effect let you rotate the image around the X, Y, and Z axes. Note that you can rotate from −720 to 720 degrees, which is the equivalent of four turns. Figure 3.2 shows how angles of rotation (in degrees) are distributed around a circle, where a positive number gives a clockwise rotation and a negative number gives a counterclockwise rotation.

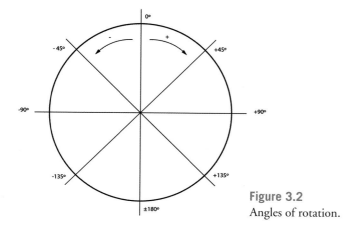

Figure 3.2
Angles of rotation.

For the following sections, load up the Exploring the 3D Warp sequence in the Lesson 03 3D Warp bin and open the Effect Editor so you can follow along.

Promoting to 3D

You can promote many effects to 3D by clicking the Promote button (see Figure 3.3) at the bottom of the Effect Editor window. For example, if you start with a PIP, you might wish to include rotation or movement in the Z space as part of your effect. When you promote a basic PIP to a 3D Warp, you will see a larger list of parameters in your Effect Editor window, as shown in Figure 3.4. As you can see, there are not only many extra parameters, but there are also extra features, such as the enable buttons, and additional toolbar buttons on the right side. (See Figure 3.5.)

Figure 3.3
The Promote button.

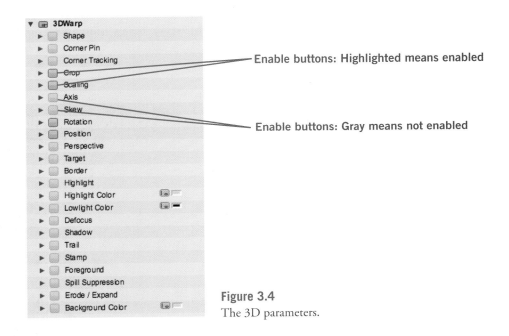

Figure 3.4
The 3D parameters.

Figure 3.5
The Direct Manipulation buttons.

Using the Enable Buttons

Next to the triangle, which you can click to expand each group of parameters, is a small enable button. Clicking this toggles the corresponding parameter on and off without resetting. If the buttons are active, they are colored with the highlight color that you choose in the Interface settings. If they are inactive, they are gray. As soon as you change a parameter, the enable button is active. If you deactivate the button, the changes are no longer applied, but they are saved. When you reactivate the button, the changes will be reapplied.

The really good thing about the enable buttons is that you can also use them to *reset* individual parameters by Option-clicking (Mac) or Alt-clicking (Windows) the button. When you do this, your changes are discarded and the parameter is returned to its default settings.

Direct Manipulation of the Image

On the right side of the Effect Editor are a series of buttons that allow you to directly manipulate the image in the Effect Editor preview monitor. When you click the different buttons, you will see the handles at the edge of the image change depending on how they function. There is also a small upward-pointing arrow in the bottom-right corner to show you the orientation of the image. If you flip the image around so you are looking at the back, it will fill with a negative of the image inside the arrow.

Note: Whenever you move the image using direct manipulation, you will create
         a keyframe at that point in time. In Lesson 2, "Animating with Keyframes,"
         you saw that if you move the sliders or thumbwheels, no keyframes are
         created if there are none to start with. However, when using the on-screen
         tools, you will create a keyframe regardless.

There are several direct-manipulation modes:

■ **Scale.** As shown in Figure 3.6, this mode gives you three handles. Grab the top-right corner for fixed aspect scaling or the top and side handles for Y only and X only. You can also move the image around with this mode.

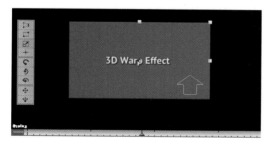

Figure 3.6
Scale handles.

■ **Crop.** This mode, shown in Figure 3.7, lets you crop top and right together and bottom and left together.

Figure 3.7
Crop handles.

■ **Corner Pin.** In this mode, shown in Figure 3.8, you can grab each corner and move it as you wish to reshape the image.

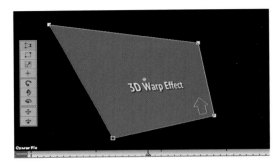

Figure 3.8
Corner Pin handles.

■ **Axis.** This mode, shown in Figure 3.9, lets you move the axis in relation to the image so you can modify how the rotation is applied.

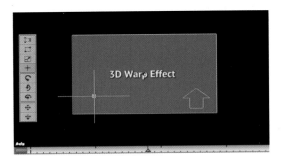

Figure 3.9
Axis shifted bottom left.

Note: The axis can also be moved in the Z direction so your image, enabling you to rotate your image in the X and Y planes so it comes in and out of the screen. You can't do this with direct manipulation mode, however. You must open the Axis group and adjust the parameter slider.

- **Z Axis Rotation.** This mode, shown in Figure 3.10, lets you spin the image around the Z axis.

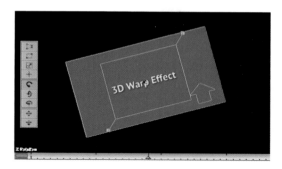

Figure 3.10
Z Axis Rotation mode.

- **X Axis Rotation.** This mode, shown in Figure 3.11, lets you spin the image around the X axis.

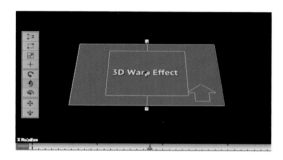

Figure 3.11
X Axis Rotation mode.

- **Y Axis Rotation.** This mode, shown in Figure 3.12, lets you spin the image around the Y axis.

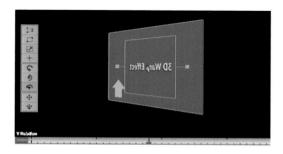

Figure 3.12
Y Axis Rotation mode.

Note: You can't change the order rotations are applied. For example you may wish to rotate in the X axis *before* rotating in the Z axis. This is not possible in the 3D Warp effect. As you will see in Lesson 10, "Introducing Avid FX," however, you can easily do this in Avid FX.

■ **XY and XZ Movement.** In addition, you can further manipulate the image in the X and Y plane or the X and Z plane, as shown in Figure 3.13 and Figure 3.14, respectively.

Figure 3.13
XY Movement mode.

Figure 3.14
XZ Movement mode.

Order of Processing the Parameters

All the parameters in the 3D Warp effect are processed in the order they appear in the Effect Editor from top to bottom. This may not be important for some of the effects you wish to create, but when you are applying movement to a PIP on certain trajectories, you will see the order that a parameter is applied does make a difference. For example, suppose rotation is applied before position; that is, you apply rotation and then move the result. Suppose further that you want to rotate an image in the Y axis and then wish to apply an animation in the X position so that the rotated picture moves across the screen. (See Figure 3.15 and Figure 3.16.)

In this example, you can see that the PIP moves across the screen but does not get further from the viewer. What you see is a change in *perspective,* not size. If you had applied a change in position first and then rotated the entire plane, including the path of the animation, the PIP would appear to move back into the screen and get smaller as it moved away from you.

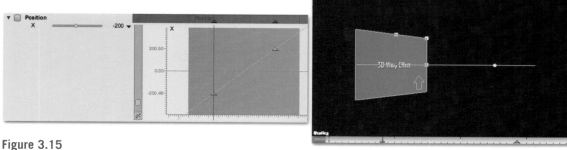

Figure 3.15
Rotated image at start of move.

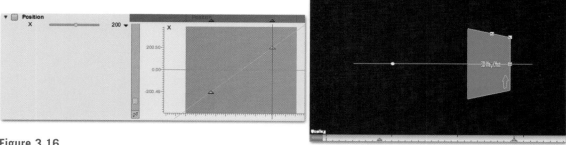

Figure 3.16
Rotated image at end of move.

In some cases you may wish to achieve that result, so you could, for example, fake this process by applying animation to the Z position so the image appears to go back into the page (see Figure 3.17). There is an element of guesswork in doing this, however. To get it absolutely right, you can use Avid FX, as you shall see later.

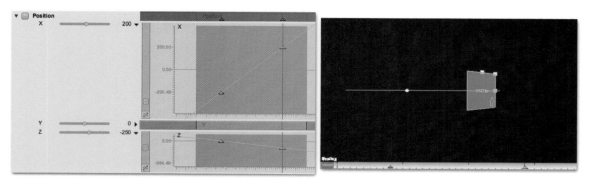

Figure 3.17
Rotated image with Z position animation.

To better understand the impact of order of processing, let's look at two parameters that appear some distance down in the parameter list, meaning they are processed after many others.

Perspective and Target

Below the basic 3D manipulation parameters you will see Perspective and Target options. Although these tend to be overlooked, they are actually quite powerful. To see how they work, load the Exploring the 3D Warp–Perspective sequence and enter Effects Mode.

Imagine you are in a TV studio looking at a stage, and you have a camera that is filming a rectangle—your 16×9 (or 4×3, if you are still in the dark ages) image. You have applied some animation in the X axis (relative to the camera plane, not the rectangle itself). For this, imagine your image is on a small track so it can move from left to right. How the image appears in the camera screen depends on two things: the camera lens angle and the camera position.

Perspective

To understand the Perspective parameters, think of the vanishing point that is always present in drawings that simulate a three-dimensional appearance. All parallel lines appear to converge at the vanishing point (see Figure 3.18). When you adjust the Perspective parameters, shown in Figure 3.19, you are moving your camera, and the position of the image is changing with respect to a vanishing point. The camera can move in or out (with the Z control), up and down (with the Y control), or side to side (with the X control). Perspective allows you to adjust your camera position so you can look at your entire animation from a different position.

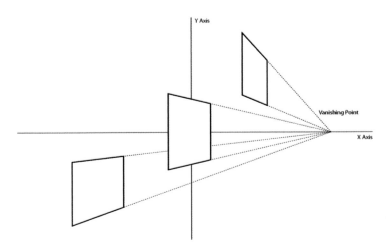

Figure 3.18
Vanishing point with three objects in three different positions.

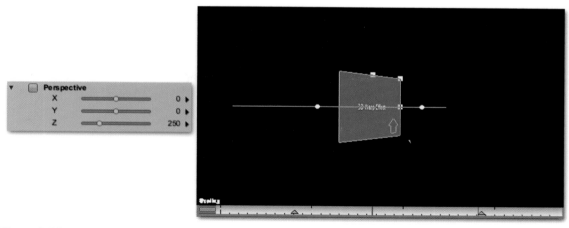

Figure 3.19
Perspective parameter in default settings.

Park your position indicator somewhere in the middle of the move from left to right and try changing the Perspective parameters. Perhaps the most obvious is the Z control; when you decrease Z, you are moving toward your image and your sense of perspective is exaggerated (see Figure 3.20). The vanishing point is very close to your image. When you increase Z, you are moving further from your image, and the sense of perspective is much reduced (see Figure 3.21). The front edge and the rear edge are almost the same.

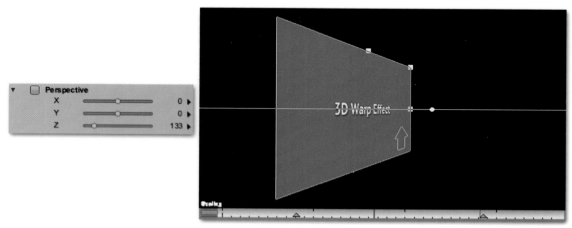

Figure 3.20
Adjusting the Perspective Z control (move in).

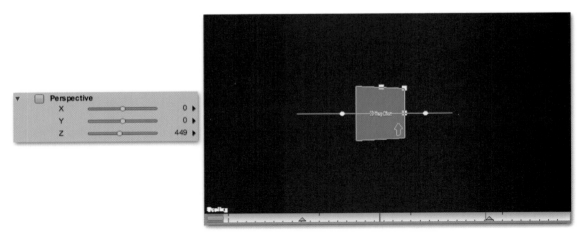

Figure 3.21
Adjusting the Perspective Z control (move out).

In a similar way, the X and Y Perspective parameters give the appearance of adjusting your camera position in the X and Y plane, but you are actually moving it in respect to your imaginary vanishing point. When you adjust the X parameter, you are moving from side to side (see Figure 3.22 and Figure 3.23); adjusting the Y parameter moves you up and down (see Figure 3.24).

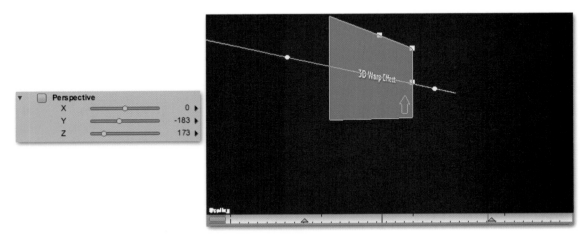

Figure 3.22
Adjusting the Perspective X control (camera moves right; image moves left).

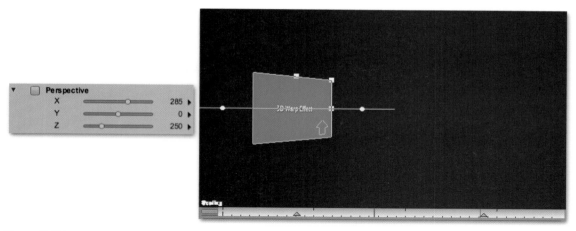

Figure 3.23
Adjusting the Perspective X control (camera moves left; image moves right).

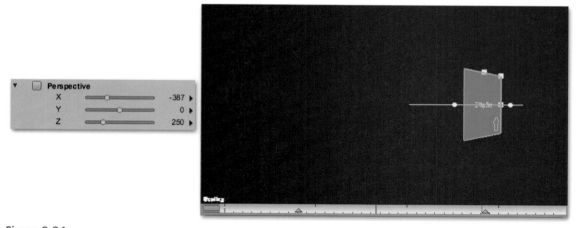

Figure 3.24
Adjusting the Perspective Y control (camera moves down). In other words, *you* are moving down and looking at the image from a lower point of view.

Target

In addition to moving your camera, you can change the lens angle. Most cameras have a zoom function, often measured in terms of millimeters. Thus, a wide angle lens might be 20mm, a standard field of view lens might be 50mm, and a telephoto lens might be anything from 85mm to 300mm or more. When you change the camera lens angle, you "zoom" into the image. This appears to make the image bigger, but the perspective is not affected; the vanishing point and all the imaginary lines leading to it are moving with the image. Think of this as a global parameter—it affects *everything*: the position of the object, including the animation, and the position of the vanishing point.

For the rotated image in the demo sequence, you can try adjusting the Target controls and see how it differs from adjusting Perspective parameters. This type of movement does not affect the perspective; whether you zoom in or out with the Size control (see Figure 3.25 and Figure 3.26), from side to side with the X control, or up and down with the Y control, you are shifting the entire image—with its animation—but not affecting the perspective.

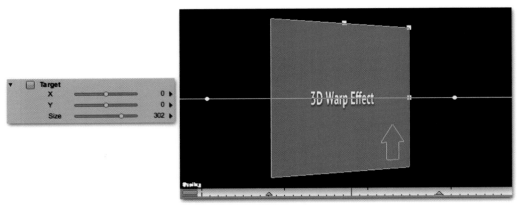

Figure 3.25
Increasing target size.

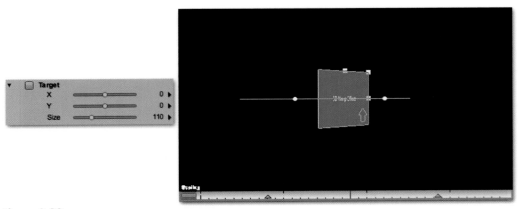

Figure 3.26
Decreasing target size.

As mentioned earlier, there is a processing order for all these parameter groups. You apply Target transformations after you have applied all the other parameters, including Position and Perspective transformations. You can adjust the Position controls to place your image, and the Perspective controls to get the required amount of perspective in an image, and then you can adjust the Target controls to make *overall* adjustments to everything in your animation.

Note: It is of course possible to animate the Perspective and Target controls to achieve all kinds of strange results. For example you can simulate a zoom and a camera move (also known as a "dolly") at the same time so the image stays the same size on the screen, but the perspective is wildly changing. (See Figure 3.27 and Figure 3.28.)

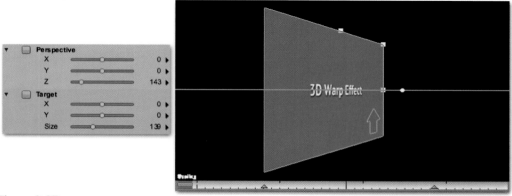

Figure 3.27
Zoom out and move dolly in.

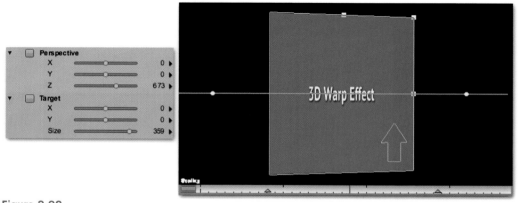

Figure 3.28
Zoom in and move dolly out.

Finally, a word about the difference between Scale and Z Position. If you scale an image, it appears to have the same effect as adjusting the position in Z space. But there is a subtle difference when you animate movement: An object moving away from the viewer appears to move more slowly as it gets further away. Conversely, as it gets closer to the viewer, it appears to move more quickly. The 3D Warp effect emulates this visual perception when an object is moved in Z. However, if an image is resized by scaling it, the rate of movement does not change. A small but important difference.

Now let's put some of this knowledge to practice.

Using the 3D Warp to Make a Mac Cover Flow Effect

If you are familiar with the Mac interface, you may have seen the Cover Flow view, where you have a series of pictures in a folder that animate as you scroll through them. (See Figure 3.29.) You are going to try to re-create this type of animation for just one picture and its reflection. This will introduce a lot of the basic concepts of the 3D Warp effect.

Figure 3.29
Cover Flow effect.

Note: In the "Exercises" section at the end of this lesson, you will take this a bit further—and look at some of the challenges when using more than one picture!

First, you need to find a picture to use for your effect. You can do this with still or moving pictures, but for this example, let's use a still image. You are going to start the image in the right side of the screen, animate to the middle, blow it up slightly, and then animate it to the left side applying some rotation as well. Then we will create a reflection to give it a touch of class!

To create the Mac Cover Flow effect:

1. Open the **LESSON 03 3D WARP** bin and locate the **COVERFLOW** sequence. This contains a 10-second still image and a black background.

2. Drag the 3D Warp onto the top clip and enter Effect Mode.

3. Crop the picture a little bit to get the proportions right at the sides, as shown in Figure 3.30.

Figure 3.30
Apply a little crop.

4. Now for the scaling. This is going to animate, so you need to start at 30 percent and go to 40 percent for the middle part of the animation. You also need to consider the timing. Let's say you'll hold at 30 percent for 1.5 seconds, animate to 40 percent during the next 1.5 seconds, and then hold for 4 seconds. Then you'll shrink back down to 30 percent during the next 1.5 seconds and then hold for the rest of the effect. To begin, add four keyframes in the Scaling parameter. Your curves should look something like what's shown in Figure 3.31.

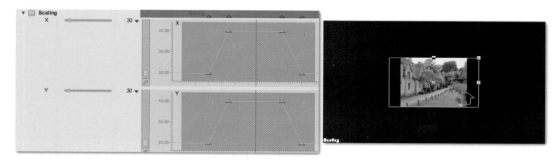

Figure 3.31
Scaling keyframes added.

Tip: Remember you can increase the scaling of your animation graph by clicking the Zoom to Curve Height button.

5. To get a true Cover Flow feel to the animation, you need to change the way the image scales. It is not a smooth increase in size but a sudden snap, followed by a smooth deceleration. To do this easily, convert your keyframes to Bézier and adjust them so they look like Figure 3.32. Remember the three modes with Bézier: asymmetrical, independent, and symmetrical. For this to work, you need to Option-click (Mac) or Alt-click (Windows) the handles to convert them to independent.

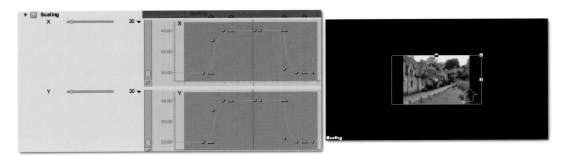

Figure 3.32
Bézier keyframing.

6. The image needs to start on the right side, move to the middle, and then end up on the left, so you need to add four keyframes in exactly the same place as for the scaling. You are only animating the X position, so open the X graph and add four keyframes directly on the graph as shown in Figure 3.33. Again, you need to use Bézier curves to get that snap effect. The X position should be set to 300 and −300 on the outside keyframes.

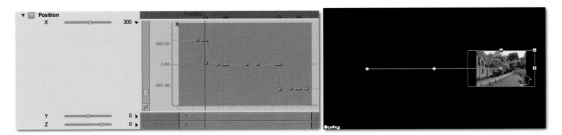

Figure 3.33
Positioning keyframes with Bézier.

7. Now you are ready for the rotation. To do this, add four more keyframes in the same place as before, with the same Bézier curve effect. This time, the rotation is going to be from −40 to 40 on the Y parameter. (See Figure 3.34.)

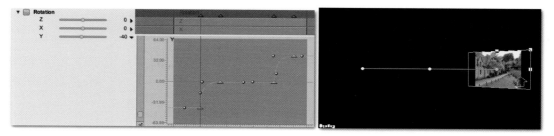

Figure 3.34
Rotation keyframes with Bézier.

8. You are almost there! But just to make it look a little more realistic, you want to adjust the perspective. If you look at Figure 3.29, you'll see that the photos in the window are quite elongated when they are at the side. Also, the tops of all the photos are completely flat. You can make this happen with a combination of Perspective and Target controls. Adjust the **Z PERSPECTIVE** control for a more exaggerated look to the perspective when the object is rotated. However, this will make the photos bigger, and you'll cut them off the screen. So use the Target control's **SIZE** parameter to make the overall size of the entire animation a bit smaller. There is no animation here; these adjustments apply throughout the whole animation.

9. Finally, you can move the **Y PERSPECTIVE** control so the top of the image is flat when it is on the side of the screen. You will also want to use the **TARGET Y** parameter to globally move the animation upward to make room for the reflection! The end result should look something like Figure 3.35.

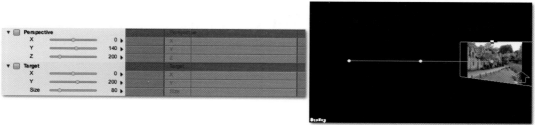

Figure 3.35
The final adjustments.

10. Play the clip. You'll see the photo animate from right to left.

11. If time permits have a go at the reflection. It is quite easy—just copy the effect and reuse it with some slight modifications. If you don't have time, there is a sequence called Coverflow Reflection that shows you the finished effect.

12. You need to copy the same effect onto track V2. The easy way to do this is to press **T** to mark the clip and press **OPTION+COMMAND+C** (Mac) or **ALT+CTRL+C** (Windows) to copy the entire clip with the 3D Warp to the Source monitor. (You'll need to leave effects mode for this.) Now edit this into track V2. Go back to Effects Mode; you will now make some minor adjustments to the effect on V2.

13. For the reflection, you will need to rotate the image 180 degrees. Before you do that, however, you will need to move the axis. You'll be shifting the Y position of the axis downward (you can turn on the Axis button so you can see exactly where it goes). Don't try to manipulate it on screen, as you'll add unwanted keyframes. Just use the slider—but watch the axis move. If you want a small gap between the image and the reflection, you'll need to move it just below the picture. In this example, –510 works well.

14. Set your X rotation to 180 and set the **OPACITY** (in the Foreground section) to around 25 percent. There you have it—a nice animation that makes good use of the Perspective and Target controls! (See Figure 3.36.)

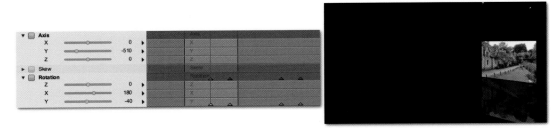

Figure 3.36
The finished effect.

Handling Transitions with the 3D Warp

Quite often you will want to have one picture animate off the screen in some way. Or perhaps you'll want to have another picture animate on the screen, or have both the outgoing and incoming picture animate. While there are many premade wipes, pushes, and squeezes in the list of effects in the Effect Palette, you have more control with 3D Warp. Let's try a simple case of making the outgoing image swoop off the screen to reveal the incoming picture.

To create the swooping transition effect:

1. Load the **3D TRANSITION** sequence into your Timeline.

2. Apply the 3D Warp effect to the transition between the first two shots.

3. Type **2.00** in the **DURATION** field at the bottom of the Effect Editor.

4. Because you want to animate the outgoing shot, you need to swap sources. Click the **FOREGROUND** triangle to display the Foreground options; then click **SWAP SOURCES**, as shown in Figure 3.37.

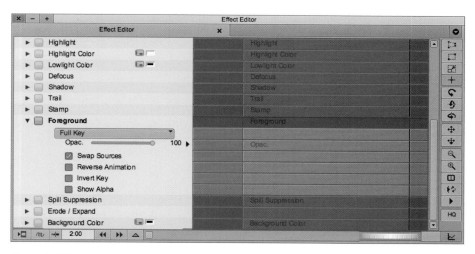

Figure 3.37
The Swap Sources check box.

5. Start by animating the size of the outgoing shot. It starts at 100 percent; you need to reduce it to around 25 percent. To begin, add a keyframe at the start and end of both the X and Y scaling, as shown in Figure 3.38.

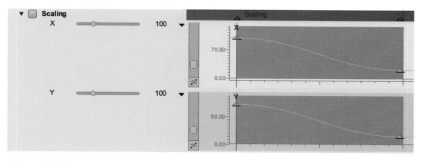

Figure 3.38
Animating the scaling.

6. The rest is up to you. Add keyframes at the start and end of the X and Y position and one in the middle. Then perform some animation with Bézier curves. (See Figure 3.39.) The idea is that you start with the shot in the center of the screen and by the end of the effect it will be off screen. The path it takes is up to you!

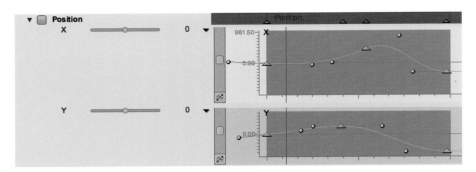

Figure 3.39
Animating the position.

7. Finally, the rotation. Experiment with different rotations in the X, Y, or Z axes. (See Figure 3.40.) You can even change the axis position if you like. Your image will lift off the screen, reduce in size, and gently swoop out of the edge of frame.

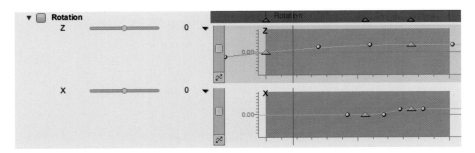

Figure 3.40
Animating the rotation.

8. If you are happy with your transition, you may wish to use it again. To save it to a bin, drag the icon in the top-left corner of the Effect Editor. Alternatively, drag the icon directly to the next transition in the sequence.

A Quick Guide to the Remaining Features

Most of the other parameter groups are fairly self-evident, but there are some useful things hidden away in various places. Load the sequence Exploring the 3D Warp–Remaining Features and enter Effects Mode to explore further.

- **Skew.** This feature enables you to distort the image by either skewing or shearing it in the X direction or the Y direction. (See Figure 3.41.)

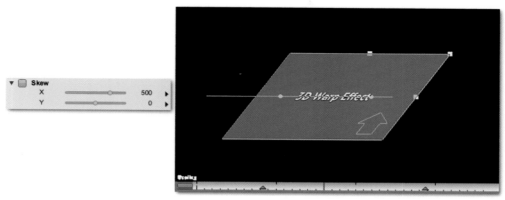

Figure 3.41
Skew.

- **Border.** While you don't get the two-tone border that comes with the PIP, you do get some simulated 3D edges to enhance your border, as shown in Figure 3.42.

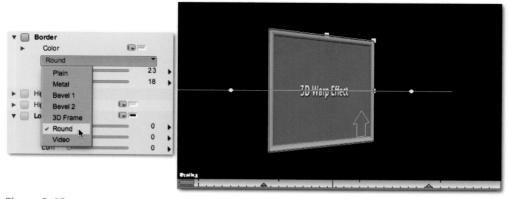

Figure 3.42
Border.

■ **Highlight.** This basically shines a spotlight onto your image, as shown in Figure 3.43. With the default settings, it may not appear to be of much use. However, by adjusting the various controls—for example, adjusting the aspect and applying a bit of animation with the X and Y controls—you can simulate a glint or flash of light across your image. As shown in Figure 3.44, the color of this highlight can be adjusted with the Highlight Color controls.

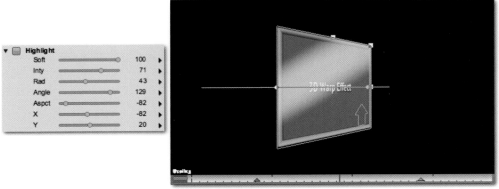

Figure 3.43
Highlight.

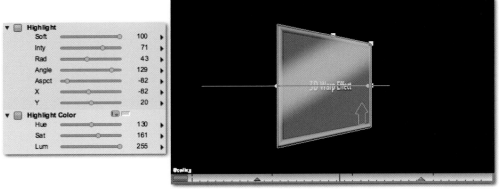

Figure 3.44
Adjusting the highlight color.

■ **Lowlight Color.** This control is a bit more subtle. In fact, when you turn it on, nothing happens, at which point most people give up. However, you can create a useful knock-back effect with this parameter. The secret is to go to the very first group: the Shape group at the top of the Effect Editor.

Hidden away in the drop-down menu is a Reverse Manual Highlight option, which you need to select. (See Figure 3.45.) This will also enable the page curl; since this isn't what you want now, deselect the Shape enable button. The lowlight will remain, enabling you to create an interest point on a specific part of the image and knock back the rest. Note that Highlight must be on for Lowlight Color to work.

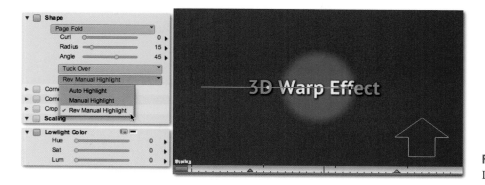

Figure 3.45
Lowlight color.

Note: The Lowlight Color can't be tracked, but you can adjust and animate the position and size with the Highlight X and Y controls. Should you wish to go one further and track a highlight or lowlight—for example, to follow someone moving in a crowd—you can do this with the Intraframe tools. For more information, see Lesson 5, "Paint Effects."

■ **Defocus.** Should you wish to apply a blur to your entire image, you can do so with this control. As shown in Figure 3.46, there are two modes: Internal and FG Only. Internal applies a small amount of defocus, whereas FG Only lets you blur your image right away. I think of them as "little blur" and "big blur."

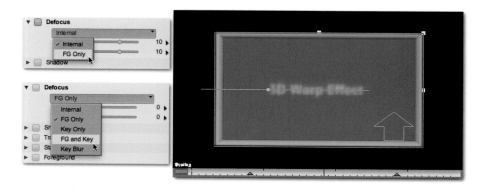

Figure 3.46
Defocus.

Note: This is a great effect when you want to blur titles in and out. You can promote
a title to 3D to animate your titles in 3D space, but you can also apply
defocus. When you go to the Defocus group, you'll see some extra options;
because your title is keyed onto the layer below, you need to choose FG
and Key so the key matte is blurred as well.

- **Shadow.** You can apply a shadow to your image (see Figure 3.47), but no
  soft edge. However, this can be achieved quite easily with a simple cheat. See
  the upcoming exercises for more details.

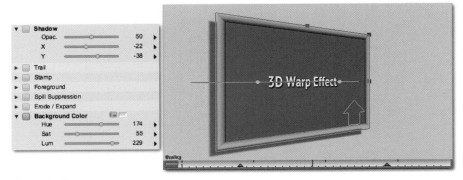

Figure 3.47
Shadow (also, background color).

- **Foreground.** This group, shown in Figure 3.48, has quite a lot of useful
  buttons hidden inside, and it's worth going through them:

  - Most importantly, this is where you can adjust the opacity of your image,
    and of course animate a fade-in and fade-out.

  - You also have various key options. Full Key is the default, but there is also
    a Luma Key and two types of Chroma Key. The most powerful of these is
    the SpectraMatte Key, which is covered fully in Lesson 6, "Keying."

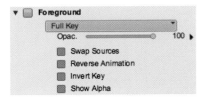

Figure 3.48
Foreground.

Note: The Spill Suppression and Erode/Expand groups below the Foreground
group are for when you apply the other default Chroma Key. SpectraMatte
has its own controls for this.

- Another very useful control is the Swap Sources check box. When you select it, your image appears as the background, and the image on the video track below appears inside the PIP, as shown in Figure 3.49. This is also very important when applying the 3D Warp as a transition effect, as you saw earlier.

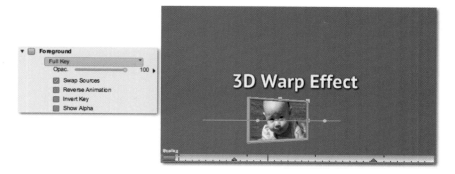

Figure 3.49
Swap Sources check box.

- If you have applied a key, selecting the Invert Key setting simply inverts it.

- Selecting the Show Alpha check box turns on the alpha channel that is keying your PIP onto the video track below (see Figure 3.50).

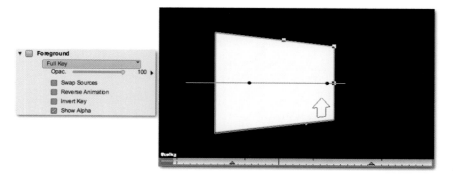

Figure 3.50
Show Alpha check box.

Third-Party Plug-ins

If you want a soft shadow for your PIP, you can also use various third-party plug-ins. For example, as you will see in Lesson 10, Avid FX will let you add a soft shadow quite easily. You can also use the BCC plug-in BCC DVE, which works like a standard effect; all the controls appear in the Effect Editor. Here you will find not just a soft shadow that can be customized in many ways, but many more options that will allow you to achieve even more effects.

- **Background Color.** At the bottom of the list is a very useful group for changing the background of your animation to a color instead of the image on the video track below. If there is no video track below, the default background color is black; with this parameter group, you can change that to any color you like.

- **Shapes, Trails, and Stamps.** The final three categories are mentioned here only in passing because you probably won't use them that much. When the 3D tool appeared in the mid 90s, page turns were all the rage. Today, however—although there are legitimate reasons you might use them—they are regarded as somewhat retro. As for the remaining shapes, they should never be used under any circumstances, except when you are trying to emulate a cheesy 70s sitcom look. (You are allowed to go there if you want to turn on Reverse Manual Highlight, however.) Trail and Stamp also have a limited appeal these days but can be used in case of extreme emergency. Just promise me you will never use Sparkle. Ever. On a more serious note, there are some excellent plug-ins that do a great job generating glows, lens flares, and a much more realistic sparkle; I'll discuss these in Lesson 9, "Third-Party Plug-ins."

Review/Discussion Questions

1. How do you reset a parameter in 3D Warp to its default settings?

2. True or false: If you manipulate an image on screen using the scale handles when there are no previous keyframes, you will not add any more keyframes.

3. How do you rotate an image around the right vertical edge?

4. Which statement best describes the working of the Z Perspective control?

   a. Using the Z Perspective control is like moving the camera nearer or further from the object.

   b. Using the Z Perspective control is like altering the lens angle.

   c. Using the Z Perspective control enlarges or reduces the size of the image.

5. What do the Target controls do? How are they different from the Perspective controls?

6. Describe the procedure for using the Lowlight Color control (fill in the blanks):

   1. Switch on _____.

   2. Go to _____ and turn on _____ _____ _____.

   3. Turn off the _____ _____ for the Shape parameters.

   4. Use the _____ controls to adjust the size and shape of the Lowlight Color.

   5. Use the _____ controls to adjust the color of the Lowlight Color.

7. If you want to show the picture underneath inside the PIP rather than the picture to which the 3D Warp effect is applied, what must you do?

8. How do you achieve a "big blur"?

9. You have a title that you wish to blur out. What steps do you need to take to achieve this?

10. Which parameter group allows you to fade in and out your PIP?

    a. Shape

    b. Foreground

    c. Background

Lesson 3 Keyboard Shortcuts

Key	Shortcut
T	Marks a clip according to the selected video tracks.
Option+T (Mac)/Alt+T (Windows)	Marks nearest edit points regardless of which video tracks are selected.
Option-click Match Frame (Mac) or Alt-click Match Frame (Windows)	Loads the clip to the Source monitor without adding a mark IN point.
Option (Mac) or Alt (Windows) Add Edit	Adds an edit on a blank track without affecting tracks with video clips.

Creating Effects

Use your newfound skills with corrective effects to improve two segments from a sequence you have been working on.

Media:

Open the 03 Exercises bin to find your material.

Duration:

60 minutes

GOAL

■ Create some effects with the 3D Warp effect and experiment with the possibilities

Swooping

Betty is back again! She is still working on her bird park project and wants some ideas for transitions. She heard that you know how to make pictures rotate in 3D space and wants to see what you can do. She has a sequence with the same four shots as before, only she wants you to make them animate in more interesting ways. Can you use the 3D Warp effect to impress her?

There are three transitions and she wants three different kinds of swoop—each two seconds in duration, but with different kinds of animation. For example, she wants the image to reduce in size and move off screen following different paths each time and with different rotations applied.

1. Load the **Exercise 01-Swoop** sequence from the bin.

2. Add a 3D Warp effect to the first transition and adjust the duration in Effect Editor Transition Duration box to 2 seconds.

3. For the first transition, you'll animate the first shot out rather than animate the second shot in. To begin, open the **Foreground** controls and select the **Swap Sources** check box.

4. You'll need keyframes for scaling, rotation, and position at the start and end of the effect, so why not add them all in one go? Open the graphs for the required parameters and use the **Add Keyframes** menu to add the keyframes at the start and end of the effect.

5. On the last keyframe, experiment with various combinations of rotations to get the desired effect.

6. You will also need to reduce the size of the image as it swoops off. Again, do this on the last keyframe.

7. Adjust the parameters for the position in both X and Y. You may find that an additional keyframe is required somewhere in the middle of the transition. Don't go crazy with the controls for now; subtle is often better for convincing effects.

8. When you are happy with the first transition, apply it to the second transition. Then just change the parameters. If you have set the effect up nicely, you will find that minor adjustments to the Position parameters will make a very different swoop effect.

9. If you like the effect, save it in the bin and give it a name—say, "Swoop Top Left."

For the final transition, Betty wants to see if you can animate the incoming shot rather than the outgoing one. If you apply the same effect from transition 2, what will you need to change to make this work? Here are a few things to keep in mind:

■ To start, uncheck the Swap Sources check box. That isn't quite enough, however. Play the effect, and you'll see that the incoming shot starts full screen and flies off at the end. You need to swap the animation curves in time as well.

■ All the animations you have created have keyframes at the *start* in the default settings, but you need the default settings (i.e., full frame, no rotation, etc.) to be at the *end* keyframe.

■ Remember, each animation curve will need to be swapped, but you can do this all in one go! Just right-click the Effect Keyframe track (the one at the top that globally affects all the tracks) and choose Reverse Keyframes. It should highlight yellow and helpfully tell you that you are applying the change to all the keyframes.

Now your final shot will swoop in rather than swoop out. Betty is very pleased, but as usual she wants more!

Adding a Flash Pan

Last night, Betty saw an effect on TV that moved both the shots out of the screen, blurred them, and made a kind of glow as well. Can you do this for her? If both shots are moving, how many layers will you need?

To start, load the Exercise 02–Flash Pan sequence, which has two shots. You'll need to set up a couple of things. First, think about timing. The flash needs to be quite short—let's say half a second. You'll need two layers to start with: one for the outgoing and one for the incoming animations. You don't need to apply the effect to the entire segment, but just the last half second, so you can use the Add Edit button to do this.

1. Scroll back from the transition exactly half a second and add an edit on the V1 track.

2. Now you need a half-second segment of the incoming shot on V2 above this. It must match frame so that it joins seamlessly with the continuing shot on V1. In the first frame of the next shot, Option-click (Mac) or Alt-click (Windows) the MATCH FRAME button to load the same frame in the Source monitor.

Tip: Normally, when you perform a Match Frame operation, you will load the frame on which you are parked into the Source monitor. Media Composer helpfully adds a mark IN point to the loaded clip. However, in this case, you don't want to mark an IN point; you want to mark an OUT point. When you match frame with the Option (Mac) or Alt (Windows) key, the clip is loaded into the Source monitor, but no IN point is added.

3. Step back one frame in the Source monitor and mark an OUT point.

4. Create a new video track.

5. You now need to mark up the half-second segment. Park your position indicator in this segment on V1 and press **OPTION+T** (Mac) or **ALT+T** (Windows) to mark it.

Tip: Pressing Option+T (Mac) or Alt+T (Windows) to mark a clip is one of my favorite hidden shortcuts. For example, suppose you want to mark a clip that is on V1, but you are on V2. Instead of messing about changing video tracks temporarily to make the standard T shortcut work, you simply use the Option (Mac) or Alt (Windows) modifier. You'll be amazed at how many other buttons change their functionality when used in combination with the Option (Mac) or Alt (Windows) key.

6. Patch your source to track V2 and edit in the clip.

7. Now apply a 3D Warp to the top segment.

8. Next, some animation. It is very simple: The shot needs to appear from the left, so the keyframe at the start is off screen, and the keyframe at the end is on screen. Use the **POSITION X** control to do this.

9. You also need to animate the clip underneath. Add another 3D Warp effect to this segment and use the **POSITION X** control to animate the clip off screen to the right so that its motion matches the incoming shot.

Now you have two shots animating: One slides in and pushes the other one out. You needed two DVEs because you are moving two shots separately. But what about the blur and color correction? For this, you need two more video tracks. You also need to create some add edits on the blank tracks at the start and end of your transition. You can Command-click (Mac) or Ctrl-click (Windows) on the Timeline to snap your blue position indicator to the start of the effect. Add edits on the blank tracks here and at the end.

Tip: Let's build on your repertoire of Option (Mac) or Alt (Windows) button modifications! Normally, when you add an edit with the Add Edit button, you will add an edit to any clip on a highlighted track. Click the Add Edit button while pressing the Option (Mac) or Alt (Windows) key at the same time, however, and you'll add an edit to all the blank tracks, whether they are highlighted or not. What's more, you'll leave the video clips untouched!

1. Add another 3D Warp, this time to the blank track above your transition. You can add an effect to a clip or the blank track. Now the effect will apply to all the tracks underneath. Your Timeline should look something like Figure 3.51.

Figure 3.51
Warp on blank track.

2. Go to the **DEFOCUS** parameters and add some **FG ONLY** blur (the big blur). You will need to play about here. Keep the Horz and Vert sliders as separate amounts. You'll need a keyframe at the start and at the end where everything is set to zero and one in the middle where you apply lots of horizontal blur.

3. Play with the animation curves to get the right effect here, as the blur doesn't kick in until the values are quite high. I found it works well when you have curves that look like Figure 3.52.

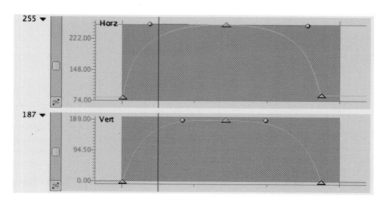

Figure 3.52
Blur animation curves.

4. You need to add one more effect on the very top track: a color effect or the color correction. Both can be animated. You will start and end with no adjustments, but the middle keyframe will have an increase in brightness and perhaps a color change. In the example in the completed exercise section, I boosted the Red and Green parameters and lowered the Blue, which gives an overall yellow look to the transition.

5. Just to keep Betty happy, edit in the sound clip to give it a nice "whoosh" feel.

You might also want to think about collapsing your tracks so your effect is nested inside a container on V1. In Lesson 8, "Refining the Composite," you'll see how to use the container to create the effect with different shots without having to rebuild everything all over again.

Applying a Soft Shadow

In the lesson, you saw that the 3D Warp effect has a shadow but no soft shadow. You can easily apply a soft shadow in Avid FX, discussed later in the book. You can also "cheat" and create a soft shadow on a PIP with the 3D Warp effect (see Figure 3.53). Here's how:

Figure 3.53
Soft Shadow 3D Warp.

1. Load the **EXERCISE 03–SOFT SHADOW** sequence. It already has an animated 3D PIP on the top track.

2. Create a new Video track.

3. Copy the clip with the effect and paste it on track V2. You can do this in a couple of ways, but perhaps the easiest is to enter Effects mode and save the effect with source by Option-dragging (Mac) or Alt-dragging (Windows) it into a bin. Then edit this effect (with source) onto track V3.

4. Enter Effects Mode again and select the 3D Warp effect on track V2.

5. Open the **BORDER** parameters. You can monitor just track V1 for the moment.

6. Create a big, wide black border—the maximum is 100.

7. Apply some softness to this border. Don't apply too much, or the entire shape will shrink too much.

8. Enable the **SHADOW** parameter and adjust the position so that you can see the shadow to the right of the image.

9. Monitor V3. Lo and behold, you have a soft shadow!

You can only do this with two duplicate layers, and there is a limit to how much you can soften the shadow. Even so, it will do the job in many cases.

Applying a Transition Effect with a Reflection

Betty was pleased with your transition effect, but she noticed you playing with your 3D tools. She would like you to add a 3D element to her animation. She likes the Cover Flow effect you did and wants you to use the idea to give her a nice transition between two shots with a reflection effect, as shown in Figure 3.54.

Figure 3.54
Reflection effect.

There is also a finished example in the completed exercises bin. The idea is that over a 2 second period, the first shot (the bird) will go from full screen to the smaller image on the right and a short while later the second shot will go from being on the left to full screen. Look tricky? Well, if you plan ahead, it is actually quite easy. In fact, you've done most of the steps before.

1. Load the EXERCISE 04–REFLECTION TRANSITION sequence and add a 3D Warp effect to the top track. There is a color correction there, so remember to add the 3D Warp effect with the Option (Mac) or Alt (Windows) key.

2. As before, you'll need to animate the scaling, the X position, and the Y rotation. You'll also need to adjust the Perspective Y and Z, Target Y, and Size controls. To begin, open the graphs for all of these parameters and add a keyframe at the start in all the open graphs.

3. Step forward 15 frames and add another keyframe to all the open graphs.

4. On this keyframe (the one you added in step 3), set the SCALING to 35, the Y ROTATION to −40, and the POSITION to 230.

5. Adjust the PERSPECTIVE and TARGET settings. This time, you need some animation because the first frame needs to be the default size and position. On the second keyframe, set the Y PERSPECTIVE control to 140, the Z PERSPECTIVE control to 200, the TARGET Y control to 200, and the TARGET SIZE control to 80.

6. To save time later, you can set the Y AXIS to −510; no animation required for this.

7. Adjust the Bézier handles to get the animation to work in an interesting way. Remember to use the Zoom to Curve Height button to max out the graph display. Experiment until you are happy. Table 3.1 shows the values I used. When you are finished, your keyframe graphs should look something like Figure 3.55.

Table 3.1   Table of Keyframe Values

Parameter	Value at Keyframe 1	Value at Keyframe 2
Scaling X and Y	100	35
Rotation Y	0	−40
Position X	0	230
Perspective Y	0	140
Perspective Z	250	200
Target Y	0	200
Target Size	100	80

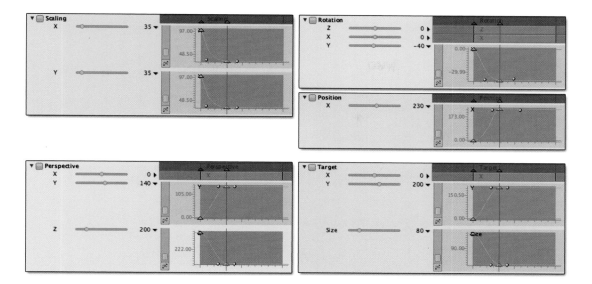

Figure 3.55
Keyframe graphs.

8. To recycle your effect, drag the effect icon from the Effect Editor window to the middle layer. You have now applied the same animation on the layer below.

9. What do you need to change? Well, you need to reverse the animation and change the initial position and rotation of the clip underneath. First, right-click the yellow **EFFECT KEYFRAME** track at the top of the Effect Editor and choose **REVERSE KEYFRAMES**.

10. Now set the **POSITION** to **–230** and the **ROTATION** to **40**.

Now you have your basic effect; let's review it. Because you are not interested in the quality, just the animation, open the Video Quality menu and choose Best Performance (yellow square), which means you can review without rendering.

Tip: The Video Quality menu, shown in Figure 3.56, is a great feature that lets you quickly preview a complex effect without having to render. The button to access this menu is at the bottom of the Timeline, on the left. There are three modes: Full Quality (green), Draft Quality (green/yellow), and Best Performance (yellow).

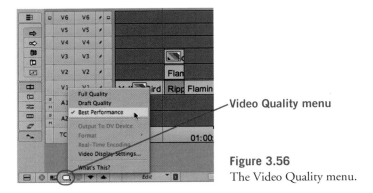

Video Quality menu

Figure 3.56
The Video Quality menu.

You are nearly there. The problem is that for the second half of the transition, the flamingo picture should be on top of the bird, but it is underneath, because that is how it is ordered in the Timeline. As with the transition in the last lesson, you need to swap the order of the clips, but you also want to add a reflection effect. You'll do that first. You need to duplicate the two layers so that they also appear on Video 4 and 5.

1. Option-drag (Mac) or Alt-drag (Windows) the two effect icons on tracks V2 and V3 to the bin. Load the first effect into the Source monitor, then patch your tracks so you can edit the effect with source onto track V4. Edit the second effect on to V5 so that the copy of the flamingos is on V4 and the copy of the yellow bird is on V5. Then go back to the Effect Editor.

2. You already set the axis, so all you need to do is set the **X ROTATION** to **180** and the **OPACITY** to **25 PERCENT** in both the clips. Easy! You can do this to the top pair of clips or to the bottom pair. It doesn't really matter. Just remember which pair you changed.

3. Now for the tricky bit. You need to split the effects in the middle and swap the order.

4. Select all four video layers and add an edit somewhere in the middle. You might want to add a couple of extra video tracks temporarily so you can swap the segments around.

5. Arrange the segments so the first half has the bird and the reflection on top and the flamingos and their reflection on the bottom. Then reverse this order for the second half.

6. Play back your effect and pat yourself on the back! In Best Performance mode, this plays back fine even on my humble laptop—five layers of HD, with animated 3D Warp and a color correction!

Betty is very happy and is cooking up some more challenges for you!

Importing Graphics and Mattes

After you have added various effects to your sequence and created some imaginative animations, it is time to look at the next stage in your workflow: importing images, logos, and animated graphics to add some extra gloss to your work.

Media Used: The media for this lesson is in the MC205 Pro Effects Project. Open the Lesson 04 Graphics bin. There is also a folder on the DVD called Graphics for Lesson 04 that contains various files for importing.

Duration: 60 minutes

GOALS

- Understand image-size adjustment
- Work with square and nonsquare pixels
- Understand color space
- Deal with aspect-ratio conversion
- Prepare images for import
- Import Photoshop layers
- Import sequential pictures and time lapses
- Import animated graphics and logos
- Learn to batch import and explore a graphic workflow

Importing Still Images

Although Media Composer can produce many amazing effects, plenty of other applications are widely used in the video industry. To name but two, Adobe Photoshop is an industry-standard image-creation program and Adobe After Effects is widely used for creating animated 3D graphics. Your workflow may also include Avid DS, which is a great finishing and compositing tool.

If you are working with a graphics department, it is important to know about the kind of files these and similar programs will produce. Avid Media Composer supports a wide variety of industry-standard image formats, such as JPEG, TIFF, TARGA, PICT, and many more, including Photoshop layered files. However, there are many things you need to check before you import a file. If you don't import a file correctly, the quality in your sequence will suffer.

In this section, you will look at some of the guidelines and techniques for importing image files and animated graphic files and making sure they are captured correctly for your final output. For example, suppose you want to import a photograph from your camera. The first consideration is the image size and aspect ratio. You also need to know about the color space. If you have an image that is going to be keyed over your sequence as a logo, for example, does it have an alpha? If you are working for a large organization with its own graphics department, it could be that your images are all carefully prepared before you import them. In many cases, however, you will need to adjust some settings to ensure that the images arrive in your bin with the correct aspect and color levels.

Organization

A key consideration when using imported images is how you organize your images. When you import a graphic—either still or moving—you do not touch the original. Instead, you create a clip in the bin with a media file. (This is known as *rasterizing* your graphic; you are converting it to a TV format.) It pays to know exactly where the original graphics are kept, and the bin into which you have the imported graphics. This is especially true if the graphics department is working on the image while you are editing. That is, the graphic you edit into your Timeline may subsequently be updated, in which case you'll need to know where to find the new version.

To help you with this, there are some useful bin columns that you can display to view important information about your graphics. It is a good idea to create a special "graphics" bin view that includes the following columns (see Figure 4.1):

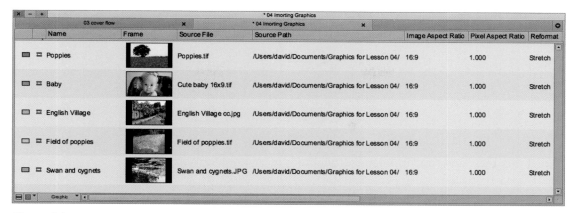

Figure 4.1
Graphics bin view.

- **Source file.** You may wish to rename your graphic after it has been imported, but the original name can be displayed in the bin so you can easily find it.

- **Source path.** This shows you the folder from which you originally imported the file. (Of course, you may choose to move it; if you do, Media Composer can't possibly know that you have done so. But at least you'll know where it was when you imported it.)

- **Image aspect ratio.** This tells you the project aspect ratio at the time you imported the graphic. If this differs from the current project aspect, you can toggle this to match, just as you can toggle the project aspect ratio. It won't change the image, but it will affect whether the Reformat column enables you to make changes. (The Reformat column is discussed momentarily.)

- **Pixel aspect ratio.** This column indicates the original *pixel* aspect ratio for the file (not to be confused with the aspect ratio of the original picture). This is discussed in more detail in the section "A Word About Nonsquare Pixels."

- **Reformat.** Here, you can change how your image is viewed if you are swapping from 4:3 to 16:9 or vice versa. This is discussed in more detail in the section "Aspect-Ratio Conversion."

Try to keep bins specifically for graphics, and make sure you have a naming convention that makes it easy for you to find your original graphic should you need to reimport.

Before You Import Your Graphics

Images come in many shapes and sizes, as do television formats. Before you even think about importing an image, you have to be clear about what your project format is. Are you planning to output in standard definition or high definition? Are you working in 4:3 or 16:9? And are you working in PAL or NTSC? This is a changing world, and many TV stations are switching to HD—but it is not happening overnight.

When you've answered those questions, you then need to look at your images. It is very likely that your image will have a different aspect ratio and will most likely be of a much higher resolution than your TV picture. Whatever dimensions your image has now, it will end up as a TV picture and thus must be cropped to fit the dimensions of your project format. You can do this before you import or you can let Media Composer do the job for you.

When you import an image into Media Composer, you will convert it from its initial size and resolution to that of your project format. This is known as *rasterizing* —you are making a media file from your image that is the same aspect and resolution as everything else in your Timeline.

Tip: If you have a very high-resolution image and you want to zoom into it during playback, you might want to consider using the Avid Pan and Zoom effect. Instead of importing the image and then zooming in, you start by linking to the image and performing the zoom; then you import the result. This will give much better quality when you zoom in because you are using the original resolution of the image rather than the rasterized import, which will be at a much lower resolution when you zoom.

Exactly how you convert the image on import depends on various settings. Before we look at the settings, you need to know a few things about your image, such as the aspect ratio, the resolution, and the color space. It isn't always possible to determine an image's aspect ratio just by looking at it. You can, however, find some details about the picture by right-clicking and choosing Get Info (Mac), as shown in Figure 4.2, or Properties (Windows). This gives you the dimensions in pixels— but does it match your project?

In the example shown in Figure 4.2, the image has a dimension of 3,888×2,592 pixels. If you get out your calculator, you'll see this is equivalent to 16×10.6667. So if you were to import it to a 16:9 project, it would be squeezed in the vertical plane. To import correctly, you would need to either crop it in an image-editing program to match your current project aspect or use the appropriate settings for import, which I will discuss momentarily. Table 4.1 gives the dimensions of various common project formats. If your image does not have these dimensions (or their equivalent), you have some cropping to do!

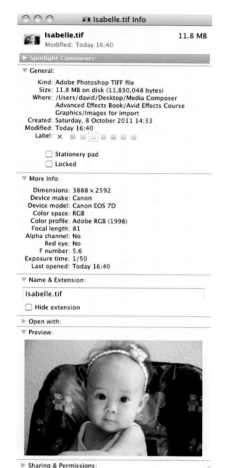

Figure 4.2
Viewing information about an image on a Mac.

Calculating the Aspect Ratio

For those mathematically inclined, you can easily convert the dimensions of an image to a simple ratio. Let's say you want to see whether the aforementioned image with the dimension of 3,888×2,592 is equivalent to 16:9. If you replace the 9 with x, the amount is expressed by the following equation:

$$x = 16 \times \frac{2592}{3888} = 10.6667$$

Thus, this image has a ratio of 16×10.6667.

Table 4.1   **File Dimensions**

Format	4:3 Square Pixel	16:9 Square Pixel	4:3 and 16:9 Nonsquare Pixel
NTSC	648×486	864×486	720×486
NTSC DV	640×480	853×480	720×480
PAL	768×576	1,024×576	720×576
HD 1080	N/A	1,920×1080	N/A
HD 720	N/A	1,280×720	N/A

Note: If you do the math, you will notice that all the dimensions in the square pixel columns in Table 4.1 have the same ratio as 4:3 or 16:9. In fact, you can create an image in any size you like as long as it is some multiple of 4:3 or 16:9. Thus, for example, an image created for square-pixel PAL will import perfectly well into an NTSC project. So why do you choose these exact numbers? Because they will result in the least amount of resampling when you import and squeeze the image to the correct nonsquare size. There is a further complication in standard definition (as if you didn't have enough to deal with already) that the number of active pixels along the horizontal line is not actually 720 but is instead 704, because you need some part of the line for analog blanking.

A Word About Nonsquare Pixels

Okay, take a deep breath. Some people may find this section somewhat disturbing. But if you can get your head around it, it will help you to import your images correctly! In Table 4.1, you saw that the standard-definition formats have a column for nonsquare pixels, while the high-definition formats only have square pixels. Why?

In the world of television, there are two possible aspect ratios for your project: 4:3 and 16:9. That's only part of the story, however. Just to spice things up a bit, you also have standard definition (SD) and high definition (HD). High definition is a bit easier to deal with because although there are many different types of HD, they are all 16:9, and they all have square pixels.

The problem is that standard definition—whether PAL or NTSC—is normally shown as a 4:3 image. But PAL and NTSC contain different numbers of lines.

PAL has 576 active lines, and NTSC has 486. The only way to squeeze the same number of lines into a 4:3 picture is to make PAL lines thinner and NTSC lines thicker—hence nonsquare pixels. (See Figure 4.3.)

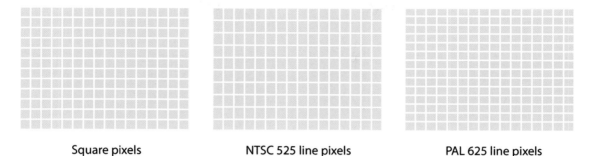

Square pixels   NTSC 525 line pixels   PAL 625 line pixels

Figure 4.3
A magnified view of NTSC and PAL pixels.

If that wasn't enough, you also have 16:9 standard definition. Many countries now transmit in 16:9 even though they are still not transmitting in HD. This is because almost every new TV set sold today is widescreen, so even if you don't have enough HD channels, you still want to see widescreen pictures on your TV. NTSC and PAL don't really cater to widescreen, however, so they cheat. Standard definition 16:9 still has exactly the same number of lines, but they squeeze them even more. That is, it appears that you get widescreen, but your lines are simply thinner. This is known as *anamorphic 16:9*. It isn't really true 16:9 like HD; it just looks like it. So you really need to know what format your pictures are going to be displayed in when you perform that import.

Because your computer works in square pixels, you need to create a file in square pixels that will then be adjusted to the correct aspect with nonsquare pixels by Media Composer when you import it. If you are preparing your pictures in Photoshop, you can also work in nonsquare throughout. Photoshop gives you special options for creating images in TV formats where the pixels are squeezed for you; you can even preview what your image will look like on TV. (This is discussed further Appendix A, "Working with FluidMotion and Photoshop.")

The good news is that standard definition is gradually being replaced by high definition. Within a few years, we will be able to eradicate this entire section of this book (and your memory). HD is much simpler; you can only have 16:9, the pixels are square, and you don't need to worry about blanking because it is all digital. You can now breathe again—but keep that nonsquare pixel information in your mind, because you'll need it to get through the next section.

Import Settings

Either you have carefully cropped your image in an image-editing program so it fits the current project format or you haven't, in which case you can let Media Composer try to sort it out for you. Either way, you'll want to check your import settings before you import the image into Media Composer. There are two ways of accessing these settings:

- **Before you import.** Open the Import Settings dialog box directly from the Settings tab in the Project window.

- **During the import process.** Choose File > Import or right-click in a bin and choose Import from the menu that appears. Then click the Options button in the Select Files to Import dialog box, as shown in Figure 4.4.

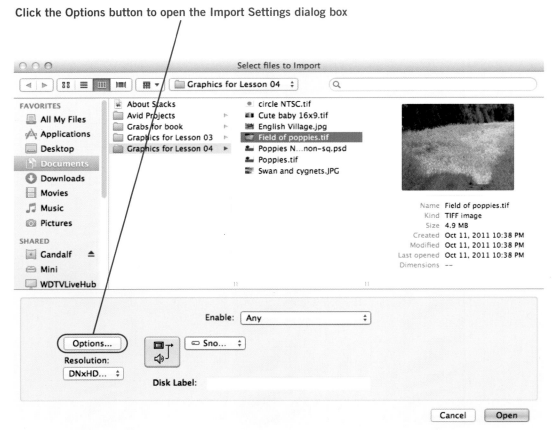

Figure 4.4
The Select Files to Import dialog box.

There are four tabs in the Import Settings dialog box, so make sure you are looking at the Image tab, as shown in Figure 4.5. To begin with, you need to look at the Image Size Adjustment section.

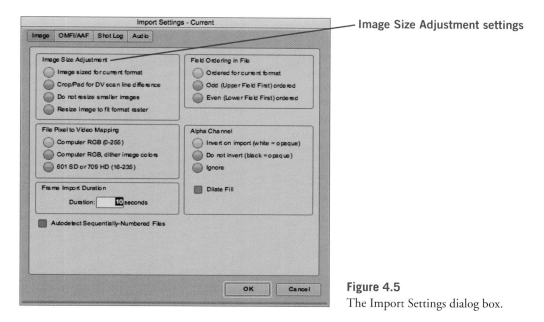

Image Size Adjustment settings

Figure 4.5
The Import Settings dialog box.

As you can see, there are four choices for image size adjustment:

■ **Image Sized for Current Format.** Use this option when your image is already correctly sized for your current project format. If you have prepared your image in square pixels according to the aforementioned guidelines (648×486 for NTSC or 768×576 for PAL), the imported image will correctly compensate for nonsquare pixels in your TV format. Alternatively, if you are working in Photoshop and you can switch to non-square pixels mode, you can make a nonsquare pixel image (either 720×468 for NTSC or 720×576 for PAL) that will also import correctly.

Note: If you are working in standard definition 16:9, you will find that preparing a nonsquare image is difficult unless you can view the image in nonsquare mode (i.e., with the lines squeezed). Otherwise, it will just look wrong because you are still really working in either 720×486 or 720×576. Photoshop allows you to view such images correctly. The section "Preparing Images in Photoshop" in the appendix will go into this in more detail. (In HD, you are always in square pixels, so if you have prepared your image in a 16:9 aspect, it will come in correctly.)

- **Crop/Pad for DV Scan Line Difference.** Just to add to the confusion, when working in NTSC DV, you will find that you have only 480 lines. In that case, you can compensate for the missing lines. If you are in a 486-line project and you have a 480-line image, Media Composer will expand the frame by adding six black lines (known as *padding*). If, on the other hand, you are working in a DV25 resolution and you want to import a full-frame 486-line image (or movie), Media Composer will crop the top four and bottom two lines. PAL people: Be thankful. You never need to use this setting because PAL DV is 576 lines, just like normal PAL.

- **Do Not Resize Smaller Images.** If your image is of lower resolution than your current format, you may not wish to blow it up further because it will look soft. If so, you can keep the image in its original dimensions and place on a black background, as shown in Figure 4.6.

Figure 4.6
A smaller image, not resized.

- **Resize Image to Fit Format Raster.** If your image has not been cropped to the dimensions of the current project format, you can still import it. When you select this option, your image's aspect will be preserved, and the image will be imported with a black background so that the largest dimension is fitted to the screen. This works for both smaller and larger images, although in the case of smaller images—unlike with the preceding setting—the image will be enlarged so that the largest dimension fits the screen. See Figure 4.7.

Figure 4.7
Two images, one tall and one wide.

Effects in NTSC DV

Working with DV footage in NTSC has additional complications because you may want to create PIP effects with your media. If you are mixing normal (i.e., non-DV) material with DV material, you may notice black lines above and below the picture in a PIP effect. This is because Media Composer uses the 480 lines for the image and adds four black lines above and two black lines below. There is a special setting to deal with this called the Effect Aperture setting. You can find it in the General settings when you click the Settings tab in the Project window. This setting lets you decide whether or not to use the six black lines when you create effects.

In a project that only uses DV media, it is best to switch to the DV 25 aperture setting. In a project using non-DV media or a mixture of both, use the ITU 601 aperture and use the Crop tools in the PIP to remove the lines.

A Quick Guide to Preparing Your Images

Let's go through some examples to demonstrate how best to prepare your image. Suppose you want to import an image of a perfect circle into your project. In all the following cases, you will create the image with the correct proportions, and the setting for import will be Image Sized for Current Format.

- **SD NTSC 4:3 (648×486 square, 720×486 nonsquare).** If you are working in square pixels, you can create an image at 648×486, which is a 4:3 ratio. If you create a perfect circle in this image, it will import correctly. Media Composer will stretch it out to 720×486, which is the correct *nonsquare* aspect, such that your circle will appear slightly elongated, but will then compensate by stretching the pixels to the nonsquare proportions required for TV.

The result is a perfect circle in 720×486 nonsquare. (See Figure 4.8.) Thus, if you crop any (square pixel) image to 648×486 before you import, it will import correctly.

Original image 648×486

Stretched out to 720×486 pixels

Result when imported

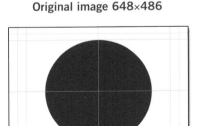 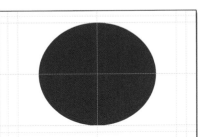 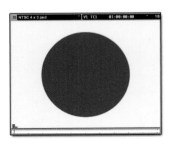

Figure 4.8
Importing for 4:3 NTSC.

Tip: If you are going to crop your image before importing, always use the 10 percent grid or safe action. Many TVs will not show the full picture but will instead zoom in so the edge is hidden. If you crop an image, try to keep the area of interest inside the 10 percent box so it will still be visible on the TV at home.

- **SD NTSC 16:9 (864×486 square, 720×486 nonsquare).** This time, create an image at 864×486, which is equivalent to a 16:9 aspect ratio. When you import it, Media Composer will *squeeze* it to 720×486 (the same nonsquare aspect), but will then compensate by *reducing* the thickness of the lines so you get your 16:9 circle. See Figure 4.9.

Original image 864×486

Squeezed to 720×486 pixels

Result when imported

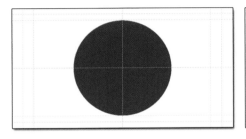 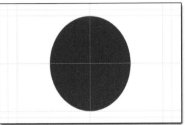 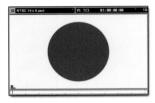

Figure 4.9
Importing for 16:9 NTSC.

- **SD PAL 4:3 (768×576 square, 720×576 nonsquare).** Importing images in PAL also distorts the pixels, only this time they are squeezed to fit. You create your image at 768×576, which is a 4:3 aspect. This is then squeezed horizontally to 720×576 (the nonsquare aspect for PAL TV) on import. When in Media Composer, the pixels are squeezed down even more to display correctly. (See Figure 4.10.) Note that the initial images are larger because PAL has more lines, but the end result is the same because Media Composer displays PAL and NTSC images in the same monitor.

Original image 768×576　　Squeezed to 720×576 pixels　　Result when imported

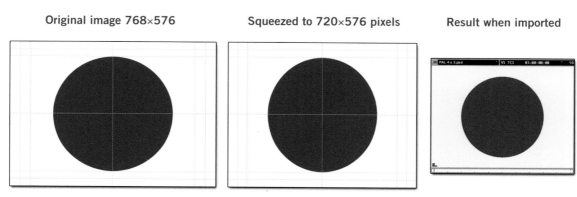

Figure 4.10
Importing for 4:3 PAL.

- **SD PAL 16:9: 1,024×576 square, 720×576 nonsquare.** This time, you create your image in 1,024×576, which will be squeezed to 720×576 nonsquare when imported. Media Composer then squeezes the lines further so the image appears correctly with a 16:9 aspect ratio, as shown in Figure 4.11.

Original image 1024×576　　Squeezed to 720×576 pixels　　Result when imported

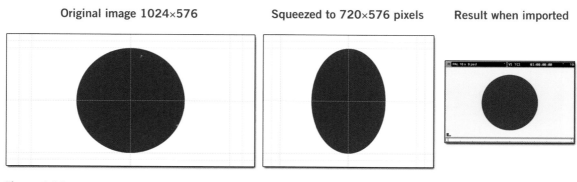

Figure 4.11
Importing for 16:9 PAL.

- **HD 720 (1,280×720).** Technically, in the world of HD, there is no PAL or NTSC. The frame size is the same the world over. Only the frame *rate* is different. And you are all using square pixels, so any image created in 1,280×720 (or multiples of this) will be imported correctly.

- **HD 1080 (1,080×1,920).** Again, with HD, the frame size is the same the world over, and square pixels rule. Any image with this dimension (or a multiple of it) will be imported correctly. Figure 4.12 shows how an HD image —whether at 1,280×720 or 1,080×1,920—looks when imported into Media Composer.

Original image at 1,280×720 or 1,080×1,920   Result when imported

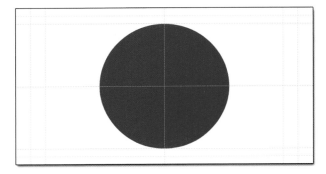

Figure 4.12
Importing HD 16:9.

Color Space

The next area of interest in the Import Settings dialog box is the File Pixel to Video Mapping section, shown in Figure 4.13. Here, you have three choices. Before I get into each choice, I want to explain why you may sometimes need to change this setting.

Figure 4.13
File Pixel to Video Mapping settings.

In the world of film and broadcast, images—still or moving—are displayed on a screen, and the image you see on the screen should match as closely as possible the way you would have seen the original scene. (Okay, in truth, we spend a great deal of time and effort enhancing the image so it actually looks *better* than the original, but that's another story.)

So how does this happen? When you capture an image or a movie, you create a media file that is then displayed on a computer screen in the RGB (short for red, green, blue) color space. In RGB, every pixel on the screen has a value expressed in levels of red, green, and blue. The most common form of RGB is 8-bit RGB, which gives you 256 discrete levels of color per channel. So, for example, in 8-bit RGB, black is 0,0,0—meaning there is 0 amount of red, green, and blue. In contrast, white is 255,255,255. Every other color is some combination of these values.

Note: You can define even more colors by using 10-bit RGB (1,024 levels) or higher. Remember, though, that more digits means more space on your hard drive.

TV screens don't work in quite the same way as computer screens. When you import an RGB image into Media Composer, it needs to be remapped to a range specified by a TV standards committee known as ITU-R BT.601 (ITU-R BT.709 for HD). It's a bit of a mouthful, so you can call it 601/709 for short. The result of this is that in 601/709, white is 235,235,235, black is 16,16,16, and everything in between is adjusted accordingly. If you don't convert RGB images to 601/709, your whites come in too hot and your blacks will be crushed. If you don't convert the images, you may find your work gets rejected.

So back to the settings. You have three choices:

- **Computer RGB (0–255).** With this setting, which is the default, your image will be remapped from 0–255 to 16–235. It will look different from the original, but it will be correct for TV.

- **601 SD or 709 HD (16–335).** If your graphics department is clued in and has already prepared everything correctly, you'll want to choose this setting to import the images without remapping them. Note, however, that if you accidentally import an RGB image as 601/709, the whites will be too hot and the blacks will be crushed.

Tip: It is a good practice to label correctly converted images as .601 or .709 so that everyone knows to leave them just as they are.

Note: Avid provides you with a folder of various line-up signals buried deep in the application folder. You can put these at the front of your sequence if you want to let everyone know you understand about video levels. These are all correctly set for TV levels, so make sure when you import them that you switch the setting to 601/709. Otherwise, you'll be in trouble! You'll explore this procedure in the exercise at the end of this lesson.

Note: Although not so common these days, you will occasionally come across animated graphics that are keyed onto a background track using a Luma key. This is where everything black in a movie is keyed out. For this to work correctly, the black must be below the normal black level (known as super-black), and you need to use the 601/709 setting so that black levels are not bumped up.

- **Computer RGB, Dither Image Colors.** This does not change the color levels but instead adds a bit of noise to randomize the levels. This can help remove banding that is sometimes apparent with graphics created in 8-bit with a gradient of some kind. (Note that real-world images never have artificial gradients, so you will not need to use this setting with photographs.)

Importing Your Image

Well, that was the hard part. The rest is easy. You have your settings correct, and now you want to put the image in your bin. There are three ways to import an image:

- Choose File > Import.
- Right-click in the bin and choose Import.
- Open the folder containing your file or files in the Mac Finder or Windows Explorer and drag them directly into the bin.

If you are dragging into the bin, you will import the image using whatever current settings you have. Using the Import menu gives you one last chance to check your settings; just click the Options button in the bottom-left corner of the Select Files to Import dialog (refer to Figure 4.4). You will also get a chance to choose a storage location and capture resolution; otherwise, it will use your current Media Creation settings.

Aspect-Ratio Conversion

Switching from 4:3 to 16:9 can be another headache. Although we live in a world in which 16:9 is becoming the norm, many TV stations still output in 4:3. You may be faced with using images (or footage) that is 4:3 in a 16:9 project. Fortunately, Media Composer is very good at dealing with aspect conversion. You can actually prepare your imported footage before editing it by using the Reformat column in the bin to set how your clips will be displayed in the Timeline. If you have created your bin view according to the guidelines at the beginning of this lesson, you have this Reformat column.

Note: If you are using the MC205 Pro Effects project, you are working in HD
       23.976 and thus you only have the choice of displaying footage at 16:9.
       However, to import the images, you need to change your project format by
       clicking the Format tab in the Project window and choosing a project type
       of 23.976 NTSC. Now that you are working in standard definition, you have
       a choice of 4:3 or 16:9. PAL people may like to create a PAL SD project for
       this section, but the principles are exactly the same as in NTSC.

To prepare to experiment with the Reformat column, import some prepared images:

1. Find the **GRAPHICS FOR LESSON 04** folder on the DVD. There are two
    files with circles—one created in standard definition at 4:3 called NTSC
    720×486 Non sq.tif and the other created at 16:9 called NTSC 864×486.tif
    (or their PAL equivalents). You may like to copy this folder to your hard
    drive or desktop.

2. Start with the 4:3 image. To import this correctly, the project aspect needs
    to match, so convert the project by right-clicking the Composer window
    and choosing **PROJECT ASPECT RATIO > 4:3**, as shown in Figure 4.14. (Of
    course, this only works in standard definition. HD projects are always 16:9.)

Figure 4.14
Changing the project aspect (SD only).

3. Open the **LESSON 04 GRAPHICS** bin and make sure your Import Settings
    dialog box is set to **IMAGE SIZED FOR CURRENT FORMAT**. The bin should
    already be set in the graphics view, as shown in Figure 4.1.

4. Right-click in the bin and choose **IMPORT** from the menu that appears.

5. Navigate to the **GRAPHICS FOR LESSON 04** folder and select the **NTSC
    720×486 NON SQ.TIF** file.

6. Double-click the file or click the **OPEN** button to import the file to the bin. Notice that the Image Aspect Ratio column says 4:3 and the Pixel Aspect Ratio setting is 0.900, indicating that the image has been stretched to fit the nonsquare project format. (PAL users would see 1.067 in this column.)

7. Now for the 16:9 image. You need to change the project aspect ratio back to 16:9. Right-click in the Composer window and choose **PROJECT ASPECT RATIO > 16:9**.

8. Right-click the bin again and choose **IMPORT** from the menu that appears.

9. In the **GRAPHICS FOR LESSON 04** folder, select the **NTSC 864×486 (16:9 SQ).TIF** file and double-click to import it. Note that this time the **IMAGE ASPECT RATIO** setting shows 16:9 and the **PIXEL ASPECT RATIO** setting is 1.200.

10. Let's examine the two files in the bin. Look at the image in the Frame column. You will see that the 16:9 image is displaying correctly but the 4:3 is stretched out. Quickly change the project aspect to 4:3. You will see that the 4:3 image is now correct, but the 16:9 image is squeezed!

11. Change the project aspect back to 16:9. Sadly, it seems you can't have your cake and eat it too!

Only one of the images is correct. If you imported your graphic correctly for 4:3, it will now display wrongly in a 16:9 project. The circle will now look like what Americans call a football (and what everyone else calls a rugby ball). Here's where the Reformat column comes to your rescue! Let's see how you can use it to display the 4:3 image.

By default, the Reformat column is set to Stretch, but if you click the word Stretch, you will see a menu with four choices:

■ **Stretch.** Choosing Stretch (see Figure 4.15) will leave things as they are. Not a good choice in this case.

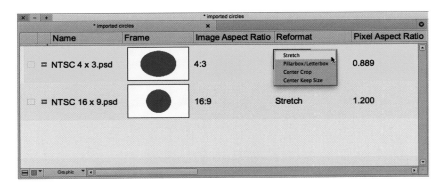

Figure 4.15
The Reformat column's default setting: Stretch.

- **Pillarbox/Letterbox.** This gives you the full image in the correct aspect, with bars along the side. See Figure 4.16.

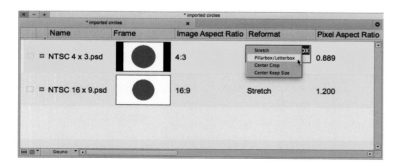

Figure 4.16
The Reformat column, set to Pillarbox/Letterbox.

- **Center Crop.** Choosing this option maintains the aspect but enlarges the image to fill the 16:9 screen. In this case, the circle is cropped slightly (see Figure 4.17). Often, this is the best option, as it fills the screen. People who've just spent money buying a new widescreen TV tend to prefer seeing the screen filled!

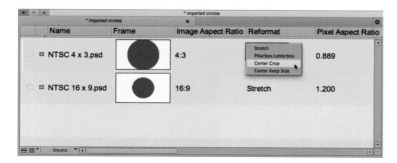

Figure 4.17
The Reformat column, set to Center Crop.

- **Center Keep Size.** This will keep the image at its original size (in this case, the same as choosing Pillarbox/Letterbox). See Figure 4.18.

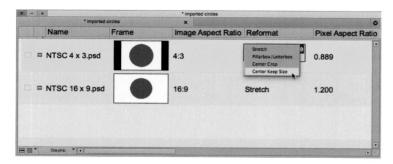

Figure 4.18
The Reformat column, set to Center Keep Size.

In the reverse situation, when you have a 16:9 image and you wish to display it in a 4:3 aspect, you will get similar results from these four choices, only you'll get a letterbox instead of a pillarbox and you'll see a center crop if you choose Center Keep Size.

Note: The Reformat column will apply an aspect conversion *before* you edit a clip into the Timeline. If you have already edited the clip and subsequently make a change to the reformat options in the bin, you will need to refresh your sequence. To do this, right-click your sequence in the bin and choose Refresh Sequence. You will see a submenu with various choices. Select Reformatting Options and your sequence will update with the new aspect conversion you selected for the clip.

In addition, the Reformat column works only if the image aspect (in the Image Aspect column) does not match the current project aspect. If you have a 16:9 image and you are in a 16:9 project, the Reformat column doesn't do anything. Finally, the Reformat column options don't work in the Interplay environment.

Importing Movie Files

Nowadays, many clips are captured from digital files rather than from tape. There are specific workflows for capturing file-based media, which are discussed in the book, *Media Composer 6: Professional Picture and Sound Editing*. Often, these workflows use the Avid Media Access (AMA) method, which involves pointing your system to some kind of file folder and viewing the files before importing by consolidating or transcoding. But what if you just have a movie file on, say, a memory stick or that you've downloaded from the Internet and you just want to import it into your project? In that case, to import a movie file, you simply drag the file into your bin or right-click in the bin and choose Import from the menu that appears. (Note that the same rules apply to moving images as to still images, and the settings work in the same way. You have to get the aspect ratio correct for your current project format, and you need to know whether you are working in RGB or 601/709.)

Fields and Field Ordering

When you are importing movie files, another consideration is field ordering. Different formats have different field ordering and if you get it wrong your footage will not play correctly.

A Word on Codecs

Avid Media Composer recognizes many digital movie formats, including MOV and AVI. Before you can import a movie, however, you also have to know what codecs were used in the creation of the movie file. A *codec* (short for "compressor-decompressor" or more simply "coder-decoder") is a small program used to encode or decode a digital data stream. It should not be confused with a compression *format* or *standard*. Just because a file is in the MOV format (QuickTime) doesn't necessarily mean you can import it. You will need the correct codecs installed on your system so that Media Composer can recognize it and play it back. If it doesn't recognize it, you will get an error message. Fortunately, Avid comes with a wide variety of codecs that are installed when you install the program. If you are missing a codec, you can go to the appropriate Web site to download it. For example MPEG-4 and H.264 are commonly used compression codecs in the HD world; these are already installed on your system. Avid uses its own DNxHD codecs for HD compression and Apple uses ProRes. Anyone can go to the Avid Web site and download the DNxHD codecs. If you are planning to play a QuickTime file on a system that doesn't have Media Composer installed, then you'll need to install the DNxHD codecs.

Avid codecs are available for free: Do a search online for "avid dnx codecs download" and you will find both Mac and PC codec bundles on the Avid Web site.

Fields

You may already know the story: Each frame in interlaced footage is actually made up of two fields. The reason for this is historical—in days of old, flicker was a problem on TV systems. To overcome this, each full frame of video was divided into two fields. For example, a frame of NTSC has 525 lines (of which 486 are active picture lines), but instead of playing these all at the same time, the lines were alternated so that lines 1, 3, 5, etc. (the odd lines) were designated as field 2, and lines 2, 4, 6, etc. (the even lines) were designated as field 1. (Don't ask me why; PAL is more logical and has odd lines as field 1.) Each field is played sequentially, which eliminates the flicker as the TV picture is now refreshed once every 60th of a second instead of once every 30th. The playing of two sets of intermingled lines like this is known as *interlacing*.

Because the fields represent a series of progressing slices of time, the order in which you play the fields is critical. The order is known as *field dominance*. If you play the odd (upper) fields first, your field dominance is said to be odd, whereas if you play the even (lower) fields first, your field dominance is said to be even.

In a perfect world, there would be no fields. They would be banished to the outer regions of the solar system to mingle with the Oort cloud and never bother us again. We would work in frames and frames alone. But this is not a perfect world, so we have to deal with fields.

You may also think that you can escape from all this by working with progressive material, as in our project, but if you are going to broadcast this on TV, your footage will be playing as fields whether you like it or not.

To make matters worse, there may be only two fields—an upper and a lower—but it seems that no one can agree which order to play them! Table 4.2 has the details.

Table 4.2   Field Ordering

TV Format	Field Order	Field Dominance
NTSC 601	Lower Field First	Even
NTSC DV	Lower Field First	Even
PAL 601	Upper Field First	Odd
PAL DV	Lower Field First	Even
DVCProHD 720i (50/60)	Upper Field First	Odd
1080i HD (50/60)	Upper Field First	Odd

Why does this matter? Well, if you are working on a 1080i 60 HD project and you try to import a movie file that was created in SD NTSC, it will come in with the wrong field order. For those in the PAL world, a 1080i 50 project will have the same problem when trying to import PAL DV. (Who thinks up this stuff?) And you may not even spot it because your Media Composer monitor will play only field one. But if you hook up a client monitor, you will see something wrong. The footage will appear to stutter, as if it is going one step forward and one step back (25 or 30 times a second). Not very nice. So always check the source of your movie file—was it PAL or NTSC? DV or not? If you get it wrong, no problem; just open the Import Settings dialog box, choose the appropriate setting in the Field Ordering in File section (see Figure 4.19), and re-import the file. You have a 50/50 chance of getting it right, so if at first you don't succeed, you will surely get it right the second time! (Okay, okay, the eagle eyed among you may see that there are in fact three choices, the first one being Ordered for Current Format.

That means you are assuming the file you are importing is correct for the current project format. But again, this can either be odd or even, so you still have a 50/50 chance in the long run!)

Figure 4.19
Field order settings.

Note: **If you are working in a progressive project format (e.g., 24P), you won't see these settings in the Import Settings dialog box.**

Importing TIFF and Other File Sequences

Occasionally, instead of importing a movie file, you will get a folder full of individual frames, all numbered. This could happen, for example, with a graphics animation or time-lapse photography. You might also be working with digital intermediaries where a series of frames from a high-resolution computer-generated file has been output at HD resolution and sent via FTP. These could be TIFF files, Targa files, PICT files, or what have you, each containing just one frame rather than a self-contained movie file. If you are faced with this situation, the Auto Detect Sequentially Numbered Files check box in the Import Settings dialog box will help you. When you check this check box (see Figure 4.20), any files in a folder that are numbered sequentially will be imported as a single movie clip. Let's try this now.

Figure 4.20
Importing sequentially numbered files.

To import the series of JPEG files in the Animated Logo JPEG folder:

1. Open the Import Settings dialog box and make sure the **Autodetect Sequentially-Numbered Files** check box is checked.

2. Right-click the bin, choose **Import**, and navigate to the **Animated Logo JPEG** folder. Inside, there are lots of files.

3. Click the first file to select it; then click the **Open** button.

4. The first 24 frames are black. If you don't want to import these, click frame 25 (or any frame between frame 1 and 25) and click **OPEN**. The import will start from the selected frame. Note that this movie does not have an alpha; it will come in as a normal clip that you can edit into the Timeline. Figure 4.21 shows the result of the import.

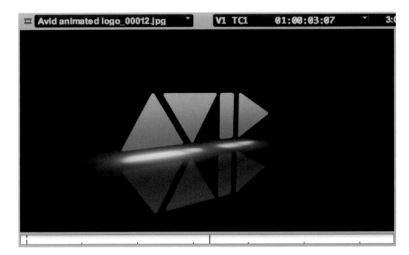

Figure 4.21
Imported files example.

Note: Whenever you have a large number of files, you don't have to start at frame number one. If you want to start at a later file, just click the file you wish to start with and Media Composer will import everything from that file onward.

Importing Animated Graphics and Logos with Alpha

Graphics files (whether still or animated) can have an alpha channel that is used to let you key it over your image. The alpha channel may be embedded in the file or it may come as a separate file as just a luma (black and white) image. Not all file formats support embedded alpha, however. Table 4.3 summarizes the different possibilities.

Table 4.3   Supported File Formats

Format	Extension	Alpha Supported	Comments
Alias	.als	No	Alpha comes in as a separate file.
AVI	.avi	No	Not all codecs are compatible with the Macintosh. It is better to use QuickTime for cross-platform movies.
BMP	.bmp	No	
JPEG	.jpg	No	CMYK images are not supported.
Photoshop	.psd	Yes	Supported: RGB images, flat or layered files. Unsupported: CMYK images and files with more than four channels. Any applied blending modes are ignored.
PICT	.pct or .pict	Yes	
PNG	.png	Yes	Graphics should not be web interlaced.
QuickTime	.mov	Some	Only the Animation, Planar RGB, and None codecs support alpha. The Avid QT codecs do not support alpha for high definition.
Softimage	.pic	Yes	
Targa	.tga	Yes	
TIFF	.tif or .tiff	Yes	Supported: RGB, grayscale images, TIFF files with layers (in Photoshop 6 or later). Unsupported: CMYK images, files with more than four channels.

Importing the File

Now let's try importing an animated graphic with alpha:

1. Change your import settings back to **Computer RGB** and **Image Sized for Current Format**.

2. Navigate to the **Graphics for Lesson 04** folder and import the **Shatter Title** file. If your file has an embedded alpha, Media Composer will automatically detect this on import. Importing will take two passes: first the video fill and then the alpha data. (See Figure 4.22.) What you see in the bin is an icon to show this is a matte key, as shown in Figure 4.23.

Figure 4.22
Importing the alpha.

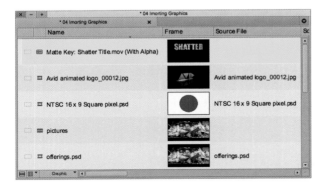

Figure 4.23
Bin view of icon and frame.

Note: When you import a file with alpha, two media files are created. The video fill is created at the resolution you set in your Media Creation settings—for example, DNxHD 115. However, the alpha is always imported as uncompressed.

Editing could not be simpler: Just put your matte key clip on a higher video track—in this case, V2—and it will key automatically so that the background track on V1 is showing underneath. You can step into this clip and see that there are two components: the Graphic Fill and the Alpha Matte, as shown in Figure 4.24.

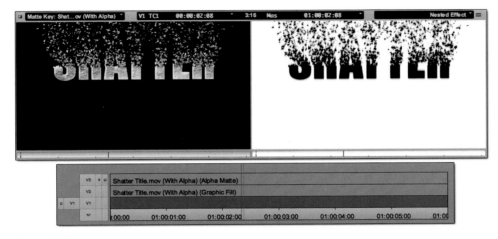

Figure 4.24
Stepping into the matte.

An alpha channel is a black-and-white (or grayscale) channel that is used to key the foreground part of the image over the video background in the Timeline. When compositing, you will come across alpha channels a lot, so it is good to understand how they work. When an image is keyed, it is the alpha channel that decides what is used in the graphic, and what is removed, revealing the background track in the Timeline.

As you might imagine, there are two possibilities:

■ Black represents opaque, in which case you are seeing the graphic, and white represents transparent, in which case you are seeing through the graphic to reveal the background layer. This is the way the film industry worked in the old days of optical effects on film. It is also the way Media Composer works.

■ White represents opaque and black represents transparent—in other words, it is the other way around. This is pretty much standard for all other applications.

You may also have gray in the alpha, which in both cases represents a degree of opacity (or transparency, depending on how you look at it). For example, you might want a soft edge to a shadow. This would be achieved by having gray in the alpha.

Thus, there is just one teensy weensy consideration you need to be aware of: Which way around is the alpha you are importing? That is where the Alpha Channel section of the Import Settings dialog box, as shown in Figure 4.25, comes in handy. In most cases the alpha channel will be inverted (as far as Avid is concerned) and normally you need to select the Invert on Import button. (Note that Media Composer helpfully gives this as the default now.)

If the file has been specifically prepared with the kind of alpha that the Media Composer recognizes, choose the Do Not Invert button in the dialog box.

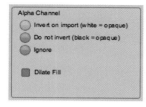

Figure 4.25
Alpha Channel options.

Tip: If you have a bin full of images or clips with alpha, they will all have the matte key icon instead of a picture icon. You can get a sneak peek at what the image actually looks like by changing the head frame when your bin is in Frame view. Just select the clip and press the 2 key on your keyboard to advance one frame, and you'll see the image rather than the matte icon.

This is only a temporary view, though; as soon as you click somewhere else in the bin, it will revert back to the matte icon. A more permanent way of viewing the matte image in your bin is to use the Frame view in your Text view of the bin. This will show you the first frame (or any frame you choose by advancing forward or backward with the 1, 2, 3, and 4 keys) of the matte key.

Importing Photoshop Layers

Adobe Photoshop is widely used to create graphics, titles, and logos. There are many workflows for using Photoshop. It is very common to prepare files by creating a series of layers in Photoshop, each with its own alpha channel so you can key it onto your sequence. If you are given such a file, you can bring in either a selection of layers or all of them at once and then create a sequence with all the layers intact. For example, you may be given a series of lower thirds, each with a different name but all using a common background element. If you have named the layers, Media Composer will recognize the name, enabling you to select the appropriate layer. If the layers use an alpha channel, Media Composer will recognize it as long as it is prepared in a particular way. (See Figure 4.26.)

Figure 4.26
Layers and channels in Photoshop showing alphas.

Note: This book's appendix contains a section on working with Photoshop to create lower thirds. There, you will be guided through the workflow for creating alpha channels in Photoshop CS5 that will import correctly into Media Composer.

Following are several points to bear in mind when working with Photoshop:

■ Media Composer will work directly with Photoshop files. You do not need to convert to TIFF, PNG, or any other format, regardless of what you may read on the Internet.

■ Media Composer does not recognize Photoshop blending operations. If your layers use a blending operation such as Overlay, Screen, or Multiply, it will not be recognized on import. Instead, you will just get a series of layers, one on top of the other.

■ People often use various Photoshop layer effects such as drop shadows, bevels, embosses, and so on to enhance layers—particularly text layers. Media Composer does not recognize these effects. Before importing, you must rasterize the effects so they are merged into the layer. (See the appendix for more on this.)

■ If your layer is not full screen but perhaps a title or lower third, you will also need an alpha channel in Photoshop so you can key this over your sequence. This may also include some kind of transparency or a soft shadow, which means you will need a soft edge alpha. Again, this is discussed in the appendix.

To import a Photoshop file:

Note: You don't need Photoshop installed on the Media Composer system for this to complete these steps.

1. Right-click in the bin and choose **Import** or choose **File > Import**.

2. Choose the **Photoshop Titles with Layers** Photoshop file in the Graphics for Lesson 04 folder and click **OK**.

3. As shown in Figure 4.27, a dialog box appears to inform you that the file you want to import contains layers and asks you what to do. You can bring all the layers in as a sequence, you can flatten the image, or you can select the layers. Choose **Select Layers**.

Figure 4.27
Importing Photoshop files dialog box.

4. The Select Layers dialog box appears, as shown in Figure 4.28. Here, you can see the name of each layer as named in Photoshop. This is especially useful if you have a series of lower thirds with names for people. Select the layers you want and Click **OK** to import.

Figure 4.28
Choosing which Photoshop layers to import.

5. You will see a series of matte key clips in your bin and a sequence. Load the sequence into the Timeline, and you will see all the layers stacked up on top of each other—and correctly keyed. See Figure 4.29.

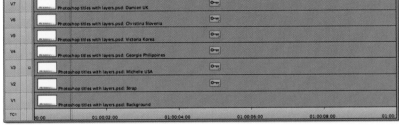

Figure 4.29
The imported Photoshop layers as a sequence in the Timeline.

6. If you have selected individual layers, you can now edit them into your sequence; they will key over your shots.

Batch Import: Graphic Workflow

Earlier, I talked about a typical workflow where the graphics department might be working on some images for you, but they might need to update them during the editing process. However, you may have already edited them into your Timeline and perhaps even applied some effects to them. For example, you might have a slide show with some animations to take you from one slide to another.

The good news is, you don't have to do all the animations all over again. This is thanks to a very useful feature called Batch Import. Batch Import enables you to automatically reimport any or all of your graphics in one go.

To use Batch Import:

1. Select your sequence. Then choose **CLIP** > **BATCH IMPORT** (see Figure 4.30) or right-click the sequence and choose **BATCH IMPORT**.

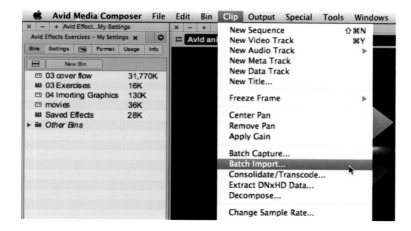

Figure 4.30
Choosing Batch Import from the Clip menu.

2. A dialog box opens, asking whether you want to import clips that are offline or all the clips. (See Figure 4.31.) If you have a lot of clips in your sequence and only a few need replacing, you can delete the media files of the ones that have been updated. In this case, choose **OFFLINE ONLY**. Alternatively, you may wish to see all the clips and choose from a list which ones you wish to import. In that case, choose **ALL CLIPS**.

Figure 4.31
Batch Import choices.

3. The Batch Import dialog box opens, as shown in Figure 4.32. There, you will see a list of the clips and the path to the original file location. If you have moved or renamed a file, you will see a question mark to the left of the path to signify that Media Composer can't find your file. Or it may be that you just wish to point to a different file. In either case, select the file, right-click it, and choose **SET FILE LOCATION**. Alternatively, select the file and click the **SET FILE LOCATION** button to choose a new path to your file.

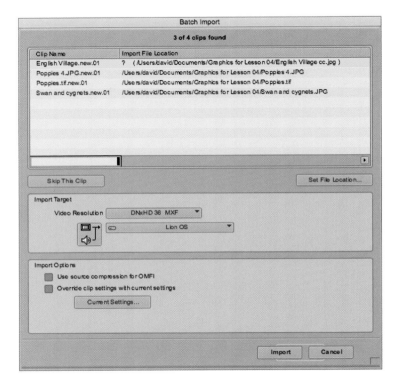

Figure 4.32
The Batch Import dialog box.

Note: Files for import can be stored on a server somewhere, and your path may be a shared drive on a different computer. Media Composer can keep track of the path to any location on your network.

4. If you have multiple files and don't wish to reimport one of them, select the file you want to skip, right-click it, and choose **SKIP THIS CLIP** (see Figure 4.33). Alternatively, select the file you want to skip and click the **SKIP THIS CLIP** button. Note that you can select more than one file. To do so, click one file and Shift-click another file to select all the files from the first to the last. Alternatively, you can Command-click (Mac) or Ctrl-click (Windows) files to select multiple files without including files in between.

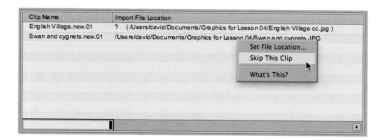

Figure 4.33
Skip the clip.

5. You also have the option to choose a resolution for import and a target drive. You can also change the import settings if you got them wrong the first time.

6. Click the **Import** button. Media Composer automatically recaptures all your graphic files and updates the sequence with the new files. If you have added any effects to the graphics, they will automatically update as well. As shown in Figure 4.34, the updated clip will be appended with .new after the original name, regardless of what the new file may have been named.

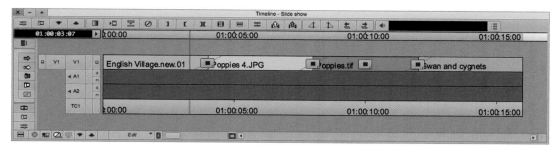

Figure 4.34
Sequence updated with new clip.

Batch Import: File Workflow

Batch Import has another very important use. You may be planning to output a high-quality movie in HD, but you need to work in an "offline" resolution during the edit. For example, suppose you were editing the Singapore clips, which were imported at DNxHD 36. Although you probably can't tell, this is meant to be an offline resolution. When you finish your edit, you will need to reimport the shots at a higher resolution. In the old days of tape, you would have redigitized all the clips from the original source tape. Now you can do the same, only with files instead. Batch Import works for imported files of any type—still or moving.

So if you wanted to import the Singapore files again—only this time at, say, DNxHD 175—you would use the Batch Import dialog box to find the original files and reimport them.

Review/Discussion Questions

1. True or false: When you import an image it is rasterized to the current project format.

2. What is the appropriate image size for NTSC SD (or PAL SD) in square pixels?

    NTSC

    a. 648×486

    b. 720×486

    c. 640×480

    PAL

    a. 768×576

    b. 720×576

    c. 1024×576

3. You have an image that is tall and thin. You want to preserve the aspect. What setting must you use for this?

    a. Image Sized for Current Format

    b. Crop/Pad for DV Scan Line Difference

    c. Do Not Resize Smaller Images

    d. Resize Image to Fit Format Raster

4. When you play back a movie file that you have imported, it appears to be flickering on the broadcast monitor. Why might this be? What can you do about it?

5. What video-file mapping should you use when importing Avid test signals?

   a. Computer RGB (0–255)

   b. Computer RGB dither

   c. 601/709 (16-235)

6. How can you convert the aspect ratio of an image imported as 4:3 when you are working in 16:9?

7. You have been given a movie file that came with an alpha as a separate video clip. Outline the steps you take to make it composite over a clip on V1.

   1. Import the two clips and create _____ extra video tracks.

   2. Edit the foreground clip on _____ and the alpha on _____.

   3. Add a _____ _____ effect to _____.

8. How do you reassign the location of a graphic on a disk when reimporting?

9. What is the difference in file aspect between NTSC D1 and NTSC DV, and how do you compensate?

10. Why are there nonsquare pixels?

Importing Files

In this exercise, you'll practice importing files.

Media Used:

Open the bin 04 Exercises. Also find the folder called Graphics for Lesson 04 on your DVD.

Duration:

45 minutes

GOAL

- Import various images and movie files and experiment with the settings

Preparing and Importing Various Images

Begin by importing some files. Open the Graphics for Lesson 04 folder on the DVD. In your MC 205 Pro Effects project, open the Lesson 04 Exercises bin. There are some images in the Graphics folder with different sizes and aspect ratios. You are going to try to import them with different settings and see the results. Your current project format is 1080P 23.976 and the aspect is 16:9. However, for the first part of this exercise, you need to work in standard definition.

1. Click the **FORMAT** tab in the Project window and change the project type to 23.976 NTSC.

2. Change the project aspect ratio to 4:3.

3. If you haven't already done so, switch to the Graphics bin view.

Note: The Pro FX User settings that come with the project on the DVD have this view created for you. Otherwise, refer to Figure 4.1 as a guide in setting up this view.

4. Locate and double-click the **NTSC 720×486 NON SQ** file in the Graphics folder to open it. You will see in Preview (Mac) or Windows Photo Viewer (Windows) that it doesn't look quite right.

5. Right-click in the bin and choose **IMPORT**.

6. Select **OPTIONS**. The Import Settings dialog box opens.

7. Choose **IMAGE SIZED FOR CURRENT FORMAT** and **COMPUTER RGB** and click **OK**.

8. Navigate to the **GRAPHICS FOR LESSON 04** folder and select the **NTSC 720×486** file.

9. Click **OPEN** and the file will be imported. Notice in the bin that it is correctly displayed.

Now let's see what happens if you choose the wrong setting.

1. Repeat the procedure, only this time choose **RESIZE IMAGE TO FIT FORMAT RASTER**.

2. Import the image again.

This time, you'll see that it has black lines at the top and bottom. This is because Media Composer is trying to preserve the original aspect of your image on the assumption that it is a square pixel image.

Now let's try to import the 16:9 image. Keep the settings the same—i.e., Resize Image to Fit Format Raster. Then follow these steps:

1. Right-click in the bin and choose **IMPORT**.

2. Select the **NTSC 864×486 (16:9 SQ)** file and import it. This time, it has the right aspect but is letterboxed. Why? The file was created as a square pixel file and the aspect is correct. The settings will try to preserve the original aspect, so the letterboxing will appear.

3. Change your settings back to **IMAGE SIZED FOR CURRENT FORMAT** and reimport the image. Does it look right? No, because this is a 16:9 image, which is being displayed in a 4:3 aspect. It has been imported to fill the frame, but you are not displaying it correctly.

4. Change your project aspect to 16:9. Now your image is displaying correctly!

If you are importing a 16:9 file, your project needs to be set to 16:9, and the import setting should be Image Sized for Current Format. Resize Image to Fit Format Raster is the wrong setting because this will cause the image to be letterboxed even though it looks like a circle when displayed as 4:3.

Now let's try some real-world images. Set your project back to 1080P 23.975 and you will be back in the world of 16:9.

1. With the settings on Image Sized for Current Format, import the 16:9 **CUTE BABY** file. Looks good, right? Well, she is very cute. Plus, the image is 16:9 and the project is 16:9, so all is well.

2. Import the **RICE PADDY BALI** file. This does not look good because the image was originally in a tall aspect. What is the correct setting for this image?

3. Change the settings back to **RESIZE IMAGE TO FIT FORMAT RASTER** and try again. All is good again.

4. Import the **OFFERINGS** image. This is also a different aspect. Think about which is the best setting for these images.

5. Look at the **SWAN AND CYGNETS** file. What aspect is this? What settings would you use here? What if you were importing it into a 4:3 project?

Note: For those in the PAL world, there are two images of circles that were created in PAL SD dimensions. You will need to create a PAL project for these, but you can try to import them and see which are the best settings.

Importing Color Bars for Line Up

If you are outputting an online master, you will need to line up your sequence correctly. You can easily create some bars for this.

1. Open the Import Settings dialog box and choose **601 SD OR 709 HD (16–235)** under FILE PIXEL TO VIDEO MAPPING.

2. Navigate to **HD/APPLICATIONS/AVID MEDIA COMPOSER/SUPPORTINGFILES/ TEST_PATTERNS/HD_1080** (Mac) or **C:/PROGRAM FILES/AVID MEDIA COMPOSER/SUPPORTINGFILES/TEST_PATTERNS/HD_1080** (Windows). Then select **SMPTE_BARS** (or any other bars of your choice).

3. Create a test pattern that you can edit into your sequence.

Note: If you have completed the MC 239 Color Grading with Media Composer and Symphony course and you are familiar with how the Y Waveform scope works, then you might like to try looking at the bars in Color Correction mode. You can use the Y Waveform scope to confirm that it is correctly imported. Try the same file with the settings on Computer RGB and see the difference in the Y Waveform.

Creating a Slide Show and Reimporting Files

Betty has sent over her assistant at Mad Dogs, Freddie Flashframe, with a small job for you. He has four photographs from the English Tourist Board, and he needs you to make a slide show in 16:9 format. First, you'll import the images. Follow these steps:

1. Because the files are not 16:9, select the **RESIZE IMAGE TO FIT FORMAT RASTER** option.

2. Navigate to the **ENGLISH TOURIST BOARD** folder to import the files. (You can import them all together.)

3. Edit five seconds of each clip into a new sequence and name it **SLIDE SHOW**. (Make sure you leave yourself some handles.)

4. To save time, you can use the transition in the bin. If you like, you can make your own.

5. Play the sequence. You'll see there is a problem with the Poppies clip; you need to crop it.

6. Add a **3D WARP** effect and crop the image so it matches the others. (A value of **755 RIGHT** and **–755 LEFT** is pretty accurate.)

Now Freddie (who is almost as ditzy as Betty) has a new file that he would rather use than the English Village shot. Of course, you could simply import it and replace the shot, but you can use Batch Import too….

1. Select the sequence in the bin, open the **Clip** menu, and choose **Batch Import**.

2. In the dialog box that opens, click **All Clips**.

3. A list of clips appears. You only want to replace the English Village clip, so select the others and click **Skip This Clip**. They will vanish from the box.

4. Select the **English Village** clip and click **Set File Location**.

5. A Finder/Explorer window will open and return you to where the files were before, but you can see in the enclosing folder there is a file called English Village 2. Select the **English Village 2** file and choose **Open**.

6. In the dialog box that appears, choose **Import**.

The file is imported, but more importantly, it is edited into your sequence with the same effect applied. Although this is a simple case, it is a useful feature to bear in mind for a complex sequence that uses imported files of any kind—still or moving.

Paint Effects

Avid Media Composer has various effects known as Paint (also known as Intraframe) Effects that allow you to draw your own shapes. These shapes can be used either to composite one image over another or to create various effects such as blurs, mosaics, clones, or spot color correction. The shapes can be animated and tracked to follow movement on the clip to which it is applied.

Media Used: The media for this lesson is in the MC205 Pro Effects project. Open the Lesson 05 Paint bin.

Duration: 60 minutes

GOALS

- Use the Paint Effect to create solid objects
- Use the paint modes to apply treatments to all or part of the frame
- Create and adjust the objects using a variety of tools
- Animate the shape of an object over time

Applying Intraframe Effects

There are two basic types of Intraframe effects:

■ **The Paint Effect.** This creates visible shapes.

■ **The AniMatte effects.** These are used to create mattes.

Note: The Paint Effect can be applied only to segments, not to transitions.
     However, the AniMatte effect can be used as a transition effect.

The most comprehensive set of effects is the Paint Effect. This is found in the
Image group of the Effect Palette. There are some subsets of this effect, which are
used for specific applications, such as Mosaic, Blur, Scratch Removal, and Spot
Color; these are also found in the Image group. All of these allow you to add various kinds of objects to the video clip. Figure 5.1 shows an example of various
paint objects grouped together to form a smiley face.

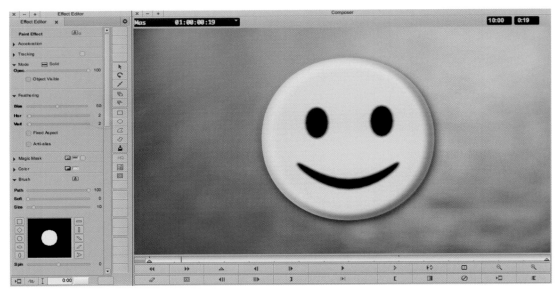

Figure 5.1
Painting with the Paint Effect.

To apply the effect, just drag it from the Effect Palette to the clip you want to
modify. If you wish to use either the Paint Effect or the AniMatte effect on just
part of a clip, you can use the Add Edit button to isolate the area you wish to treat.
There is a sequence in the Lesson 05 Paint bin called Paint Effects–Shapes that
you can use to try out the Paint Effect.

As shown in Figure 5.2, the Paint Effect offers a wide variety of modes for overlaying the shapes. Depending on the mode you use, the shapes can overlay a specific color or somehow modify the image underneath in a variety of ways. The various modes will be discussed in more detail later in this lesson, along with the standalone effects—Blur, Mosaic, Spot Color, and Scratch Removal.

Figure 5.2
The Paint Effect modes.

The AniMatte effect is also an Intraframe effect. Although it shares many of the features of the Paint Effect, it is specifically used for drawing mattes and is found in the Key group.

Note: All the Intraframe effects allow you to animate the shapes you draw, but they do not use keyframe graphs. Instead, the keyframes are added directly on the Composer window effect Timeline.

Shape Creation

As shown in Figure 5.3, there are five tools for creating shapes: the Rectangle tool, the Oval tool, the Polygon tool, the Curve tool, and the Brush tool. You'll learn about all these tools next. Find the Paint Effects–Shapes sequence in the Lesson 05 Paint bin and try the following examples.

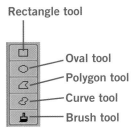

Figure 5.3
Shape tools.

The Rectangle and Oval Tools

The Rectangle and Oval tools allow you to create rectangular and oval objects, respectively. Use the Paint Effect–Shapes sequence if you haven't already loaded it.

To draw a rectangle or an oval:

1. Apply the **PAINT EFFECT** to the soft water clip and enter Effect mode.

2. Select the **RECTANGLE** or **OVAL** tool.

3. Click anywhere on the image. The cursor will change to a cross.

4. Drag the cursor down to the right and release the mouse button to create your shape. (There is no way to constrain the shape to a square or circle.)

Custom-Made Shapes

The Paint Effect has basic shape-creation tools. More complex shapes need to be designed from scratch using the Polygon, Curve or Brush tools. However, you will see later that certain third-party plug-ins have many more premade custom shapes. For example, Sapphire's Shape plug-in Boris's 3D shape tool called BCC Extruded Spline let you create polygons with as many sides as you like and apply all kinds of transformation to make stars and other shapes.

When you have created the shape, the Paint Effect will automatically revert to the Selection tool so you can move or resize the shape. You can create as many shapes as you like by clicking the Rectangle or Oval button again. While the Selection tool is active you can also click to select the object and press the delete button to delete it.

The Polygon Tool

This tool enables you to draw irregular closed shapes. You can draw straight-line objects, curved objects using Bézier curves, or a combination of both.

To draw a polygon with straight lines:

1. If you haven't already done so, use the **SELECTION** tool to select any shapes you have and delete them.

2. Select the **POLYGON** tool.

3. Click the image to create the first point. The cursor will change to a cross.

4. Move the cursor to the next point on your shape (just move, don't drag) and click again to create the next point.

5. Continue clicking different points until you have your shape.

6. Click on or very near the first point to close the shape. Alternatively, you can double-click the penultimate point to close the shape. Figure 5.4 shows an example of a straight-line polygon.

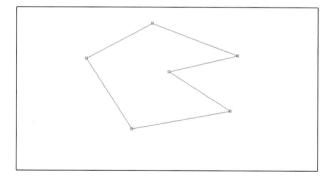

Figure 5.4
An example of a straight-line polygon.

Note: In all the illustrations for drawing shapes, the image has been inverted from what Media Composer will display for clarity. Black is white and white is black.

To draw a polygon with Bézier curves:

1. If you haven't already done so, use the **SELECTION** tool to select the shape you have just drawn and delete it.

2. Select the **POLYGON** tool.

3. Place the cursor where you want the curve to begin; then click and drag in the direction you want to go, as shown in Figure 5.5. As you drag, you create the first handle and you pull the handle in the direction you drag. Make sure the direction you drag is tangential to the curve you are creating. The length and angle determine the shape of the first section of the curve.

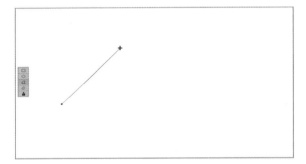

Figure 5.5
Create the first handle.

4. Release the mouse button when you are happy with the direction.

5. Move (don't drag) the crosshair to the position where you want to create the second anchor point. As you move your mouse, you will see the arc of the first section follow your current position.

6. Click to add the anchor point; then drag (without letting go) to create the next handle (see Figure 5.6). As you drag, you not only set the direction for the next section of the curve, but you also determine the shape of the preceding section because the handles are symmetrical.

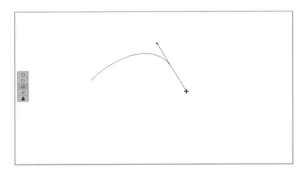

Figure 5.6
Create the next handle.

Note: Sometimes, you may need different types of curves on each side of a point, but you will need to finish the entire curve before you can adjust the individual curve segments. You can't make any corrections to what you have done till you finish drawing.

7. Continue adding points until you have your shape. (See Figure 5.7.)

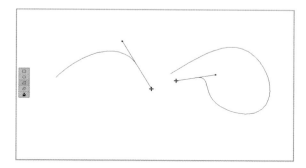

Figure 5.7
Two stages in drawing a curve.

8. Position your mouse pointer on or near the first handle and click to close the shape (see Figure 5.8). Alternatively, double-click the penultimate handle to close the shape.

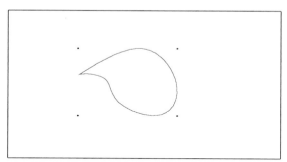

Figure 5.8
The finished curve.

Understanding Bézier Curves

You first came across Bézier curves in the section "Working with Animation Curves" in Lesson 2, "Animating with Keyframes." The same principles apply here. You are drawing an arc between two points that is controlled by the Bézier handles. You can move either the point or the direction handle to reshape your object. The angle and the length of the handles determines the shape of the curve. The direction lines are always tangential to the curve at the anchor point. Figure 5.9 shows examples of Bézier curves.

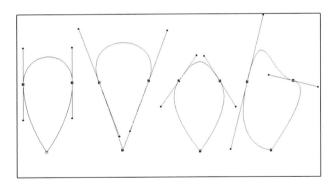

Figure 5.9
Bézier curve examples.

Bézier Drawing Tips

If you have not used Bézier curves before, you may find it a little difficult to draw your shape at first. After some practice, it will become quite natural to draw Bézier shapes. In the meantime, keep these tips in mind:

■ When you drag your direction handles, the leading edge always needs to be in the direction you are heading (see Figure 5.10), not the direction you came from. If you drag in the wrong direction, you will cause the curve to twist.

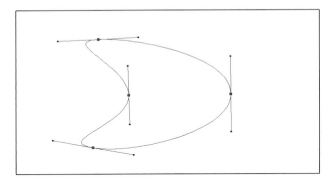

Figure 5.10
Draw in the direction of the curve.

■ When drawing a series of varying curves, try to place the anchor points at the beginning and end of each curve where the direction of the curve is changing. This will enable you to draw the shape more efficiently and uses fewer anchor points.

■ Use as few anchor points as possible. The more anchor points you use, the less smooth the curve will be.

■ You may not always get your shape right the first time. In the next section, you'll learn how to edit the shape.

The Curve Tool

This tool lets you draw freeform closed shapes. When you finish drawing a shape with this tool, the shape is converted to a Bézier curve that you can edit point by point, as shown in Figure 5.11. (See "The Reshape Tool" which is covered in the next section.)

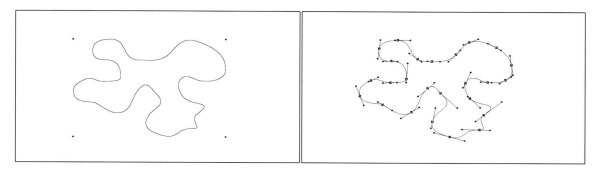

Figure 5.11
A freeform shape selected (left) and showing the Bézier points (right).

Tip: If you want to draw shapes with the Curve tool, you'll find it works much better with a pen and tablet than with a mouse.

To draw freeform shapes:

1. Click and hold the mouse button (or touch the pen) on the location where you want start your shape.

2. Keep the mouse button held down and drag to create your shape. To complete the shape, return to the starting point.

3. When you have completed the shape, release the mouse button (or lift the pen). The shape will close and the Selection tool will activate.

The Brush Tool

This tool allows you to draw a stroke rather than a filled shape. You can also change the size and shape of the brush for particular jobs. This makes it very useful for touching up images or scratch removal, as you'll see later.

To draw with the Brush tool:

1. Select the **Brush** tool. By default, the brush has a round shape.

2. Click and hold the mouse at the point where you wish to begin drawing your shape.

3. Keep the mouse button held down and draw your shape.

4. Release the mouse button when you are finished.

Note: This is the one tool where you don't have to create a closed shape. You are drawing a stroke with a pre-defined brush that doesn't fill when you complete the shape. Also, you don't automatically revert to the Selection tool when you are done. The Brush tool stays selected, so you can use this tool to create multiple lines, blobs, scratch marks, etc.

There are some special parameters for the Brush tool that allow you to select and even design various brush types. As shown in Figure 5.12, these parameters offer you 10 choices of brush shapes, which you can select before you start to draw your shape. You can change the size and softness of your brush, and even the angle of the brush shape. For example, if you wish to create a calligraphic style for a handwriting effect, you can choose one of the shapes on the right side, as shown in Figure 5.13. (In this example, the writing also has a soft shadow and a highlight. This is easy to do: Just copy and paste to duplicate the layer twice, and then add softness to the duplicates and change the color—one to black and one to white. See the next section, "Object-Manipulation Tools," for more details on how to change a shape.) You can also change a brush type after you have drawn the shape by selecting the shape and clicking on one of the other brush types to select it.

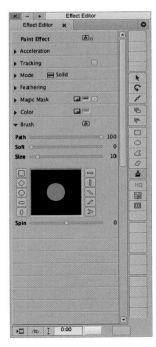

Figure 5.12
The Brush parameters.

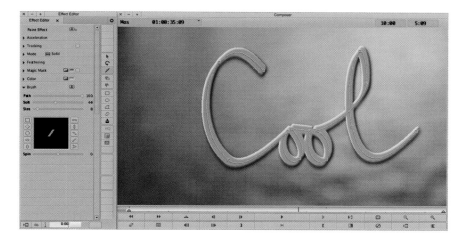

Figure 5.13
Changing the brush type.

Tip: You can actually make your own brushes. If you select any of the existing brush shapes and increase the size to more than 20, you will see that the brush becomes a Bézier shape! You can now tweak the Bézier points and handles to create your own brush. (See Figure 5.14.)

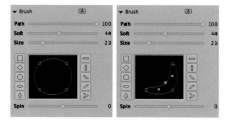

Figure 5.14
Designing your own brush.

The Brush tool also has a Path parameter, which is very useful. This lets you create write-on effects by animating the amount using keyframes, as shown in Figure 5.15. A value of 0 is the first frame of the write-on, and 100 is the fully written shape.

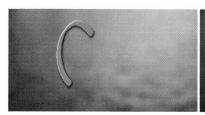

Figure 5.15
Animating the path to create a handwriting effect.

Object-Manipulation Tools

After you have drawn an object you may wish to edit the shape—for example, rotating it, changing the color, or changing the size. For these, you will need the object-manipulation tools—the Selection tool, the Rotation tool (also called Z Rot), and the Reshape tool—which are shown in Figure 5.16.

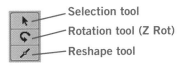
Selection tool
Rotation tool (Z Rot)
Reshape tool

Figure 5.16
Object-manipulation tools.

The Selection Tool

To make any changes to an object, you will first need to select it. To do so, simply click the Selection tool, and then click the object. When you do, you will see four manipulation handles—one at each corner of your object.

If you have multiple objects and some are stacked on top of the others, then selecting an object is not always easy because you can't see which object is which. If this is the case, then read on....

Working with Multiple Objects

If you have multiple objects, you can select all of them by lassoing. You can then choose which ones to select by selecting one and Shift-selecting others. To change your selection from one object to another, click the Fast Forward or Rewind button or click the Go to Next Edit or Go to Previous Edit button.

Note: If you have not selected an object before you click the Go to Next Edit button, Media Composer will take you to the next edit, which may be undesirable. Best to stick to Fast Forward and Rewind!

Tip: You can get a much better idea of what is going on with multiple objects by deselecting the Outline/Path button at the bottom of the Effect Editor window. When you select an object, it will highlight in blue, as shown in Figure 5.17.

Figure 5.17
The result of deselecting the Outline/Path button.

Moving Objects

You can easily move an object by simply dragging it with your mouse. You can also nudge an object incrementally with the Trim buttons—the M, comma (,), period (.), and forward slash (/) keys by default.

When using the Trim buttons, clicking the Trim 10 Frames Left (the M key) will move the object 10 pixels left, clicking Trim One Frame Left (the , key) will move one pixel left, and so on. Pressing Option+M (Mac) or Alt+M (Windows) will move 10 pixels up, pressing Option+/ (Mac) or Alt+/ (Windows) will move the object 10 pixels down, and so on. This also works when you have selected multiple objects.

Tip: You can use the Nudge buttons to move control points as well as the entire object when you are in Reshape mode.

Copying and Pasting Objects

You can select an object and then copy and paste it to create a duplicate at the same position. The objects can be stacked in this way—and you can use this technique to create soft shadows, highlights, and so on, as shown in Figure 5.18.

Figure 5.18
A circle duplicated a few times, softened, and nudged.

Tip: Not only can you copy and paste shapes within a Paint Effect, but if you want to use the same shape in a *different* Paint Effect, you can copy from one to the other. For example, if you spent a lot of time drawing a shape to apply some kind of color correction, but you decide you want to use the same shape in the Spot Color effect, you can copy the shape in the Paint Effect, go to the Spot Color effect, and paste it in.

Changing the Stacking Order of Selected Objects

As you create more and more objects, they will appear one on top of the other, in the order that you drew them. You may wish to change the order of these objects, however, because an object affects all the objects underneath it as well as the background video. To change the order of a selected object, use the Bring Forward and Send Backward buttons, shown in Figure 5.19. As shown in Figure 5.20, each click of the button will bring the object (in this case, the purple triangle) backward one step.

Bring Forward button
Send Backward button

Figure 5.19
The Bring Forward and Send Backward buttons.

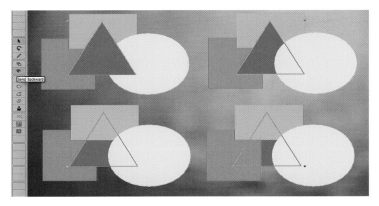

Figure 5.20
Changing the stacking order of the selected object.

Tip: To bring an object directly to the front of a stack, Option-click (Mac) or Alt-click (Windows) the Bring Forward button. Likewise, Option-clicking (Mac) or Alt-clicking (Windows) the Send Backward button sends an object straight to the back, without passing Go and without collecting $200!

Resizing an Object

When you have selected an object, you can resize it by grabbing one of the corner handles and moving it in the direction you wish to expand (or contract) the object. (Again, there is no way of constraining the resize to preserve the dimensions.) By default the object is anchored so that the expansion is centered from the opposite corner handle to the one you select.

Tip: When you resize an object, you might wish to expand the object from its center rather than from a corner. You can resize from the center of the shape by
Option-dragging (Mac) or Alt-dragging (Windows) one of the corner handles.

The Rotation Tool

When you click the Rotation button, you will see a small cross (representing the axis of rotation) and a handle. You can use the handle to rotate the object, as shown in Figure 5.21.

Figure 5.21
Moving the axis and rotating the shape.

There is a limitation to keyframing rotation. Media Composer animates the movement of each point in the object in a linear (not circular) direction. Although this gives the impression of rotation for a small angle of rotation, it will distort your object for larger angles.

The Reshape Tool

Regardless of how you draw your shape, chances are you will want to reshape it. Even a simple oval can be reshaped to better fit a face. This is the tool for doing that.

When you select an object, you will see the four corner handles, which allow you to manipulate the shape as a whole by stretching or resizing it. When you click the Reshape button, however, these corner handles disappear, and instead you will see the shape defined by a number of anchor points. Depending on how you originally drew the object, you can have two types of anchor points: corner points, which do not have handles, or Bézier curve points, which do. (See Figure 5.22.) If the points are on a curve, they will have their own pair of Bézier handles. These anchor points (and their associated handles) allow you to change the shape of your object in a much more precise way.

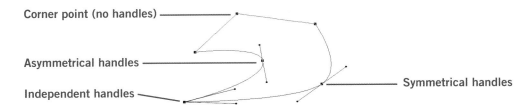

Figure 5.22
Types of anchor point.

Selecting a Point

To refine the shape precisely, you will need to edit individual anchor points—either by moving them or converting them from corner points to curve points so you can adjust the shape of the curve.

To move an anchor point or alter the curve associated with it you must first select it. When you select a point, it turns from a hollow square to a solid square. (See Figure 5.23.) If your point is a curve point with handles, you will only see them when the point is selected. You can select as many anchor points as you like by Shift-clicking subsequent points.

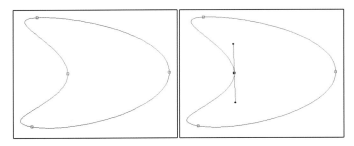

Figure 5.23
An unselected anchor point (left) and a selected anchor point (right).

Moving from Point to Point

If you have selected a point, you can select a different point along the path by clicking the Fast Forward or Rewind button. Clicking Fast Forward takes you clockwise around a path, and clicking Rewind takes you counterclockwise.

Nudging Points

You can grab a point and move it, or you can use the Trim buttons to move a point in incremental steps. The same buttons and keyboard shortcuts apply here as when nudging the entire shape. You can move single points or multiple points.

Adding and Deleting Points

If you have a curve and you want to add a point, you can do so by Option-clicking (Mac) or Alt-clicking (Windows) anywhere on the path that you wish to add a point. To delete a point, select it and press the Delete key.

Note: **When working with Bézier curves, it is a good idea to have as few points as possible. This makes it easier to achieve a smooth curve. It also makes life much easier when you animate point positions. However, if you are planning to animate your shape, you should not add or delete points during the animation. The number of points cannot change over time.**

Converting Points

We have discussed moving points, but what about changing the shape of your curve? For example, you might have drawn a square or a polygon shape, but now you want to round the corners. You can convert a corner point to a Bézier curve (see Figure 5.24) by Option-clicking (Mac) or Alt-clicking (Windows) the point itself.

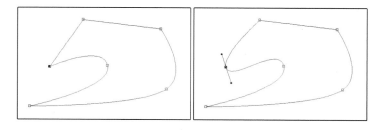

Figure 5.24
Option-clicking (Mac) or Alt-clicking (Windows) converts a point from corner point to Bézier curve.

Note: **The exact position of your mouse is critical when trying to convert a point. If you are not in the exact center of the point, you will see the curves, but they will revert to a corner point when you let go. Don't give up, though; it may take several attempts, but you'll get it!**

Adjusting Bézier Curves

The usual rules for adjusting Bézier curves apply. With the anchor point selected, drag the handle away from the point to increase the amount of curvature and drag toward the point to decrease the amount of curvature. (See Figure 5.25.) If you drag the handle so that it is on top of the anchor point, you will get a straight line. You can also rotate the handles to change the shape of the curve altogether, as shown in Figure 5.26.

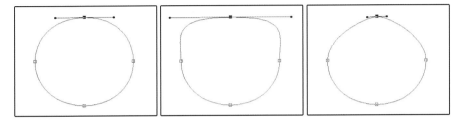

Figure 5.25
Adjusting the curvature.

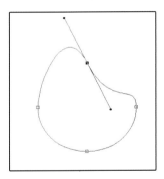

Figure 5.26
Rotate the handles to change the curve.

Changing the Handle Type

As with keyframe graphs, there are three possible modes for Bézier handles: symmetrical, asymmetrical, and independent. By default, Bézier curves are symmetrical. To toggle the handle type from symmetrical to asymmetrical, Shift-click the handle (see Figure 5.27). Note that in asymmetrical mode, you can adjust the *length* of the handles independently, but the *direction* will still be linked.

To break a Bézier curve so that you have two independent handles, Option-click (Mac) or Alt-click (Windows) the handle (see Figure 5.28). This lets you move either of the two handles without affecting the other. To return the curve to symmetrical handles, Option-click (Mac) or Alt-click (Windows) the handle again.

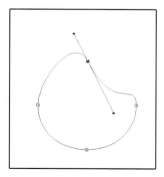

Figure 5.27
Shift-click to toggle between
symmetrical and asymmetrical
handles.

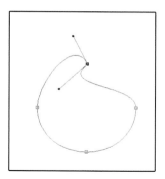

Figure 5.28
Independent handles.

Note: In Bézier language, an anchor point with independent (or broken) handles
is known as a *cusp*.

Object Parameters

At this point, you have drawn an object (or several objects) and have edited the
shape and size. What next? Well, you can do lots of things with your objects—for
example, change the mode, feather them, and change the color. The following
parameters let you do this.

Acceleration

Remember that the Intraframe effects have no animation graphs. Any animation you
apply to the position of an effect by default uses a linear interpolation—meaning
if you keyframe its motion, you will see it move steadily from one position to
another. If you want to apply some ease in and ease out (as if using a Spline curve),
you can use the Acceleration parameter, shown in Figure 5.29, to achieve this.

Figure 5.29
The Acceleration parameter.

Note: You should use acceleration only when you are moving an object independently from the background. If you are trying to track an object to follow a
point on the background shot, then you can't use acceleration.

Modes

An object need not just be a colored shape. Each object can have various effects applied to it so that it interacts with other objects or the background in some way. (See Figure 5.30.) Note that when certain modes are chosen, additional parameters may appear. These will vary from mode to mode. For example, if you choose Color Adjust, you will get the various color controls that you would find in the Color Effect. You can also adjust the opacity of each object in the Mode parameter, as shown in Figure 5.31. Finally, you can turn on or off the object with the Object Visible button. If you wish to try the various modes, you can use the Paint Effects–Modes sequence in the bin. It has a Paint Effect already applied and a shape has been added.

Figure 5.30
The many modes
of the Paint Effect.

Figure 5.31
Adjusting the opacity and
visibility of an object.

Following is a detailed description of the modes:

■ **Solid.** This is the default mode. As shown in Figure 5.32, it applies a color to a shape. Use the Opacity setting to apply a color wash to a portion of the image.

Figure 5.32
Various shapes with colors
and opacity adjusted.

■ **Erase.** This cuts a hole in all the other shapes below to reveal the background video, as shown in Figure 5.33. This mode is very useful for restoring the original image inside a shape. You can also use the Opacity setting to mix back the lower objects.

Figure 5.33
The triangle is set to Erase.

■ **Outline.** This mode, shown in Figure 5.34, converts the shape into a crude two-pixel outline. It is really only used for previsualization purposes.

Figure 5.34
The green square is set to Outline.

■ **Clone.** This basically takes a snapshot of the image underneath (including other objects) and lets you move it to another part of the frame, as shown in Figure 5.35. It is used to remove unwanted parts of the image by replacing them with another area of the image. This mode will be discussed in more detail later in this lesson in the section "Using Scratch Removal."

Figure 5.35
The square is now set to Clone and shifted.

- **Colorize.** This will let you tint the image. If you experiment with the Opacity slider and the Hue, Saturation, and Luminance sliders in the Color parameters, you can actually achieve some very nice color filters. In the example in Figure 5.36, a sepia effect was applied by setting the Opacity to 50 percent, the Hue to 32, the Saturation to 200, and the Luminance to 200. Be careful not to exceed the allowed limits for chroma values. Always use an external scope to check the results.

Figure 5.36
Part of the image is colorized
(with the Opacity setting reduced).

- **Hue.** This is similar to Colorize, except that the tint is applied in proportion to the saturation of the pixels in the original image. Thus, it only affects the more saturated colors in the original. (See Figure 5.37.)

Figure 5.37
Hue applied.

- **Saturation.** With this mode, shown in Figure 5.38, all the saturation values in the video are replaced with a single (high) saturation value. This produces highly pixilated noise on your image, which is really only any use if you want to make some kind of effect.

Figure 5.38
Saturation applied.

■ **Luminance.** With this mode, shown in Figure 5.39, all the luminance values in the video are replaced by a single luminance value that is determined by the Lum(inance) level slider in the Color parameters. Basically, what you are left with are just the chrominance values. If you want to use this, it is best to set the Hue and Saturation sliders to 0. One possible use of this is if you reduce the opacity, you can put a gray wash over an image, from which you can then cut out a hole with another shape set to Erase, as shown in Figure 5.40.

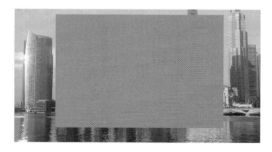

Figure 5.39
Luminance applied.

Figure 5.40
An example in which a hole is cut in a luminance "wash."

■ **Darken Only.** This acts as a low-pass filter and is used in conjunction with the Color parameters. (For best results, set Hue and Saturation to 0 and adjust the Luminance slider.) Pixels in the video that are of higher value than the Luminance setting in the Color parameter group are set to the selected luminance value. The result is like a luma clip, only the chroma values are also affected. (See Figure 5.41.)

Figure 5.41
Darken Only, with Luminance set to 120.

- **Lighten Only.** This acts as a high-pass filter and is used in conjunction with the Color parameters. (For best results, set Hue and Saturation to 0 and adjust the Luminance slider.) Pixels in the video that are of lower value than the Luminance setting in the Color parameter group are set to the selected luminance value. The result is also like a luma clip, only the chroma values are also affected. (See Figure 5.42.)

Figure 5.42
Lighten Only, with Luminance set to 120.

- **Darken.** This uniformly lowers the luminance signal, as shown in Figure 5.43. It's used in conjunction with the Amount (Amt) slider in the Mode group. The values in the Color group do not affect this mode. Note that this mode can lower the luminance below legal levels, so always use it with an external scope.

Figure 5.43
Darken applied.

- **Lighten.** This uniformly raises the luminance signal, as shown in Figure 5.44. It is used in conjunction with the Amount slider in the Mode group. The values in the Color group do not affect this mode. Note that this mode can lower the luminance below legal levels, so again, always use it with an external scope.

Figure 5.44
Lighten applied.

- **Add.** This raises the luminance levels by adding the luminance and hue values of the object. That means you can add a tint to a picture, as shown in Figure 5.45, by adjusting the Hue, Saturation, and Luminance sliders in the Color parameters.

Figure 5.45
Add applied with Hue at 120, Saturation at 130, and Luminance at 100.

- **Subtract.** This lowers the luminance levels by subtracting the luminance and hue values of the object. Thus, as shown in Figure 5.46, your tint will have the opposite hue to the original color of the shape.

Figure 5.46
Subtract with the same color values.

- **Invert.** This simply gives you a "negative" image (see Figure 5.47) by inverting the luminance and chrominance values. The color sliders have no effect.

Figure 5.47
Invert applied.

■ **Mosaic.** This effect applies a mosaic to the selected area, as shown in Figure 5.48. Because this is an effect with specific applications, it has been broken out into its own freestanding effect: the Mosaic effect. This is covered in more detail later in this lesson in the section "Applying Mosaic and Blur Effects."

Figure 5.48
Mosaic.

■ **Blur.** This applies blur to the selected area, as shown in Figure 5.49. Because this is also an effect with specific applications, it has been broken out into its own freestanding effect: the Blur effect. It is covered in more detail later in this lesson in the section "Applying Mosaic and Blur Effects."

Figure 5.49
Blur.

■ **Median.** As shown in Figure 5.50, this removes detail, or high-frequency information in the image. It can be used to remove grain or video noise, or simply to apply a very subtle posterizing effect. The amount of filtering is controlled with the Opacity slider.

Figure 5.50
Median.

- **Unsharp Mask.** As shown in Figure 5.51, this increases the detail, or sharpens the selected area. It is good for enhancing detail on soft camera sources. It will also increase contrast. Note that it may set the luminance to above legal levels, so again, always use it with a scope.

Figure 5.51
Unsharp mask.

- **Gradient.** This is similar to Solid in that you use the original color of the shape, only with Gradient, a gradient to transparent is applied (see Figure 5.52). You can change the angle of the gradient and the overall opacity. This mode is good for adding a color gradient to the sky, for example.

Figure 5.52
An orange gradient applied
to the top half of the image.

- **Emboss.** This mode, shown in Figure 5.53, creates a bas relief effect, which gives a kind of texture to the image. You can adjust the angle and the opacity for interesting effects.

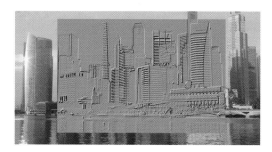

Figure 5.53
Emboss applied.

■ **Scratch Removal.** This mode, shown in Figure 5.54, lets you remove small scratches or tape drop-out from the background. It is similar to the Clone effect. Scratch Removal, which even has its own button, is covered in more detail later in this lesson in the section "Using Scratch Removal."

Figure 5.54
Applying the Scratch Removal effect to remove film dirt.

Blending Operations

There are some excellent plug-ins that allow more complex blending operations than the Paint Effect. Using Sapphire MathOpps and/or Boris BCC Super Blend, you can perform blending operations that allow you to composite one clip over another using some of the modes that you may be familiar with from other graphics applications such as Add, Multiply, Screen, etc. You'll learn more about third-party plug-ins in Lesson 9, "Third-Party Plug-ins," found in PDF form on the DVD accompanying this book.

Spot Color Modes

The remaining modes are broken out from the Color Effect. Each of the parameter groups in the Color Effect can be applied to a part of the image instead of the entire image. The shape you have drawn dictates the area affected. You can apply the effects as individual modes within the Paint tool, or you can use the Spot Color effect—a separate effect within the Image category of the Effect Palette. The advantage of using the Spot Color effect is that it has all the following modes from the Paint Effect, but they can all be applied at the same time:

■ **Color Adjust.** Use this to change the brightness, contrast, hue, and saturation of part of the image. You can also invert luma and chroma separately. (See Figure 5.55.)

Figure 5.55
Color Adjust.

■ **Luma Range.** This setting, shown in Figure 5.56, is used for adjusting the gamma, white point, or black point of part of an image.

Figure 5.56
Luma Range.

■ **Luma Clip.** This setting allows you to clip the luminance at video black or video white, as shown in Figure 5.57.

Figure 5.57
Luma Clip.

- **Color Style.** This setting, shown in Figure 5.58, lets you posterize part of the image.

Figure 5.58
Color Style, set to the maximum value.

- **Color Gain.** This setting is for adjusting the color balance of an image. (See Figure 5.59.)

Figure 5.59
Color Gain.

- **Color Match.** This setting provides a spot color match. The controls here are the same as for the RGB Color Match control, available in the Curves tab of the Color Correction mode. It is useful for changing the color of part of the image—for example, when you have a lighting change in a shot that is inside, but has a window looking outside with a totally different color balance.

In the Avid Learning Series

Using the Color Correction mode is covered in detail in the Avid Training Series book *Color Grading on Media Composer and Symphony 6.*

Using Color Match

To use Color Match, you have two color match swatches: on the left is the input color and on the right is the output color. Simply click the input color and drag the eyedropper to sample a color inside your shape that you want to change. Then, click the output color and drag the eyedropper to sample a color outside the shape that you want to change your color *to*. Finally, click Enable Color Match to see the result. (See Figure 5.60.) It is a good idea to use Natural Match; this is designed to match the hue without affecting the luminance and saturation. It gives a much more realistic color match.

Figure 5.60
Using the color swatches to adjust color.

Feathering

The Feathering controls are an essential part of the Paint tool modes, giving you a soft edge to your shape (see Figure 5.61). Note that even if you don't need to feather your shape, you should always enable the Anti-alias setting because this will give a smoother edge, particularly to curved shapes. Feather bias is simply a way of controlling whether your feathering is on the inside or the outside of your shape. The default is 50, which centers the feathering.

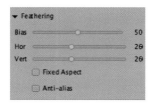

Figure 5.61
Feathering controls.

Note: You will see a big difference in the quality of your shapes by toggling the Video Quality menu at the bottom of the Timeline. Remember, you can choose Full Quality (green), Draft Quality (yellow/green), or Best Performance (yellow). The default Draft Quality provides good playback performance but shows quite a lot of pixilation at the edge of a shape. If you switch to Full Quality, you will see a much sharper edge.

Figure 5.62 shows a simple "vignette" effect. This effect is created with two shapes: an outside shape, which is a Color Correction, and an inside shape, which is an Erase with a large amount of feathering applied to give a soft edge to the erase. (Remember, once you have created your effect, you can save it by dragging the icon in the Effect Editor into a bin. Now you can apply a vignette to all your clips. And it is a real-time effect!)

Figure 5.62
Vignette effect.

Magic Mask

Magic Mask is a powerful tool for recoloring an object in the scene. Rather than drawing a complex, precise shape around the object(s), you can use it to make the selection based on the chroma and luma values of the objects. Think of it as a kind of chroma key in which you replace a chosen color from the image with the color of your shape.

To use the Magic Mask tool:

1. Draw a shape and set it to **SOLID**.

2. Choose a color for your shape.

3. Turn off the visibility for a moment.

4. Use the eyedropper in the Magic Mask to select a color—for example, the color of a shirt.

5. Turn on the visibility again.

6. Adjust the **MAGIC MASK** controls to key out the shirt color (or whatever you chose) and replace it with the shape color. Note that you can use this in conjunction with any of the other modes—for example, Gradient. Figure 5.63 shows an example where an interviewee's shirt color has been changed using the Magic Mask. You will perform this correction in the exercise at the end of this lesson.

Figure 5.63
Magic Mask used to change a subject's shirt color.

Choosing Pixels

Magic Mask can work quite well in certain instances, but not as well in others. Even so, the concept is worth bearing in mind. The ability to selectively affect certain pixels—which is to say, certain parts of the image—is quite powerful. Many Boris BCC plug-ins and many filters in AvidFX include a Pixel Chooser parameter, which lets you select pixels on the basis of luminance, color, etc., and even create masks that you can draw. Then you can apply any of the effects just to those pixels.

Color

Near the bottom of the controls in the Paint Effect are the Color controls. When you are using Solid Color mode, the Color controls let you choose the color of the basic shape. However, you can also affect how many of the other modes work as well by adjusting the different sliders to achieve different effects. Finally, you can use an eyedropper to select a color from part of your image.

Animating Shapes

So far, you have created a shape and you have played with the multitude of possible effects. Now you are ready to animate your shapes. In the real world, of course, the background image never stays still, and you often need to match your shape to the action in the background. There are several ways of doing this:

- You can animate the size and position of your object.
- You can animate the shape of your object.
- You can track your object.

Note: All shapes can be tracked in various ways so that the object you draw
follows the action of the footage underneath. This is particularly useful for
tracking shapes that need to obscure the image below, such as with the
Mosaic effect discussed in this lesson. Tracking is a fairly complex subject,
however, and is covered in Lesson 7, "Tracking and Stabilizing." For now,
you will just look at the first two options.

The first thing to remember is that the Intraframe effects have no keyframe graphs.
That means when you add a keyframe, it will affect all the parameters you have
changed. This can occasionally have undesirable consequences, so it is important
to understand the way animation works.

Animating Size and Position

Let's look at an animation of the size and position of a simple shape. Load the
Paint Effects–Animation sequence, which already has a Paint Effect added, and
open the Effect Editor. Start by drawing a simple shape—in this example, a heart,
as shown in Figure 5.64. (If you want to look just at the shape and not be dis-
tracted by the image underneath, turn off the video monitor on the Timeline.)

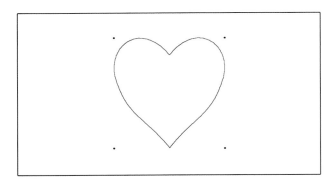

Figure 5.64
A simple heart.

To animate the size or position of the shape:

1. Select the first keyframe or create a keyframe where you want the animation of the shape's size or position to begin.

2. Move to another place in the Timeline and, with the shape selected (with
   the Selection tool, not the Reshape tool), adjust the shape to the desired
   size or position. Remember, if you hold down the Option (Mac) or Alt
   (Windows) key as you move the handle, the shape will resize from the
   center of the object.

3. Select or create a new keyframe and adjust the size or position again, as shown in Figure 5.65. Now you have a shape that will change in size from the first keyframe to the second. In this example, the heart is growing in size. If you scroll the Timeline or play the effect, you will see the heart grow on the screen.

Figure 5.65
Size animated: first and second keyframes.

Note: By default, you have a start keyframe and an end keyframe, and both are selected. As soon as you select just one keyframe, any changes you make are applied only to that keyframe. If you move to a place where there is no keyframe, any new adjustments you make will automatically create a new keyframe and your adjustments are applied to the new keyframe.

Keyframe attributes can be copied and pasted like any other keyframes. For example, you could animate a "heartbeat" by having a series of keyframes half a second apart. Alternate keyframes would be the small heart and the keyframes in between would be the big heart. As you play back the clip, the heart will shrink and grow each second.

Animating the Shape

In the previous section, you saw that you could change the size of an object by making an adjustment to the corner handles. This method allows you to enlarge, stretch, or squeeze the overall shape. This is done by selecting an object with the Selection tool. However, you have also seen that if you click on the Reshape tool, the corner handles disappear and the object now has various points along the edge of the shape. These points define the shape of the curve—and can be corner points or Bézier points with their associated handles. You can animate the shape of the curve in a more precise way by adjusting the position or the handles of these points using keyframes.

To animate a shape (here, a simple heart):

1. Select the first keyframe or create a keyframe where you want the animation of the shape to begin.

2. Click the **RESHAPE** tool and adjust the position of the individual points or their Bézier handles until you are happy with your shape.

3. Move to the next keyframe and adjust the position of the points or their handles for any or all of the points.

4. Repeat step 3 on subsequent keyframes or the frames between two existing keyframes to create a new keyframe. The shape will now animate between keyframes. (See Figure 5.66.)

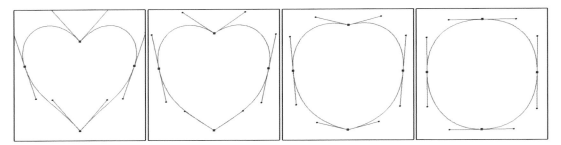

Figure 5.66
The shape animating between two keyframes in four stages.

Note: As before, if you select just one keyframe, any changes you make are applied only to that keyframe. If you move to a place where there is no keyframe, any new adjustments to the points or their handles you make will automatically create a new keyframe, and your adjustments are applied to the new keyframe.

Following are some points to bear in mind when working with animations:

■ Adjusting the size and adjusting the shape are considered two separate animations. Thus, you can make an adjustment to the overall size and position of a shape, and you can also use the Reshape tool to adjust the position or the handles of individual points. Adjusting one at a particular keyframe will not affect the other.

■ There is no way to separate out animations from one shape to another. If you have multiple shapes, you really need to keep track of which keyframe is affecting which object.

■ Don't add or delete points during an animation.

Rotoscoping Strategies

In the real world, you may be tracing a shape—for example, someone's body shape—that is moving on the video below. There are various strategies for this kind of work. One is to draw a shape to create some kind of mask or effect by tracing a moving object in the frame—something known as *rotoscoping*. You might have a simple shape, such as a car, that is moving around the frame, or you might be trying to trace someone walking, which is much more complex. Sometimes, you will be working with many complex shapes in the same effect. Regardless, here are a few guidelines to consider:

- Plan ahead with your Bézier points. Try to add as many points as necessary at the outset before attempting animation. Scroll through the image to see where the shape is most complex and decide how many points you need. Adding points during the animation is not a good idea because if a point suddenly comes into existence, there will now be a discontinuity in the shape, which will cause the shape to move in unpredictable ways between the keyframes.

- Shapes in your video image naturally evolve over time. Look at the motion of the shape you are tracing and see if there are any abrupt changes, or whether it is a gentle evolution over time.

- If you have a complex shape, like someone walking, think about breaking the shape into simpler components such as arms or legs that will cross over each other as the person walks and a less complex shape for the torso.

- Don't try to trace the shape frame by frame. Use the fact that the Media Composer applies a natural interpolation between the shape at each keyframe to make your life easier.

- Use the Outline/Path button to view the image underneath. This is especially useful with multiple shapes.

- You can zoom into the image for a clearer view by clicking the Enlarge button. Alternatively, you can Command-click (Mac) or Ctrl-click (Windows) to zoom into a specific region.

Interpolation between keyframes can be used to make the rotoscoping process more efficient. For example, suppose you are trying to trace a shape—perhaps someone's face—that changes throughout your clip.

To trace a shape:

1. In the first frame of video, trace a shape using the Polygon tool.

2. Move to the last keyframe (or to an earlier frame if there is an abrupt change) and adjust your shape at that frame. You'll see that there is a fairly natural interpolation between the first keyframe and this one.

3. Now move to a frame halfway between your two adjusted frames, and adjust your shape so that it fits at that frame. The interpolation will now smooth out the differences between your keyframes.

4. Continue adjusting the shape by making new keyframes at the halfway point between existing keyframes. Each time you do this, the amount of tweaking required should be less and less. I call this "animating by halves."

Note: You will find in most cases that you don't need to have a keyframe on every frame. One every few frames will suffice.

Keyframing Multiple Objects

Because working with multiple objects can get confusing, it is good to plan ahead when creating keyframes. One possible strategy is to create paint objects on different layers (by nesting or layering). However, although this can make life easier in some cases, you will lose the interactivity between multiple objects if you put them on separate layers. For example, if you have one shape that is a solid and another that is an erase, the erase will only work if it inside the same Paint Effect as the solid.

If you are working with multiple objects, here are some points to bear in mind:

■ Remember to use the Outline/Path button to more easily keep track of your shapes.

■ Break down the motion of each shape before you begin any keyframe.

■ Animate the shape that requires the fewest keyframes first.

■ Animate the other shapes going in order of complexity.

■ You can use the Fast Forward and Rewind buttons to cycle through the different shapes.

■ Always check that the current shape and its keyframe are active before making any adjustments. You can always undo an action, but you may not notice your mistake until several steps later.

■ If you select several keyframes and make an adjustment, that adjustment will be applied to *all* the selected keyframes. You may wipe out a lot of work if you are not careful when selecting keyframes!

Subsets of the Paint Effect

Earlier, I mentioned that some features of the Paint Effect have been separated out into their own freestanding versions to simplify their use. These are Mosaic, Blur, Scratch Removal, and Spot Color. In addition to these is AniMatte, which is used to key one video layer on top of another. This will be discussed in the Lesson 6, "Keying."

Applying Mosaic and Blur Effects

Both these effects work in exactly the same way, only one blurs part of the image and one adds a mosaic effect. These are very useful effects for hiding the identity of a person in a video clip.

To apply a Mosaic or Blur effect to an image:

1. Drag the **MOSAIC** or **BLUR** effect from the Image category of the Effect Palette onto the clip in the Timeline.

2. Select either the **OVAL** or the **RECTANGLE** tool and draw the shape over the face you intend to hide.

3. Use the appropriate sliders to change either the size of the mosaic squares or the amount of blur applied.

4. Apply feathering (see Figure 5.67). This is often neglected, but it makes the difference between a good-looking effect and one that looks cheap and nasty. Always use feathering if you want to impress your director/producer!

Figure 5.67
A mosaic with feathering applied.

Tip: To really make this effect look great, you can apply tracking. Faces naturally move, and the blur/mosaic needs to move with the face. Tracking is covered in Lesson 7.

Using Scratch Removal

This is a very useful tool for removing unwanted artifacts and scratches (for those that still use film!) and for replacing a portion of a video frame by cloning another area—be it another area of the same frame or another area of a different frame. Again, you can use the controls in the original Paint Effect, but Scratch Removal is also its own effect. For very specific cases, it even has its own button, shown in Figure 5.68.

Figure 5.68
The Scratch Removal button.

Typically, you apply the Scratch Removal effect to a segment; thus, it will affect several frames of video. The Scratch Removal button is a special case. It performs scratch removal on a single frame, using the video on the *previous* frame as a source for removing scratches. Thus, if you have a scratch that only appears on a single frame (or field), the button is the best way to go. If you need to remove an artifact that covers more than one frame (or field), then use the Scratch Removal effect.

Fields and Frames

If you are working with field-based material, you can choose to replace both fields or just one field of the area that your shape is covering. To do so, use the Frame Processing button. When this button is enabled, two fields will be replaced; when it is turned off, just one field will be replaced. If you are working with progressive material (as in these examples), the button is not available.

Using the Scratch Removal Effect

The Scratch Removal effect works by cloning an area of your image and placing this cloned material inside a shape that you draw. If you are choosing to clone some material from a different frame, you have three options (see Figure 5.69):

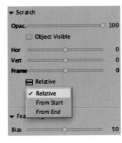

Figure 5.69
Scratch Removal parameters.

- **Relative.** This means that you will use a frame that is offset from the current frame by a fixed amount that is determined by the Frame slider. Thus, you could use material from up to five frames earlier or five frames later. If your effect is applied to more than one frame, the offset is always the same, so if you have an artifact you are trying to remove that lasts for more than five frames, then you will still see the artifact inside the shape that you draw—only five frames later.

- **From Start.** This is the default setting. This will replace the contents of your shape with the same area in the first frame of your effect. So if the first frame is "clean," then this frame can be used for removing the artifact. However, you are replacing with a still frame of video, so this will only work for areas of your image that don't move.

- **From End.** This means that instead of replacing the contents of your shape with material from the first frame, you are using the last frame of your effect. Likewise, this is a still frame, so this will only work if there is no movement in that part of the frame.

Load the Scratch Removal sequence from the Lesson 05 Paint bin and scroll through the sequence. You'll see a swing appear in the top-right corner about two-thirds of the way through, lasting about one second. (There are some markers to show the affected frames.) It's rather distracting, so you need to remove it by drawing a shape around the swing and replacing the contents with something from an earlier frame—in this case, the sky. You could use some sky material from the same frame, but as the sky is not uniform, you would not get a good result. Instead, you will use the Scratch Removal tool to "borrow" some sky from the frame before the swing appears. You won't be able to offset the frame by a fixed amount because the swing appears for more than five frames. That's fine here, however, because the sky is quite still. Note, too, that you don't need to apply the effect to the entire segment, just to the affected section with a clean frame at the beginning.

To apply the Scratch Removal effect and explore its main parameters:

1. Click the **ADD EDIT** button to add an edit just before the swing is in shot, and again to add an edit just after the swing leaves the shot.

2. Apply the **SCRATCH REMOVAL** effect to this portion of the clip. (See Figure 5.70.)

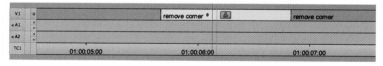

Figure 5.70
Timeline showing add edits and the effect applied.

3. Click the **REDUCE** button to see outside the frame and add a circle to cover the affected area.

Note: When you draw the circle, you will find that if you try to move it, you will move the image inside the circle to a new location. This is how cloning works. If you move the shape you can reset the movement by setting the Hor(izontal) or Vert(ical) sliders back to 0.

4. You want to replace the inside of the circle with another instance, from a different frame. In this case, the swing is in the shot for nearly a second, and the effect only allows you to grab up to five frames earlier or later (10 fields if you are working with interlaced material). Thus, you we need to set the frame to From Start. Click the **FAST** menu and choose **FROM START**, as shown in Figure 5.71. This should be the default setting and it holds the first frame of the clip inside the shape for the duration of the effect.

Figure 5.71
The effect applied,
with the first frame held.

5. Scroll through the clip to check that the swing has gone. You will see there is another section a second later that needs the same effect applied; if you want to, repeat these steps to fix it.

Using the Scratch Removal Button

As mentioned, you can use the Scratch Removal button to perform scratch removal on a single frame, using the video on the *previous* frame as a source for removing scratches. If you have a scratch that only appears on a single frame (or field), the button is the best way to go.

Note: Actually, the Scratch Removal effect is applied to two frames; it uses the previous frame as a source for the clone. But you can treat it as if it is affecting just the frame with the dirt or scratch.

To use the Scratch Removal button:

1. Load the **SCRATCHY BIRD** sequence.

2. Scroll through the sequence. Note that there are lots of scratches and film dirt throughout this shot.

3. Select one dirty frame and click the **SCRATCH REMOVAL** button. You are taken into Effect mode and the Scratch Removal effect is applied to two frames—the one you want to clean and the previous frame.

Note: If the button is not in your Composer window, you can find it in the Fast menu or in the FX section in the Command palette. If you are planning to use it a lot, you should map it to the row of buttons under the Record monitor or to your keyboard.

4. Choose the **BRUSH** tool and change the brush size if necessary.

5. To fix a small speck, simply click it. To fix the larger hairs or scratches, paint over them; then gasp in wonder as they all magically disappear!

6. If there is movement in the frame—for example, if you find a frame where the bird is moving—you can adjust the position of the grabbed scratch as well. To do so, drag the **HOR** and **VERT** sliders in the Scratch parameters to adjust the position of the material inside the replacement shape.

7. Choose another frame and repeat the procedure until you are happy. Figure 5.72 shows a before and after.

Figure 5.72
Before and after.

You will often get dirt grains on consecutive frames. Although this makes scratch removal more difficult, it is still possible to do. Clicking the Scratch Removal button will automatically create a two-frame effect—the dirty frame you want to tidy up and the previous frame you are using as a reference. The effects steal a portion of the picture from the previous frame, but if you already have an effect on that frame, you must *nest* the effect so that you can steal a portion of the previously treated frame. To do this, add an edit at the end of the frame you want to clean; then Option-click (Mac) or Alt-click (Windows) the Scratch Removal effect (rather than the button) so it will nest on *three* frames—the two with the previously cleaned effect and the next frame with new dirt. This will allow you to replace the dirt with the first frame rather than the second frame, which had some dirt before you replaced it.

Note: Getting hold of film-originated footage is getting harder and harder these days. However, it is very easy to fake film dirt. The bird shown in Figure 5.72 was of course shot on video, but I was able to achieve the film look very easily using the excellent Film Damage Sapphire effect. For more information on Sapphire effects, see Lesson 9 (found on the DVD accompanying this book) or visit Sapphire's Web site at www.genarts.com/software/sapphire/avid.

Review/Discussion Questions

1. Which of the following five shape-creation tools does not require that you close the shape after you've finished drawing it?

   a. The Rectangle tool

   b. The Oval tool

   c. The Polygon tool

   d. The Curve tool

   e. The Brush tool

2. You have a stack of five objects in a Paint Effect. What is the best way to view them so you can select one?

3. How do you bring one object to the top of the stack?

4. How do you cycle your selection of different objects?

   a. Option-click (Mac) or Alt-click (Windows) the Select button.

   b. Use the Fast Forward and Rewind buttons.

   c. Use the Trim Edit buttons.

5. What are two ways to change the shape of an object?

6. How do you break the Bézier handles so they are independent?

   a. Shift-click on the handle and drag it.

   b. Command-click (Mac) or Ctrl-click (Windows) the handle and drag it.

   c. Option-click (Mac) or Alt-click (Windows) the handle and drag it.

7. True or false: You can copy a shape from the AniMatte effect and paste it into the Paint Effect.

8. You want to remove a line of drop out from a single frame of video. Fill in the gaps below.

1. Park your blue position indicator on the frame and click the _____ _____ button.

2. Select the _____ _____.

3. Draw a _____ _____ that exactly covers the line of drop out.

4. _____ in wonder!

9. What is feathering?

10. When would you use Spot Color effect and when would you use the Color Effect?

Lesson 5 Keyboard Shortcuts

Key	Shortcut
A	Go to previous object selected (in Paint tool).
S	Go to next object selected (in Paint tool).
M and /	Nudge Paint shape 10 pixels left and right.
, and .	Nudge Paint shape one pixel left and right.
Option+M and Option+/ (Mac)/Alt+M and Alt+/ (Windows)	Nudge Paint shape 10 pixels up and down.
Option+, and Option+. (Mac)/Alt+, and Alt+. (Windows)	Nudge Paint shape one pixel up and down.

Using Paint to Enhance Your Footage

Now you are ready to try a few examples on your own. First you'll practice drawing the Bézier shapes and then you'll use some of the modes in the Paint Effect to improve some shots.

Media Used:

Open the bin 05 Exercises in the project.

Duration:

30 minutes

GOAL

- Draw Bézier shapes and use them to perform spot color correction and scratch removal

Learning to Draw Bézier Shapes

Load the Bézier Shapes sequence in the 05 Exercises bin and you will see three clips, each with a shape that you can trace. Consider the following:

- The first clip shows where to start and end the shape. Use the direction lines to help you set the length of the direction handles you create. Place your anchor points where indicated by the white dots.

- The second clip also shows you where to start and end the shape. This time, however, the direction handles are only shown in the first half of the shape.

- Many of the directions handles have different lengths on each side of the anchor point. Because you cannot adjust the length of each side of the anchor point until after you draw the shape, choose one of the two sides when you draw the shape. After you finish drawing the shape, go back and adjust the direction lines until your shape matches the one in the slide.

- The third clip only suggests where you should place some of the anchor points. Draw the shape using the white dots to place the first anchor points. Use your judgment to place the remaining anchor points and adjust the curve handles as necessary.

Using Magic Mask to Perform Secondary Color Correction

Now you have perfected your drawing techniques, let's put them to good use! In this first example, you have been given an interview clip; Betty thinks the color of the man's shirt needs to match the shirt he is wearing in the next scene, which is green. It is quite easy to add a color tint to the entire picture, but you only want to change the shirt and nothing else. For this you need to do two things: Draw a shape that just covers the shirt and use the Magic Mask feature to affect only the area of the picture that is gray.

Start by looking at the footage, which you will find in the Running the Sahara Interview sequence in the 05 Exercises bin. Here you can see the man with the gray shirt, shown in Figure 5.73.

Figure 5.73
Man with gray shirt.

Your mission is to turn the shirt green without affecting any other part of the image.

1. Apply the **PAINT EFFECT** and enter Effect mode.

2. Begin by drawing a shape with the **POLYGON** tool that roughly covers the man's shirt. He doesn't move much, and you can make the shape slightly larger than the shirt, so it is quite easy. The default shape is solid red; you can leave it like that while you draw the shape.

3. If you want, use the **RESHAPE** tool to refine the shape. If necessary, animate the shape to ensure that the man's shoulders don't stray outside as you scroll along the Effect Editor Timeline.

Tip: It is easier to see what is going on underneath the edge of your shape if you switch your Paint Effect mode to Colorize and set the Opacity to 50% in the Mode pane. However, this tip comes with a warning: If you have already started to animate and have some keyframes in your Timeline, make sure all your keyframes are selected when you make any adjustments to the opacity or color of your shape. If only one keyframe is selected, the opacity color will animate between the keyframes!

4. Now you need to enable the Magic Mask. The eyedropper needs to sample the color of the shirt, not the red color of the shape, so temporarily disable the shape by deselecting the **OBJECT VISIBLE** button in the Mode pane, as shown in Figure 5.74.

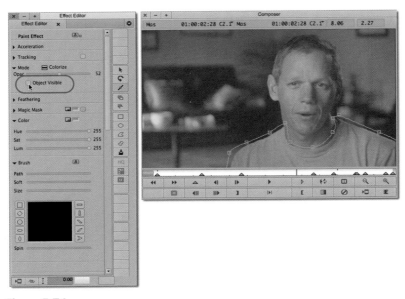

Figure 5.74
Deselect the Object Visible button.

5. Open the Magic Mask pane and enable the eyedropper by positioning the mouse over the color selection box and dragging the eyedropper over to the man's shirt. You need to select a mid gray color from anywhere in the shirt.

6. Now re-enable the **OBJECT VISIBLE** button in the Mode pane. This will bring back the red colorized shape. For the moment, the red color is applied to the entire shape, not the man's shirt. To fix this, you'll need to play with the gain and soft controls for the Magic Mask. Again, if you have applied any animation to the shape, make sure all your keyframes are selected when you make any adjustments. You want the same mask key for all the keyframes.

7. You will have to play with the controls to get the best compromise between including all of the man's shirt and coloring the area outside the shirt. You may also find that adjusting the **HUE**, **SATURATION**, and **LUMINANCE** controls of the Magic Mask key color will affect how good the key is. The area to watch is the bit of shirt under the right side of the man's head at the back. This is very low saturation and difficult to key. You may find it impossible to get a perfect key; increasing either the Gain or the Softness to cover the entire shirt will inevitably cause some spill on the background. However, a pretty good compromise can be achieved by setting the controls to those shown in Figure 5.75.

Figure 5.75
Fine-tuning the Magic Mask.

8. Now you can change the color of the shirt. The default is red; we need green. The Colorize mode will do fine for this, but you can also experiment with Color Gain. If you use Colorize, the color of the shirt is derived from the settings in the Color pane. You can choose a nice subtle green—remember: not too much saturation and also reduce the Opacity in the Mode pane. This will remove any spill of the green color onto the area outside the shirt. Alternatively, with Color Gain, the settings in the Color pane are ignored. Here you just adjust the sliders in the Mode pane, which will switch to Red, Green, and Blue. Reduce the **RED** and **BLUE** and boost the **GREEN** until you have a nice color. Either method will give good results, though in a slightly different way.

9. Finally, play through the effect to ensure that the shirt is green throughout the clip and the background surrounding the shirt is not affected. Figure 5.76 shows what you should have.

Figure 5.76
Final result.

The Magic Mask will enable you to achieve some quite spectacular results with a combination of careful shape animation and fine tuning of the Magic Mask controls. You may come across situations that can't be corrected convincingly; for that you may need to use the Secondary Color Correction tools in Avid Symphony. But you might be surprised at what this somewhat hidden feature can do with a bit of patience. And don't forget: This is all real time!

Change the Background in Boat Quay

Betty Blooper has a nice shot of some houses by the riverside, but she wants to make it more punchy. The modern buildings in the background need to be darker and the houses need to be brighter and perhaps more yellow to reflect the early morning sun. This time, the shape you'll need to draw is more complex, but the shot is static so no animation is involved.

1. Load the **BOAT QUAY CORRECTION** sequence in the 05 Exercises bin.

2. Apply the **SPOT COLOR** effect and enter Effect mode.

3. Select the **POLYGON** tool and draw a shape along the rooftops of the buildings, starting at one side and tracing all the way to the other. Then draw two more points, one in the very top right and one in the very top left of the frame and close the shape by double-clicking. Don't worry if you don't get it right first time; you can correct it later.

4. Click the **ENLARGE** button or press **COMMAND+L** (Mac) or **CTRL+L** (Windows) to zoom in; then press **OPTION+COMMAND** (Mac) or **ALT+CTRL** (Windows) to pan around. Finally, use the **RESHAPE** tool to get all your points in exactly the right position. Figure 5.77 shows the result.

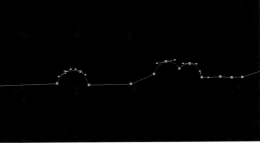

Figure 5.77
Fine-tuning the shape.

5. Convert any corner points to Bézier rounded points if necessary.

6. To improve the shape, Option-click (Mac) or Alt-click (Windows) to add points or press the **Delete** key to delete a selected point.

7. When you are happy with your shape, apply a very small amount of feathering (just one or two units will be fine) and enable the **Anti-alias** setting.

8. Experiment with the Color Correction tools. Use **Luma Adjust** to reduce the brightness and contrast of the background buildings. Perhaps use **Color Gain** to make them a bit more blue.

9. Now let's try to correct the houses. You can use the same shape, only adjusted to cover the houses. To begin, select the first shape, and copy and paste it. Notice that the copy has the same attributes as the original.

10. Click the **Reduce** button or press **Command+K** (Mac) or **Ctrl+K** (Windows) to zoom out so you can see outside of the frame. Then move the top two points to the very bottom of the frame. The rest can stay where they are. Figure 5.78 shows the result.

Figure 5.78
Move the points on the duplicated shape.

11. Change the **Luma Adjust** controls to increase the brightness and contrast for the houses.

12. Perhaps use the **Color Gain** controls to make the houses a bit more yellow.

13. Zoom back in and admire your work.

14. If time permits, use the same shot with a Paint Effect to experiment with some of the other Paint modes. Draw a big square shape and try out some of the different effects.

Wire Removal

Your final mission is to perform some wire removal on another clip from *Running the Sahara*. Load the sequence Running in the Desert in the 05 Exercises bin, and you'll see that you have a nice shot of some runners in the desert—but there are some wires at the top of the screen that are ruining the aesthetics. (See Figure 5.79.) Betty wants you to remove them.

Figure 5.79
The clip has been stabilized and now needs the wires removed.

You could resize the shot to crop out the wires, but that would ruin the nicely balanced frame, with the runners on the lower third of the frame and the flat blue sky on the upper third. Scratch Removal is an effect that allows you to copy replacement material from one area of the frame and paste it to another area. Typically, this is used to remove scratches, but it can be used for more general purposes, too. You'll use it here to remove the wires.

When you played the segment, you may have noticed there is no camera movement in the shot. That's helpful because we won't have to track or keyframe the paint strokes, but it's not by accident. The segment already has a Stabilize effect on it, as you can see in the Timeline. Any camera move will cause the paint stroke to be misaligned from the wires. With the shot locked down, we can add the Scratch Removal effect, but you need to add this on top of the Stabilize effect.

1. Hold down the **OPTION** (Mac) or **ALT** (Windows) key and drag the **SCRATCH REMOVAL** effect (in the Image category in the Effect Palette) onto the clip in the Timeline so it appears on top of the Stabilize effect.

2. Click the **EFFECT MODE** button to open the Effect Editor. To cover the wires with the fewest number of shapes and paint strokes, you'll be using the drawing tools to replace large areas of the wires first and then use the Brush tool for small, detailed areas. So the plan is to draw a rectangular shape over a clean area of the blue sky and this will be used as the replacement material. You'll then copy that replacement material over the various wires to cover them up.

Note: Scratch Removal is not a real-time effect. It needs to be rendered before you can play it. When using the Scratch Removal effect, it's beneficial to use the drawing tools as much as possible because they render much faster than a series of brush strokes from the Brush tool.

3. Select the **POLY** tool from the Effect Editor window.

4. In the Effect Preview monitor, click and draw an approximate rectangle from the left edge of the frame, between the bottom two wires where there is a nice section of blue sky, along to the right until you reach the white structure. The shape you draw should be large enough to partially replace one of the wires but should not include any of the white structure in it. The wires run at a slight angle to the ground, so your shape should reflect this.

5. Drag the rectangle down and position it so it covers the bottom wire, starting from the left edge of the frame, as shown in Figure 5.80.

Figure 5.80
Draw a shape above the wires (top) and drag it down to cover the bottom wire (bottom).

Tip: Although the rectangular shape's onscreen outline may be difficult to see, you can still drag and position it by clicking the shape in the Effect Preview monitor.

6. Now that you have covered part of one wire, you can use the same shape to cover the other two. With the shape still selected, press **COMMAND+C** and **COMMAND +V** (Mac) or **CTRL+C** and **CTRL+V** (Windows) to copy and paste it. The copy will appear exactly on top of the original.

7. Drag the new shape up to copy the next wire. Repeat the process for the top wire. Figure 5.81 shows the three shapes selected so you can see where they are.

Figure 5.81
Three copies of the shape covering the three wires.

Now you need to deal with the right side of the frame. You will do the same thing, only with a shape that covers the wires to the right of the white structure—in this part of the image there are only two wires to deal with.

8. Again, select the **POLY** tool from the Effect Editor window.

9. In the Effect Preview monitor, click and draw an approximate rectangle from the right edge of the frame, just between the two wires, along to the left until you reach the white structure. This rectangular replacement material will be used to partially cover the two wires on the right.

10. Drag the rectangle down and position it so it covers the bottom wire, starting from the right edge of the frame, as shown in Figure 5.82.

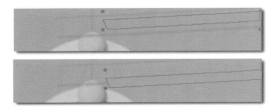

Figure 5.82
Create a second rectangle on the right side (top) and drag it down to cover the wire (bottom).

11. Copy and paste the shape and drag the new one up to the top wire. The largest areas are covered.

   The remaining portions of the wires require more finesse, so you'll use the Brush tool. Since you'll be using a small brush, you'll enlarge the frame in the Effect Preview monitor so you can see more detail.

12. Under the Effect Preview monitor, click the **ENLARGE** button twice to scale the frame to two times actual resolution. To pan the frame, press and hold down the **COMMAND+OPTION** (Mac) or the **CTRL+ALT** (Windows) keys as you drag so you see the wires. Now you'll be able to paint with more accuracy. (See Figure 5.83.)

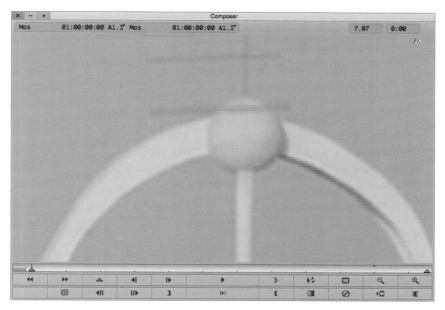

Figure 5.83
Click the Enlarge button and then pan the frame to see the remaining wires at the top.

13. Select the **Brush** tool from the side of the Effect Editor and then click the triangular opener for the **Brush** parameter group.

14. Click the **Brush Shape** button that is second from the bottom on the right side. This brush style has an angled front face that will allow you to get in closer to the round sphere. (See Figure 5.84.)

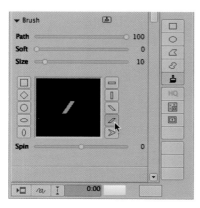

Figure 5.84
Select the brush shape second from the bottom in the Effect Editor.

15. Set the **Brush Size** to **3**.

16. The workflow for the Brush tool in Scratch Removal is slightly different from the shape tools. Using the Poly tool, you draw a shape around the replacement material and drag it to the area you want to cover up. With the Brush tool, you first Option-click (Mac) or Alt-click (Windows) to select the replacement material and then begin painting over the area you want to cover up. As you move the brush, the replacement material is offset by an equal amount in the same direction. Option-click (Mac) or Alt-click (Windows) an area of blue sky (for example, just below the arch) to select where to start the replacement material.

17. Start painting along the remaining bottom wire on the left side of the frame and end as close to the white sphere as possible, as shown in Figure 5.85.

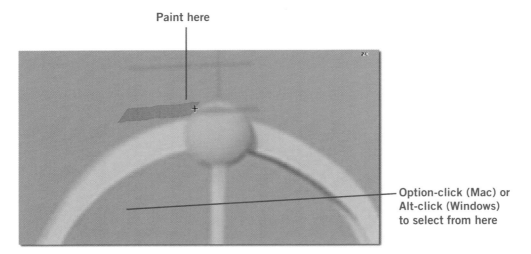

Figure 5.85
Paint out the bottom wire.

Tip: If you want to undo an error created while painting, choose Edit > Undo New Shape and try again or press Command+Z (Mac) or Ctrl+Z (Windows).

18. Now the wire above. Change your brush to a vertical wedge shape (second from the top on the right side) so that you can get closer to the antenna emerging from the white structure.

19. Option-click (Mac) or Alt-click (Windows) another area of clean sky to select a source for the replacement material.

20. Start painting along the remaining top wire on the left side of the frame, ending as close as possible to the antenna.

21. Now use the same brush to remove the wires on the right side; again, get as close to the antenna as possible. (See Figure 5.86.)

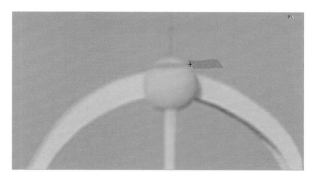

Figure 5.86
Remove the wires on the right side.

22. Now for the orb. This is a bit trickier and may require more than one stroke. A small round brush (size 2 or 3) should do it. Select an area for replacement by Option-clicking (Mac) or Alt-clicking (Windows) just below the bit where the wire crosses. You may need to try a few times before getting it right. Remember, you are looking at an enlarged view, and the final result will look much better at the default size. You should end up with something like Figure 5.87.

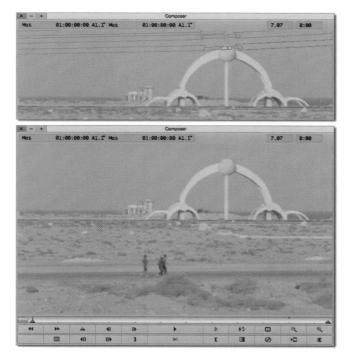

Figure 5.87
End result, with all the shapes selected and deselected.

Remember, the Scratch Removal effect is not a real-time effect. To play it, you must render the effect. However, you can see a real-time review of what you have done if you click the Play button or loop-play while in the Effect Editor.

Being able to complete intricate intraframe work on a shot is often the difference between being able to use the shot in a project and not being able to. Scratch Removal is just the tip of the iceberg when it comes to Media Composer's intraframe capabilities, but it certainly is one of the most useful.

Betty is full of admiration and offers to buy you lunch!

Keying

Often, when you composite different video layers to create some kind of effect, you will need to use a key. A *key* is a mask that removes an area of the foreground and reveals that part of the background. There are various kinds of keys available in Avid Media Composer. This lesson discusses the different keying techniques.

Media Used: The media for this lesson is in the MC205 Pro Effects Project. Open the Lesson 06 Keying bin.

Duration: 60 minutes

GOALS

- Use the SpectraMatte keyer
- Import a matte key and apply in the Timeline
- Modify the fill and the matte of an imported matte
- Use a luma key
- Use the AniMatte effect

Keying with SpectraMatte

Chroma keying is very integral to any kind of effects workflow and is widely used in most movies and many TV shows. In a chroma key, you set up the shot in a studio where you have precise control of the background: a flat, uniformly lit colored screen, usually either blue or green (see Figure 6.1).

Figure 6.1
Chroma key shot.

Why Blue or Green?

Usually, you key people over a background such as a spaceship or an exploding building where it would be difficult to put them in real life. Because the color of the human face is in the pink-to-orange segment of the color wheel, and blue is on the exact opposite side of the wheel, blue is an easy color to remove from the foreground. Also, in the film world, the blue emulsion layer has the finest crystals and thus the best detail, making it easier to get a good key edge. In the digital world, however, green is very popular because of the way the color signal is encoded; more information is kept in the green channel than in the blue channel or red channel. The more color information you have in your picture, the easier it is to key out. In certain cases, however—for example, when shooting objects that are either blue or green—it is perfectly possible to use red as the key color.

Obtaining the Best Results When Keying

It is challenging to get a good key unless your source material is of the best possible quality. Here are some considerations for getting good results:

■ The background should be flat, well lit and of a uniform color.

■ The subject should be well lit and should not be wearing clothes that contain the key color.

■ If shooting on video tape, it should be of a component or component digital format such as Betacam or Digital Betacam. Composite should never be used.

■ If your material originated on film, the dub should always be to a component format.

■ When capturing to Avid, you should always use component input—again, never composite.

■ For modern-day, file-based formats, you will get best results with 10-bit RGB video, which Avid now supports. Long GOP compression formats with a very low bit rate such as HDV, AVCHD, and XDCAM HD will not be ideal, because much of the color information is missing.

Remember that almost all video formats compromise to squeeze the data rate down so that files can be smaller. Although modern compression codecs offer excellent quality, their color information is usually much less than the luminance information because they use a system called *chroma subsampling*. (The technical aspects of this are beyond the scope of this book, but there are some excellent articles on the Web.) The bottom line is that you will come across various subsampling schemes depending on the formats used. If there is little detail in the color, keying is always very hard. If you have any input into the production of the key shots, select a format that includes color information. Table 6.1 outlines various color subsampling schemes.

Table 6.1   Color Subsampling Schemes

Type	Quality	Examples of Formats
4:4:4 RGB	Best	Sony HDCAM SR Dual Link
4:2:2	Acceptable	AVC-Intra 100, Digital Betacam, DVCPRO50, DVCPRO HD, XDCAM HD, and Canon MXF HD
4:1:1	Poor	DVCPRO SD, NTSC DV, and DVCAM
4:2:0	Poor	HDV SD, PAL DV and DVCAM, AVCHD, AVC-Intra 50, H.262, MPEG-2, MPEG-4, and JPEG

Nevertheless, it is possible to get good keys with Media Composer. You can also improve a key that you make in Media Composer through the use of additional plug-ins including Sapphire S_MatteOps and BCC Matte Cleaner. You may also want to look at the keyer in Avid FX; it gives excellent results, but it is not real time. There are several types of keyers in the Effect Palette, but by far the best results are obtained from the SpectraMatte, which is discussed next.

Applying the SpectraMatte

There are two ways to apply the SpectraMatte. One is to apply it directly from the Key group in the Effect Palette; the other is to promote any other key to 3D and choose the SpectraMatte from the drop-down menu at the top of the Foreground parameters. In both cases, you need to set up your Timeline so that the background clip is on V1 and the key clip is on V2.

To take a look at the interface and go through the various controls:

1. Open the **06 Keying** bin and find the **Chroma Key** sequence. This is a shot that you can follow along with. Don't worry that the camera is moving around; you will deal with that later. For now, we are going to key the shot onto a neutral background (gray is always a good background for this).

2. Find the **SpectraMatte** key in the Key section of the Effect Palette. Then apply the **SpectraMatte** key to the top track.

3. Enter Effect mode and look at the interface, shown in Figure 6.2. You don't need the graphs for now, so you can reduce the size of the Effect Editor window.

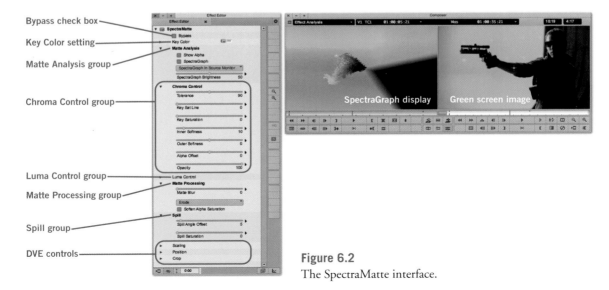

Figure 6.2
The SpectraMatte interface.

Tip: Although you may have been using a single monitor for working in Effect mode, you may want to use two monitors for SpectraMatte because you get to see two different displays. If you have enough space on your desktop, consider creating a workspace for SpectraMatte that looks a bit like the view in Figure 6.2.

There are several groups of parameters in the Effect Editor window. Let's look quickly at what they do:

- **Bypass check box.** This is the all-important check box to turn your key on and off.

- **Key Color setting.** This is where you choose the color you are going to key out.

- **Matte Analysis group.** Here, you can turn on various displays to help you get a good key.

- **Chroma Control group.** These are various tools for improving the quality of your key.

- **Luma Control group.** This is a fairly specialized section for fine-tuning difficult keys.

- **Matte Processing group.** In this group, you can blur, dilate, or erode your matte.

- **Spill group.** Here, you can remove the green or blue spill. (The color from the background that often "spills" onto the foreground.)

- **DVE controls.** These are for scaling, moving, or cropping your key.

Using the SpectraMatte Controls

So how does it all work? The SpectraMatte keyer uses the SpectraGraph as its core tool for refining the key. Before you go through the tools in more detail, it pays to understand what this graph, shown in Figure 6.3, is telling you.

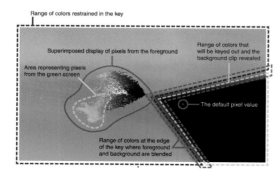

Figure 6.3
The SpectraGraph display.

The Vectorscope

When you broadcast a TV image, you separate the luminance information (the Y signal) from the color information (CrCb). This color information is encoded in such a way that it can be expressed as follows:

- A value that represents the amount of saturation
- An angle that represents the hue

The actual numbers don't matter, but if you imagine a clock, then red is coming up to 11 o'clock, blue is around half past three, and green is about half past seven. The further out from the center, the more saturated the color.

If you analyze the different pixels in any image, they will turn up somewhere on this vectorscope display, and you can superimpose them on a CrCb color space diagram, which is exactly what the SpectraGraph is. In this example, which is on a green screen, you can see that there is a big clump of pixels in the green sector of the color wheel. This is the area that you need to key out. By default, however, the key is set to blue, so at the moment you see a big dark wedge on the blue sector. Let's fix that.

Choosing the Key Color

The first thing you need to do when setting up a key is choose the key color.

To choose the key color:

1. Click the **COLOR PREVIEW** window in the Key Color section. (It is the little blue square on the right.) Your pointer will turn into an eyedropper.

2. Drag the eyedropper to your key shot and click a green bit. Click somewhere that is fairly representative of the key color—don't go too near the edge or choose somewhere that is too dark. A nice bright green near the man's arm will do nicely.

Note: The key is set to blue by default, which is a bit of a gotcha. You might be lulled into a false sense of security if you put the key on some blue-screen material and it automatically keys it out. But no two key backgrounds are the same, and you should *never* assume that the key has chosen the exact shade of blue as your shot. If you are keying a blue shot, *always* check the Bypass check box so that your key is turned off. That way, you can see the blue background and choose the exact shade of blue that best represents your key. Now uncheck the Bypass check box again.

Choosing the key color is vital to getting a good key. If you don't get this right, then the fine-tuning controls discussed in the next section will not all work correctly. Notice that the dark wedge has now moved to the green sector. This shows you the area that is going to be keyed out. However, you still need to be sure that the key color is properly centered in hue with relation to the background tones.

If you look very closely at the vectorscope display, you will see a highlighted pixel in white somewhere in the blob of green pixels, as shown in Figure 6.4. This is the actual pixel you chose out of all the million possibilities! If you chose well, your white pixel should be somewhere near the center of the crowd. However, there are so many to choose from that you may have chosen a pixel that wasn't terribly representative, meaning your little white pixel may be near the edge of the crowd. In that case, you can try choosing the key color again, or you can open the Key Color controls and nudge the Red slider so that the pixel you chose moves closer to the center, as shown in Figure 6.5.

The chosen pixel

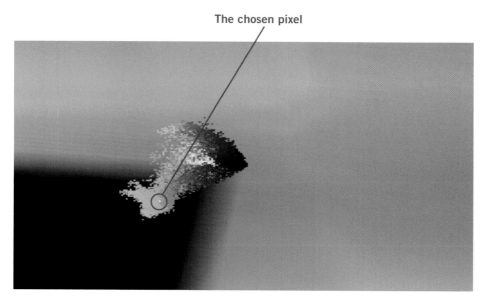

Figure 6.4
The chosen one.

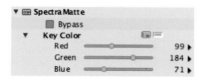

Figure 6.5
Adjusting the key color.

Note that as you move the Red slider, the pixel moves too. But you are not quite done…. Your pixel needs to be in the middle not just of the hue range but also of the saturation range. To adjust this, you need to adjust the Green slider (or the Blue slider if you are keying on blue). As you do, you will see the pixel move toward or away from the middle of the color wheel, as shown in Figure 6.6. When it is in the middle of the crowd, you have chosen a representative pixel! Now you are ready to analyze and refine the key.

Figure 6.6
The chosen one in the middle of the crowd.

Matte Analysis

To analyze your matte, you have three options:

- You can display the result of the key.
- You can display the SpectraGraph.
- You can display the alpha (the matte).

You can also choose to display the alpha or the SpectraGraph in the Source monitor while you see the result in the Record monitor, as shown in Figure 6.7.

Note: Underneath the menu for choosing the type of display is a slider that lets you adjust the brightness of the SpectraGraph display, but this will not have any effect on your output. You can see the SpectraGraph Brightness slider in Figure 6.2.

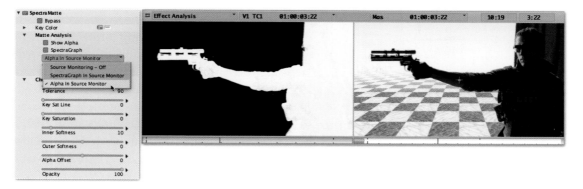

Figure 6.7
The choices for displaying the SpectraGraph or the matte.

When you look at the SpectraGraph, you can now clearly see what is being keyed out, what is being retained as the foreground image, and the area where you will find some kind of blend where the pixels will be partially keyed out. This is the all-important key edge, and the quality of the key depends on how you modify the edge. The idea is that you want the edge to be smooth but at the same time preserve as much detail as possible, such as in hair or details in clothing. To improve how the edge area blends the foreground and background, you use the Chroma Control group.

The Chroma Control Group

You can use the sliders in the Chroma Control group, shown in Figure 6.8, to modify how the edge of the key is working. They are as follows:

■ **Tolerance.** This slider is how you control the *range* of hues that are keyed. When you adjust it, the angle of the wedge will change—the bigger the angle, the more shades of green are going to be keyed out. You can get a clue as to the range of colors you are excluding from the foreground by looking at the SpectraGraph. When you increase the tolerance, you are aiming to get as many of the green (or blue) pixels into the wedge as possible. Note that increasing tolerance will clean up the black part of your alpha so that it becomes nice and solid. The idea with the Tolerance control is that you increase it until the blacks in the alpha are clean with no gray bits. If you increase it too much, however, you will start to lose detail in the sharper edges. If you look at the gun (magnify this part of the image), you will see that the key is reflected on the shiny bits of the gun; thus, increasing the tolerance will start to key out the detail in the gun.

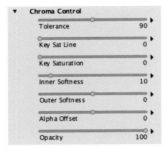

Figure 6.8
The Chroma Control group.

Note: In a good key, the actual color of the green screen should not change. In theory, the tolerance can be quite small. However, in practice, it depends a great deal on the lighting. In the exercise later in this lesson, you will deal with some shots that have poor lighting and in which the green background is not actually green, but yellow. In this case, the tolerance will have to be increased to include yellow shades of green in the key.

Tip: When making adjustments to any of the controls, it is a good idea to toggle the alpha on and off so you see the result. You are aiming for good clean blacks in the key area, good clean whites in the foreground, and a nice clean edge.

■ **Key Sat Line.** In the bits of your key background that are in the shadow, the saturation will be lower, which can make it difficult to key. The Key Sat Line slider (where *Sat* is short for *Saturation*) is how you control where the key kicks in at low saturations. When you increase the Key Sat Line setting, you remove background pixels with the less saturated color. Typically, increasing this setting will clean up the whites, because the low saturation values will be retained in the key. Try not to increase it too much, however, or you won't key out the shadows in the green areas. Ideally, it should be as low as possible, but having it too low will tend to increase the spill effect—where the key color is reflected on the foreground subject. In the end, you need to strike a balance. The top part of Figure 6.9 shows the result of setting the Key Sat Line too low; the white part of the key is dirty. The bottom part of Figure 6.9 shows the result of setting the Key Sat Line too high; while the white part is clean, the lower-left corner of the black area is starting to bleed through because these pixels are darker and therefore less saturated.

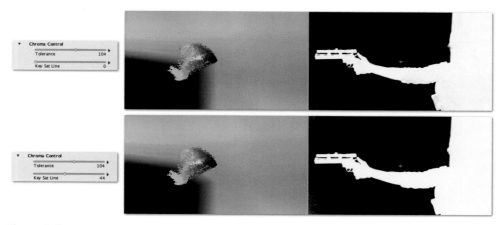

Figure 6.9
Key Sat Line, low and high.

■ **Key Saturation.** This is similar to Key Sat Line. The difference is that you are not controlling the position of a line where the key kicks in but are instead shifting the entire wedge in and out from the center. Again, this should be a fairly low value. Start at 0 and bring it up a little to further clean up the white areas. If you start to see some gray appearing in the blacks, pull it back down a bit. Check this again, only looking at the result of the key rather than the alpha. You will see that at the very low values, you key out areas of detail such as the gun, which you should be retaining. As you increase the slider, you will restore these areas, but adding too much will increase the green spill. (See Figure 6.10.)

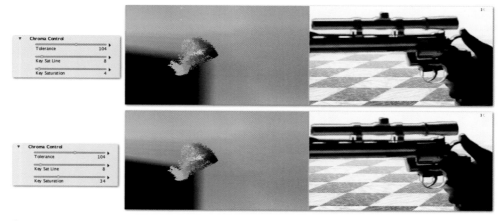

Figure 6.10
Key Saturation, low and high. Note the green spill in the gun when the value is too high.

■ **Inner Softness.** This is where you control the falloff (from opaque to transparent) of the keyed region. You can restore or remove regions that should be partially transparent in the key. If you look at the wedge displayed on the SpectraGraph, you will see that the region at the edge of the wedge becomes thinner as you increase from the default value of 10 and thicker as you decrease. If you look at an area of detail in the result (for example, the gun), you will see that you start to lose the detail as you increase the Inner Softness setting because you are increasing the transparency of the partially transparent regions. So again, toggling between the alpha and the result, you increase until the blacks are good, and you pull back a little to restore the fine detail. (See Figure 6.11.)

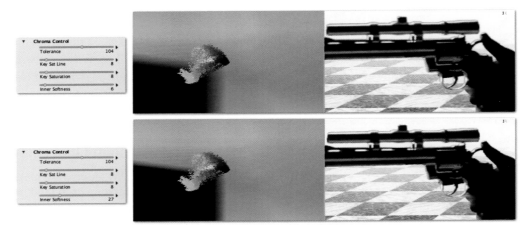

Figure 6.11
Inner Softness, low and high. The first value is about right, but the second value is too high; detail in the gun is disappearing from the key.

■ **Outer Softness.** This is similar to the Inner Softness setting, except it affects the edge of the wedge where the key is being retained—in other words, the pixels just beyond the keyed region. Increasing this setting will increase the transparency of the partially transparent regions on the outside edge of the key. Looking at the alpha, you will notice that you start to introduce some gray bits in the white regions as you increase this. Usually, you will adjust this in conjunction with the Inner Softness setting until you have a balance between the fine detail and the uniformity of the blacks and the whites in the alpha. (See Figure 6.12.)

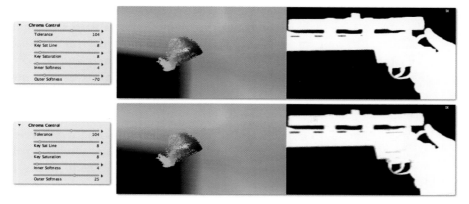

Figure 6.12
Outer Softness, low and high. The first setting is about right, but the second setting is too high; the gun is starting to key through.

- **Alpha Offset.** This setting is almost exactly the same as the Key Saturation setting. It moves the entire wedge in or out from the center. The difference is, this setting allows you to move the wedge *beyond* the center of the color display and into the region of the complementary color, as shown in Figure 6.13. Why you should ever want to do this is beyond me, but Avid has kindly given you the option. The bottom line here is that you can think of it as a coarse version of Key Saturation. Best to leave well enough alone!

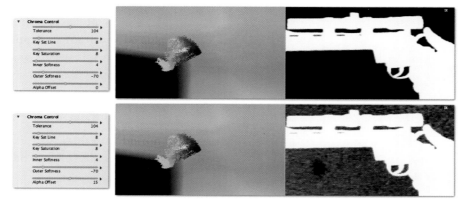

Figure 6.13
Alpha Offset, at the default and at 15.

- **Opacity.** This setting simply adjusts the overall opacity of the foreground. It's not often used, but if, for example, you want to fade your key completely away, then this is the control for you.

When you are happy with your adjustments, you should play through the whole clip. Remember that you are working with moving video. What may work perfectly for one frame may not work on a different frame. For example, you may have some hair appear in the image that wasn't there on the frame you were adjusting, so you continually need to review your work and look at the entire effect.

The Luma Control Group

The Luma Control parameters, shown in Figure 6.14, are rather specialized and only for use on a very difficult key. Think of these as extreme expert mode, or perhaps geek mode.

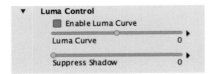

Figure 6.14
The Luma Control group.

Essentially, what you are doing in a key is creating a transition from an area that is white (the part of the foreground that is retained) to an area that is black (the part that is keyed out). All the controls in the previous section are refining this edge area of the key so that you get a good key. However, you can create your own transition from white to black using a repurposed graph: the luma curve. When you turn this on, you are not actually doing any animation. Rather, you are using the shape of the graph to define the edge of the key (or the thickness and falloff of the wedge). You typically start with a keyframe at 100 and end with a keyframe at 0; if you add one more keyframe between the two, you can adjust the shape of the luminance transition from the white to black, as shown in Figure 6.15.

Note: It is very unlikely that you will get a better result using this than from adjusting the controls in the Chroma Control group, but if you feel like giving it a go, then feel free to try!

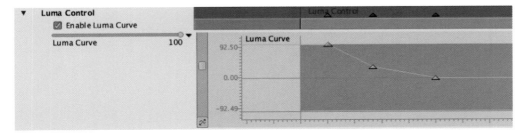

Figure 6.15
The Luma Control graph with a keyframe added in the middle to allow adjustment.

The other control in this group, Suppress Shadow (see Figure 6.16), enables you to suppress shadows cast by foreground objects or people. It works by increasing the saturation values of the shaded pixels for the purposes of calculating the key. The fact that the pixels are shifted does not, however, affect the output. I rather like this control because of the way it affects the SpectraGraph: You get an interesting display that looks like someone has just thrown a hand grenade in the middle of the vectorscope display and all the pixels have been blown outward!

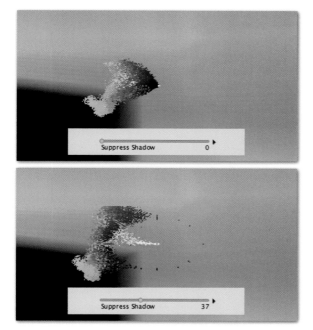

Figure 6.16
Applying the Suppress Shadow parameter.

The Matte Processing Group

Occasionally, you will need to soften the edge of your alpha. The Matte Processing controls, shown in Figure 6.17, let you do that. Most often, you will need to blur the matte very slightly; you can adjust the amount with the Matte Blur control. You can also shrink (erode) or expand (dilate) your matte by choosing the corresponding settings from the menu. What this does is blur either the inside or outside of your alpha only. This needs to be used very sparingly.

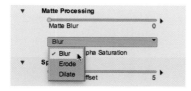

Figure 6.17
The Matte Processing controls.

Note that there is one extra setting here: the Soften Alpha Saturation check box, which is checked by default. Its function is to change the alpha values of a small range of colors at the thin end of the wedge (so to speak). If you turn this off, you may see a slight softening in areas of fine detail, which can improve the key. Always worth a try!

The Spill Group

Spill is where the key color spills onto the figure in the foreground. For example, if you zoom into the gun or along the guy's arm, you will see that the edge of the key is slightly green. There are two steps to removing spill. First, you use the Spill Saturation control to create a zone where you will apply the correction. Next, you use the Spill Angle Offset control to replace pixels inside that zone that might be affected by the key color (in this case, green) with pixels that have not been affected. These controls are shown in Figure 6.18, and described further here:

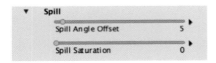

Figure 6.18
The Spill controls.

- **Spill Saturation.** As mentioned, you adjust this parameter first. Note, however, that it only works if you have increased the Key Saturation control in the Chroma Control group. Doing so softens the edge of the key but also tends to add more spill. As mentioned, Spill Saturation—which suppresses the spill by restoring the saturation values seen by the keyer—works in conjunction with the Spill Angle Offset parameter (described next). Typically, you will increase this setting to around the same value as the Key Saturation slider.

Note: If you have not adjusted the Key Saturation setting, changing the Spill Saturation control will have no effect.

- **Spill Angle Offset.** After you have defined the spill area (and removed some of the spill) with the Spill Saturation control, you can tidy up with the Spill Angle Offset setting. As you increase the value of this parameter, you restore the original color by replacing pixels inside the spill zone with pixels from outside the zone (the safe area). As a result, greeny-orange pixels are replaced with orange pixels, and greeny-blue pixels are replaced by blue pixels. Don't push it too far, though, as you might color-correct the *entire* foreground, which is not desirable. Increase it until you start to see a color change; then pull back a bit. You may need to go back to the Spill Saturation control, but between the two, you can achieve good results.

Figure 6.19 shows the result of a spill correction. The top image is the "before" view, before any correction has been made. Notice the green spill on the gun. After spill correction, the green has gone, as shown in the bottom image. See how the green pixels on the SpectraGraph have been shifted round. Those pixels in the edge areas are no longer green.

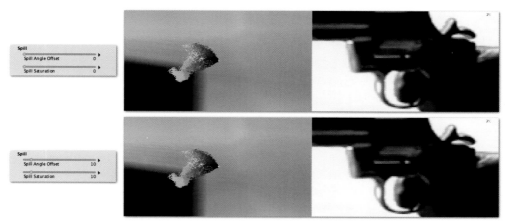

Figure 6.19
Removing the spill.

The DVE Controls

These controls, shown in Figure 6.20, are provided so you can make adjustments to the position and scaling of the key if required. You can also crop the edges if there are objects on the stage that are not meant to be there. You may have other objects to key out that cropping won't remove (these are known as garbage); those are discussed in the AniMatte section that wraps up this lesson.

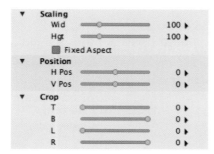

Figure 6.20
The DVE controls: Scaling, Position, and Crop.

Note: If you wish to go beyond the basic DVE tools, you can promote the key to 3D where you have all the 3D controls such as rotation and corner pin.

Workflow with VFX: Keying in the Real World

Although it is possible to get extremely high-quality keys with the SpectraMatte, you may not always be aiming for a broadcast output. If you are working on a movie, you might not be doing the final key in Media Composer, but your director will often want to get a good idea if the composite works before handing over to the VFX department. It is quite likely that you won't have the background plate; it could be a computer-generated (CG) image that doesn't exist yet.

Another issue is that in the real world, your camera is not locked off but is likely to be moving. That is why there are lots of little white crosses on the green screen. They will be used for the 3D tracker so that the background plate moves with the foreground. Although you won't be expected to perform 3D tracking, you can make some pretty impressive key mockups using the tracker to create a realistic movement of the background to match the foreground. This is discussed in Lesson 7, "Tracking and Stabilizing."

If you don't have a background plate, you can always create a mid gray graphic using the Title tool. This can be edited into the Timeline under the key clip. Gray is a great color for trying out a key because it shows any mistakes. If you can key your foreground on gray, you can key it on anything!

Motion Effects and Chroma Keys

Although you can pull a key from a source clip that has had a Motion effect applied, not all render methods will work.

Always use either VTR style or both fields (if you are working in progressive) as the render method for Motion effects that you intend to key.

Never use interpolated field, blended interpolated, blended VTR, or fluid motion as the render method. All these methods create new field information by merging existing fields, making it virtually impossible to fully isolate foreground from background after a Motion effect or time warp has been added.

In the Avid Learning Series   For more information on Motion effects, see the book *Media Composer 6: Part 2–Essential Effects.*

Matte Keys

In the previous section you saw that you can generate a chroma key from color information in the foreground shot, but you can also key shots using a matte that has been provided for you in advance. This type of key is known as a *matte key*. A matte key has two components: a foreground element, which is the image you want to see on top of something else, and a matte, which is a black and white (and occasionally gray) element that defines which part of the background you are seeing. They are typically used to add animated graphics, lower thirds (see Figure 6.21), or 3D animations to a video layer.

Figure 6.21
Animated lower third.

Types of Matte Keys

There are two basic types of matte keys. In one type, the matte element is already combined with the foreground, and you import them together in a file. In the other type, the matte element and the foreground are provided to you in two parts, as separate files or tapes. Avid Media Composer supports both types of matte keys. If you import a key as two separate clips, you will need three layers on the Timeline to composite them: the foreground, the matte, and the background. Hence these are referred to as *three-layer mattes*; they will be discussed momentarily. In the days of tape, using two separate clips was the only way you could make a key of this sort.

Importing or Capturing Matte Keys

Before importing a key, you need to check your import settings. Lesson 4, "Importing Graphics and Mattes," talked about the various settings for importing files, whether still or moving. These settings apply here too. The Import Settings dialog box is shown in Figure 6.22. The import settings are found in the Settings tab of the Project window, or by clicking the Options button in the Import dialog box when you right-click in the bin to import a file.

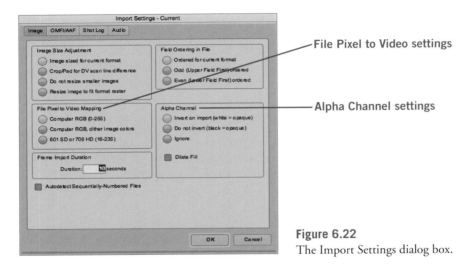

Figure 6.22
The Import Settings dialog box.

When you import a file with a combined matte key, the main settings to check are the Alpha Channel section (to determine whether the key is white transparent or white opaque) and the File Pixel to Video Mapping section (to make sure your matte is imported at the correct video levels). If you are importing a file that came from an RGB source, make sure you are mapping the pixels as RGB. If your blacks are not true blacks and your whites are not true whites, you will not get a good key, as it will regard your matte as gray. If you have a separate matte element that has been captured incorrectly, you can apply a Color Effect before you attempt to key it. The Color Effect has W Point (white point) and B Point (black point) parameters that you can adjust (in conjunction with a waveform monitor) to set the levels correctly, as shown in Figure 6.23.

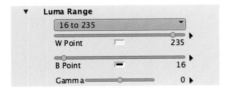

Figure 6.23
Color Effect settings.

Everything discussed in Lesson 4 concerning frame sizes applies here. If you are importing graphics, you need to make sure your graphic file has been correctly created in the aspect that matches your current project format. Field ordering is also important for interlaced video. Many graphics are created as frames rather than fields, but if you have fields in your graphic, you need to ensure that your field ordering is correct for your project format. If you get it wrong you will see artifacts and jittering on your broadcast monitor output. (Refer to Table 4.2 in Lesson 4 for more information.)

Note: If you are using the project on the accompanying DVD, it is 24P, so there are no fields and nothing to worry about! If only it were always so....

Once you have correctly configured your import settings, you are ready to import your graphic files. You saw in Lesson 4 how to import a file with a combined alpha. You will do this again—first a lower third with a combined alpha and next the same file, only with a separate alpha.

To import a file with a combined matte key:

1. Open the **GRAPHICS FOR LESSON 6** folder and locate the **1 ANIMATED LOWER THIRD_COMBINED.MOV** file. It is a QuickTime movie.

2. Check your import settings. They should be set to RGB mapping.

3. Import the file by dragging into the bin. Media Composer will combine the different layers into a matte key file, and you'll see the matte icon in the bin.

4. Edit a clip of your choice into the Timeline or use the **BACKGROUND FOR KEY** sequence.

5. Edit the animated lower third on track **V2**. It will key over the background clip automatically, as shown in Figure 6.24.

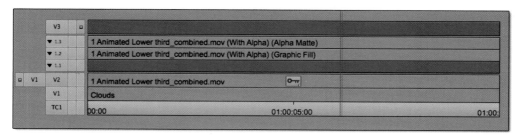

Figure 6.24
Lower third keyed over the background clip and stepped in to show the alpha matte.

Next, you are going to import another version of this file, which comes with a separate alpha layer, and combine them together with the Matte Key effect.

To import a second file and combine them:

1. Open the GRAPHICS FOR LESSON 6 folder and locate the **2** ANIMATED LOWER THIRD.MOV and **3** ANIMATED LOWER THIRD ALPHA.MOV files. Both are QuickTime movies.

2. Check your import settings. They should be set to RGB mapping.

3. Import the two files by dragging into the bin.

4. Edit a clip of your choice into the Timeline or use the BACKGROUND FOR KEY sequence.

5. Put the lower third on track **V2** and the lower third alpha on track **V3**.

6. Add the MATTE KEY effect (in the KEY section of the Effect Palette) to the alpha track.

7. The key is the wrong way around, so enter Effect mode and invert it. To do so, click the INVERT KEY button in the FOREGROUND tab of the MATTE KEY controls. (See Figure 6.25.)

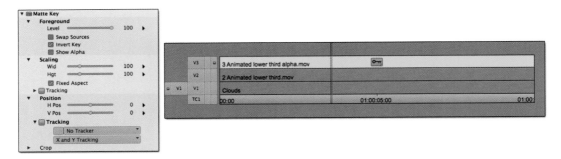

Figure 6.25
The matte key applied to track 3.

Using Three-Layer Mattes

The second example in the preceding section is called a *three-layer matte* because when your graphic comes with a separate matte, you create a three-layer composite with the background at the bottom, the foreground next, and the matte layer on top. But you can use any black-and-white image (or grayscale image if you want some degree of transparency) as a matte layer. Indeed, you can make some interesting key effects by using a normal picture or texture—perhaps using the Color Effect to make it grayscale and increasing the contrast to make it more black and white. In this example, you'll use a black-and-white animated shape to key one layer over another.

To key one layer over another:

1. Open the **06 KEYING** bin and play the **ANIMATED HEART** clip. Shown in Figure 6.26, it is a white animated heart on a black background. You are going to use this to composite two other clips together.

Figure 6.26
Animated heart.

2. Load the **MATTE KEY** sequence into the Timeline. It has two layers: a background and a yellow bird on layer V2.

3. Press **COMMAND+Y** (Mac) or **CTRL+Y** (Windows) to create a new video track.

4. Edit the animated heart clip onto video track 3.

5. Drop the **MATTE KEY** effect (from the **KEY** group in the Effect Palette) onto video track 3. You will see the video on layer 2 outside the blob. This is because the alpha is the wrong way around; as before, you can easily invert it.

6. Open the Effect Editor and reveal the **FOREGROUND** parameters.

7. Click the **INVERT KEY** check box to select it, as shown in Figure 6.27. Now your composite is the correct way around.

Figure 6.27
The result of checking the Invert Key check box.

Promoting to 3D

The Matte Key effect has some additional controls for resizing and moving the matte. You can also crop it if necessary. In addition, you can promote the effect to 3D and perform further modifications, such as applying a rotation to the key. You can also blur the key with the Defocus parameters. With these parameters, shown in Figure 6.28, you have choices: You can blur the foreground, you can blur the foreground with the key together, or you can blur just the key.

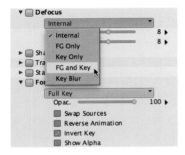

Figure 6.28
Defocus controls when promoted to 3D.

A Word About Premultiplication

Some programs generate keys by combining the foreground and the key layer. This is known as *premultiplication*. Media Composer does not support premultiplication. A sign that you may have a premultiplied file is when you have a gray halo around the edge of soft-edge key. Hard-edged keys are not affected by premultiplication issues. If you see a dark halo, get your graphics department to re-export the graphic as a straight alpha. For example, After Effects will export premultiplied foreground layers by default. The settings need to be changed as shown in Figure 6.29.

Figure 6.29
Correct setting for exporting files from After Effects.

Modifying the Contents of a Key

If you have imported a graphic with a combined key and foreground, you can still modify how the key behaves and even replace the foreground image. If you have applied the key onto your Timeline, you can step into it. In Lesson 4 you imported the Shatter graphic. Here, you will modify this graphic by replacing the fill.

To replace the fill:

1. Load the **SHATTER 2** sequence into the Timeline. This sequence has a background layer and a "Shatter" title on video 2.

2. Click the **STEP IN** button to step into the shatter video layer (track 2) and reveal the two layers: an alpha matte on top and a graphic fill on the bottom, as shown in Figure 6.30. This works just like the separate matte key, only the layers are combined within the effect. Notice that the top layer has a little lock icon to show that it is not editable.

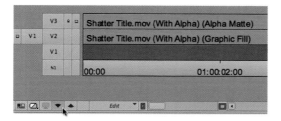

Figure 6.30
Step into the effect.

3. To replace the foreground of this effect, choose another picture from the **FOOTAGE–BACKGROUNDS** bin and load it into the Source monitor.

4. Patch your video tracks so that V1 on the source side is aligned with the graphic fill layer (V2) on the recorder side.

5. Press the **T** key to mark an IN point and an OUT point.

6. Edit in the picture and step out again. You now have the same shatter effect with a new video fill!

Note: You used this same technique to replace the fill in a title in the second exercise in Lesson 1, "Effect Design and Techniques."

Tip: Actually, you can unlock the alpha layer. The trick is to mark the alpha layer, then press Option+C (Mac) or Alt+C (Windows) to copy it into the Source monitor. Now you can edit it back in the Timeline just like any other matte track and it will no longer be locked.

Luma Keys

Luma keys are not so common nowadays, but if you are still in the world of tape, you may come across them from time to time. Lesson 4 discussed getting the levels correct; it is important for a successful luma key that you import the blacks correctly as "super black."

Avid systems obey the ITU-R BT601 digital video specification, which lets you capture information down to –48 mV (PAL or HD) and .74 IRE (NTSC). When capturing or importing, ensure that you maintain the gap between key black and video black; improper capturing will prevent you from achieving the desired key. The correct setting is 601/709 (16-235) in the Import Settings dialog box, as this will not lift the blacks.

Another consideration with luma keys is that it is impossible to key a soft edge or a drop shadow. The edge of the foreground must be clean, with a distinct pedestal between the background black and the dark parts of the foreground.

You can use the Luma Key effect in the Key group of effects, but you have a greater range of controls in the 3D Warp effect. As with the chroma key, you can either apply the 3D Warp directly or promote the Luma Key effect to 3D. Let's try it out.

To apply a 3D Warp luma key:

1. In the **Lesson 06 Keying** bin, find the **Luma Key** sequence.

2. Load the **Luma Key** sequence to the Timeline. It has a background layer and a Luma Key clip on track 2. This clip was imported using the 601 color mapping settings to ensure that the black in the background stays black.

3. In the Effect Palette, choose the **3D Warp** effect from the Blend group and apply it to video track 2.

4. In the Effect Editor, open the drop-down list at the top of the **Foreground** parameter group and choose **Luma Key**, as shown in Figure 6.31.

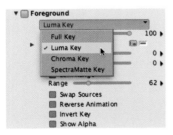

Figure 6.31
Choose Luma Key in the Foreground group.

Tips for Good Luma Keys

Two parameter groups contain controls for adjusting the luma key: the Foreground group and the Erode/Expand group. The Foreground group, shown in Figure 6.32, is where you start, by setting up the key.

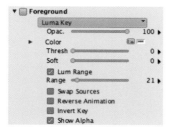

Figure 6.32
Foreground controls.

To set up the key:

1. Drag the **THRESH** (short for *threshold*) slider to **0**.

2. Drag the **RANGE** slider, starting at 0 and raising it until the black appears to be keyed out. This setting controls which levels of black are keyed out and which are kept. The slider goes from 0 to 255, but in most cases you will be entering a fairly low value here.

3. Zoom in on the round logo in the left side and check that it animates cleanly. There should be a small black line along the bottom of the strap; a value of about **37** on the **RANGE** slider seems to be good.

4. Click the **SHOW ALPHA** check box to select it in order to display the matte that is being used and thus exactly how your image will be keyed.

Note: Unless you are using the Luma Key effect to create a special effect (see the upcoming section "Additional Uses for the Luma Keys"), you probably won't need to adjust the Soft slider. In the Foreground group, the Soft control is not really blurring the matte but is including a range of pixels with values slightly above or below the key cutoff level as set by the Luma Range.

At this point, you have make a key, but it is still not looking that great. The result is quite pixilated. To improve the key further, you can use the second group of parameters: the Erode/Expand controls.

To improve the key:

1. First you need to soften the edge of the matte. Adjust the **ERODE/EXPAND** controls, shown in Figure 6.33, for further refinement. These controls are as follows:

Figure 6.33
Erode/Expand controls.

- **Filter.** This setting controls the number of pixels at the matte edge that are affected by the key. Think of it as a subtle softening of the matte, as it gets rid of "dancing pixels" when set to higher levels. Try the maximum setting of 7 first; if you see there are sharp corners in your matte that are starting to round off, then you can reduce it a little. For this strap, a setting of 3 is good.

- **Center.** This setting controls the amount of erosion or expansion of the matte. The center position is 127; dragging the slider to the left erodes and dragging it to the right expands. You will need to increase it slightly for this example.

- **Soft.** This setting blurs the edge of the matte. A setting of around 100 is good.

2. Click the **SHOW ALPHA** check box to deselect it and make final adjustments to the **CENTER** and **SOFT** controls in the **ERODE/EXPAND** group until you are happy with your key. See Figure 6.34.

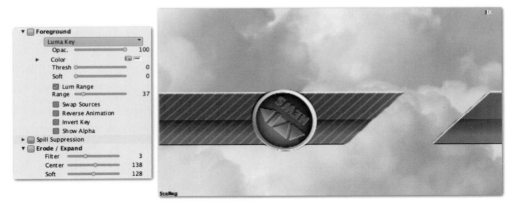

Figure 6.34
Final result.

Additional Uses for the Luma Key

Avid Media Composer does not come with blending operations—the kind you get in Photoshop, where you can merge layers in many different ways (such as by adding, subtracting, multiplying, color dodging, etc.). However, you can achieve some quite interesting blending effects by applying a luma key to any clip. Experiment with changing some of the controls, such as hue, gain, and particularly softness, to see how you can merge two video layers together. (See Figure 6.35.)

Figure 6.35
Two images blended with a luma key.

Using AniMatte

So far, you have seen various types of keyers that make use of an alpha channel that has been either imported or derived from some property of the clip such as a chroma key. There is another option, however: creating your own key. For this, you use AniMatte (see Figure 6.36), which has various shape tools that let you draw a key that can be used to composite one video element over another. As well as for drawing a shape, you can use AniMatte, a subset of the Intraframe (Paint) Effects (discussed in the previous lesson), to animate the shape over time.

Note: The Intraframe (Paint) Effects that include AniMatte do not have keyframe graphs. Animation is done with the shape-creation tools. When you add the AniMatte effect, keyframes are automatically added at the start and end of the effect.

Figure 6.36
AniMatte.

In this lesson, you will consider two main uses of AniMatte:

■ Drawing a matte that lets you key one image on top of another.

■ Removing garbage from an existing key.

Note: AniMatte shares many features with the Paint Effect. The same drawing and reshaping tools are available to create shapes. The only difference is that you have only one mode: a key that is defined by the shape you draw.

Drawing a Matte

Like many effects, the AniMatte effect can be applied as both a segment effect and a transition effect to allow you to create a shape that reveals another shot.

To apply AniMatte as a segment effect:

1. Edit a clip that will act as your background track into your sequence—for example, on V1.

2. Edit the foreground clip that you want to key over the background on the video track above the background—for example, on V2.

3. Apply the **AniMatte** effect (from the Key group) to the foreground clip in the sequence.

4. Enter Effect mode.

5. Use the shape-creation tools to draw a shape around the object you wish to key. As shown in Figure 6.37, the area inside the shape is now keyed over the background (keyed in), and the area outside the shape is removed (keyed out).

Figure 6.37
AniMatte applied to the bird shot to key over the sky.

6. Edit the shape using the shape-editing tools and create more shapes as desired.

7. Add feathering if required to soften the edge of the matte.

To apply AniMatte as a transition effect:

1. Apply the **AniMatte** effect to the edit point between two clips. (Remember, as with any transition effect, you'll need some handles on your clips.)

2. Enter Effect mode and make sure your blue position indicator is on the first frame of the effect.

3. Using the shape-creation tools, draw the initial shape of the wipe you wish to create. The initial shape should either be completely off screen or completely on screen.

4. Move to the last frame.

5. Adjust the shape to create the final shape of the wipe, which should either be completely on screen or completely off screen. Figure 6.38 shows an AniMatte wipe.

Figure 6.38
AniMatte custom wipe.

Using AniMatte to Create a Shape

Earlier I outlined the workflow for using AniMatte to create shapes. In this section, you'll reinforce what you've learned. Here, you'll create a simple shape that will let you key the image on track V2 over the background.

To use AniMatte to create a shape:

1. Load the **ANIMATTE SHAPE** sequence into the Timeline. Note that there is no key applied; the sequence is just one background clip on track V1 and one clip on track V2.

2. Apply an **ANIMATTE** effect to **V2** and open the Effect Editor.

3. Select the **OVAL** tool and draw an oval around the bird's head, as shown in Figure 6.39.

Figure 6.39
Bird's head with oval shape drawn.

4. When you finish drawing the shape, the Oval tool changes to the Selection tool, and your shape will have four handles—one at each corner—that you can use to change the shape. Drag the handles as needed to adjust the shape.

5. Scroll around to make sure the bird's head stays inside the shape. If it doesn't, reposition the shape as needed.

6. Open the **MODE** menu and choose **KEY OUT**. You will see that the key is inverted and the water is inside the shape instead of outside. Now choose **KEY IN**. (Notice that you can achieve the same result by clicking the Swap Sources button.) The correct setting in this case is Key In, which is the default.

7. The shape has a very hard edge. To fix that, use feathering. First, make sure the shape is still selected. Then drag the **HOR** slider in the **FEATHERING** controls (see Figure 6.40) to adjust the feathering. (The Fixed Aspect setting should be enabled.)

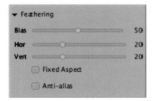

Figure 6.40
The Feathering controls.

Tip: Even if you are not using feathering, you will always get a much smoother edge if you turn on the Anti-Alias setting in the Feathering group. Figure 6.41 shows the difference between this setting being on and being off.

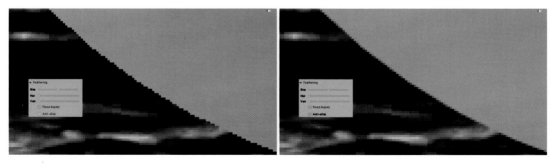

Figure 6.41
Enlarged shape edge with anti alias off and on.

8. Experiment with the **Bias** slider in the Feathering group to move the feathering from inside the shape to outside. Then return it to its default, which is in the middle (**50**). Figure 6.42 shows various Bias settings.

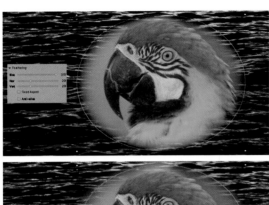

Figure 6.42
The Bias control set to inside (top left), outside (top right), and middle (bottom).

Note: Feather bias is particularly important when you are creating matte shapes. Usually, you need to choke a matte slightly so that you cannot see any of the pixels immediately around the element for which you are creating the matte. You usually set the Bias control to nearly maximum while working with the shape and then adjust back when you are done.

Creating a Garbage Matte

When you create blue or green screen keys with the SpectraMatte, you will often find areas of the foreground that are not meant to be in the composite—light stands, cables, etc. These are known as *garbage*. Sometimes it is sufficient just to crop the edge of a key, but for more complex cases, you can remove garbage using the AniMatte effect. There are two general approaches:

- You can draw a shape to enclose the area you want to keep. Any garbage outside this shape will be excluded from the key. In this case you set the key mode to Key In.

- You can draw a shape (or multiple shapes) around the garbage. In this case the garbage inside the shape is removed and the rest of the image is retained in the key. In this case you set the key mode to Key Out.

Sometimes you will have objects in the image that move (or the camera moves), in which case the garbage matte can be animated and even tracked. You'll learn about tracking in the next lesson.

To use AniMatte to remove garbage from a chroma key:

1. Load the **Garbage Removal** sequence into your Timeline. You will see that it already has a SpectraMatte applied to it, and that there is stuff around the edge that is not meant to be there. In this case you could also crop to remove the garbage, but I want to show you how you can do this with the AniMatte effect.

2. Option-drag (Mac) or Alt-drag (Windows) the AniMatte effect from the Effect Palette to apply it on top of the SpectraMatte.

3. Enter Effect mode to open the Effect Editor.

4. Click the **Oval Tool** button on the right side of the Effect Editor.

5. Draw an oval around the mad puppet. Then drag the oval outside the screen at the bottom so that you are viewing just the top half. As shown in Figure 6.43, the garbage will disappear, and you'll see a shape around the puppet.

Figure 6.43
A shape is drawn around the puppet to remove the garbage.

Note: This is an example of a very difficult key, with feathers and hair that are very hard to key out—especially when the background is so badly lit. Even so, the principle for garbage removal remains the same.

Real Time

Technically, both SpectraMatte and the AniMatte are real-time effects. When you combine the two together, the system still tries to play back in real time, but you may notice dropped frames on slower systems—particularly when working in HD. If you see dropped frames, you may need to render the top layer.

Animating Shapes

It is possible to create and animate multiple shapes. All keyframes apply to all shapes, however, which can make complex moves on multiple shapes challenging. To accomplish this, it is easier to animate the shapes individually on separate, duplicate copies of the clip. Use "key in" on each one to minimize unwanted interaction between the shapes.

Adjusting the Foreground Element

The AniMatte effect does not have any DVE controls, but you can easily step into the effect and apply a Resize or a 3D DVE to the foreground clip. You will then be able to independently move or resize the foreground clip.

Tip: If you are using the 3D Warp, it is a good idea to enable the background color and set it to a contrasting color so that it is obvious when you move your image too far and accidentally reveal the edges of the foreground element. See Figure 6.44.

Figure 6.44
Foreground with 3D Warp added and resized, with red background to reveal unwanted edges.

Review/Discussion Questions

1. What is the order of layers of a three-layer matte key?

2. Why is proper capture from tape critical for luma key elements?

   a. Because if the footage is grainy, the soft edges will not key so well.

   b. Because component footage will not give a good key.

   c. Because the black levels in the background must be kept well below the blacks in the image.

3. Which of the following statements is *not* the case when shooting chroma key elements?

   a. Both the foreground and background should be well lit.

   b. The subject should not be wearing clothes of the same color as the background cloth.

   c. The background should never be red.

   d. There should be no composite signal anywhere in the capture process.

4. What is the SpectraGraph display used for and how does it display the key?

5. Why might it be necessary to tweak the key color you initially chose when setting up the SpectraMatte key?

6. True or false: Key tolerance is the amount of hue variation that is acceptable when defining a chroma key.

7. Fill in the gaps:

   1. _____ is when the color of the background is reflected on the edges of the foreground.

   2. You can remove it by first adjusting the _____ _____, which creates a zone to define the pixels that need to change.

   3. Then you adjust the _____ _____ _____, which replaces the pixel values inside the zone with colors from the edge of the SpectraGraph.

8. What effect do you use to draw a shape around an object to key it over a background?

9. Which of the following is true for the AniMatte effect?

    a. Key In will keep the foreground inside the shape and Key Out will remove it.

    b. Key In will keep the background inside the shape and Key Out will remove it.

10. How do you adjust the position or scaling of the foreground element when using the AniMatte effect?

Lesson 6 Keyboard Shortcuts

Key	Shortcut
Command+Y (Mac)/Ctrl+Y (Windows)	Add new track
Option+C (Mac)/Alt+C (Windows)	Copy marked tracks to Source monitor
Command+A (Mac)/Ctrl+A (Windows)	Select all Keyframes (in Effect Editor)
Option+Command+A (Mac)/Alt+Crtl+A (Windows)	Deselect all Keyframes (in Effect Editor)
T	Mark clip

Using Different Keying Techniques

In this lesson, you will practice using different keying techniques.

Media Used:

Open the 06 Exercises bin. Also locate the Graphics for Lesson 06 folder if you wish to try importing the files for yourself.

Duration:

30 minutes

GOALS

- Try a few different keying techniques
- Use the SpectraMatte to obtain a good chroma key

Creating a Luma Key

First you are going to make a luma key:

1. Create a sequence and edit in a background clip of your choice. There are three clips in the **06 EXERCISE** bin for this.

2. Create a new video track and edit in the **ANIMATED LUMA KEY PARROT** clip.

3. Apply the **3D WARP** effect to the luma key clip and enter Effect mode.

4. Open the **FOREGROUND** tab and choose **LUMA KEY**.

5. Drag the **THRESHOLD** and **SOFT** sliders to **0**.

6. Adjust the **RANGE** setting until you get a good key.

7. Refine the key with the **ERODE/EXPAND** settings.

Creating a Green Screen Key

Now you are going to use the SpectraMatte keyer to get a green screen key. Betty Blooper has a video clip of one of her former FCP editors who has been reprogrammed to use Avid. She wants to put him on a background.

1. Load the **MAN IN CHAIR GREEN SCREEN** sequence into the Timeline.

2. Add the SpectraMatte key and enter Effect mode.

3. Follow the directions in the "Using the SpectraMatte Controls" section in this lesson to create a good key, as shown in Figure 6.45.

Figure 6.45
Finished key.

Using AniMatte to Remove Garbage

There is some garbage in the right side of the foreground, which you need to remove. Follow these steps:

1. Add the **AniMatte** effect on top of the SpectraMatte by Alt-dragging (Mac) or Option-dragging (Windows) the effect onto your key from the last exercise.

2. Enter Effect mode and scroll along the clip to see where the object enters the frame.

3. Select the **Oval** tool and draw an oval on the right side of the screen to cover the black object.

4. Zoom out a little and reposition and rescale the shape to make sure it covers the object. You will need to go outside the frame.

5. Of course the camera moves, so you will need to animate this shape so that it covers the object at all times but doesn't obscure the man. To begin, add a keyframe a few frames in; then reposition your shape.

6. Move down the clip about 10 frames, add another keyframe, and reposition your shape.

7. Continue moving down the clip 10 frames at a time, making sure the shape is in the right place each time. (See Figure 6.46.)

Figure 6.46
Keyframed shape.

Creating a Custom Wipe with AniMatte

Betty Blooper now wants you to create a custom wipe. She has a shot of some fountains and wants to create a wipe based on their shape. To begin, load the sequence AniMatte Wipe in the bin 06 Exercises. Then do the following:

1. Add an **AniMatte** effect to the transition between the two shots and enter Effect mode.

2. Draw a shape that follows the fountains. Use the **Polygon** tool to reshape if necessary. (You may find it easier to zoom out a bit.) It should look something like Figure 6.47.

Figure 6.47
Fountain shape.

3. Apply some feathering to make the shape softer.

4. Next, you need to animate the shape. Select the first keyframe; then use the **Selection** tool (not the Reshape tool) to select the shape.

5. Squeeze the shape by dragging the corner handles so that it is off the frame at the bottom. (You may need to step out some more to do this.) See Figure 6.48 for guidance.

6. Select the last keyframe and stretch the shape vertically by dragging the corner handles so that it covers the entire screen. You may need to move it as well as stretch it. It should look something like Figure 6.48.

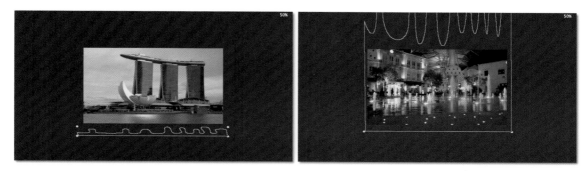

Figure 6.48
The first and last keyframes.

7. Zoom back in to normal size and play back the effect.

Tracking and Stabilizing

Media Composer can track the motion of a part of your image over time. This tracking information can be used to control the motion of effects such as a DVE, a Paint, or an AniMatte object. For example, you might use tracking to obscure the face of a person who is moving around the screen, or to place a picture in a TV screen. To do this and much more, you'll use the Tracking tool. This lesson looks at how to obtain the best results when performing a track.

Media Used: The media for this lesson is in the MC205 Pro Effects project. Open the Lesson 07 Tracking bin.

Duration: 60 minutes

GOALS

- Use the Tracking tool to obtain tracking information
- Use offset tracking and set a tracking reference frame
- Apply tracking to obscure a face
- Use more than one tracking point
- Apply a corner pin track
- Apply tracking data to different objects
- Stabilize your footage

Tracking Workflow

When you track something, you search for a distinctive group of pixels in the image—for example, someone's eye, or even a tracking reference point (some kind of mark added to the background at the time of shooting) and follow its motion over a series of frames. As shown in Figure 7.1, you can use the Tracking tool to analyze this motion using a special device called a *tracker*. Trackers (you can use more than one to better analyze the motion) generate a series of tracking data points, which can be associated with an effect parameter to control how the effect moves over time.

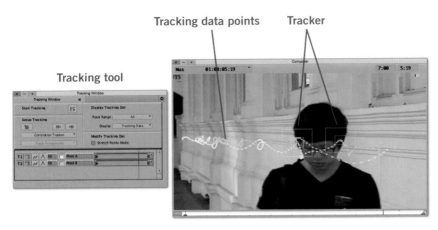

Figure 7.1
The Tracking window showing two trackers and their generated tracking data points.

Tracking is not always a straightforward operation. For example, if you're tracking a person, her face will inevitably change over time—her head may turn, it will appear larger as she approaches the camera, or it may become obscured if she walks behind a tree. Tracking is more of an art. Understanding the Tracking tool will help you overcome these and other problems that you may encounter.

There are many steps to getting a good track. We will be discussing these in detail during this lesson:

1. Choose the effect that will work best with what you have in mind.

2. Decide on how many trackers you will need.

3. Decide on the reference points in the image that you will use to generate the tracking data.

4. Create some trackers and customize how you will use them.

5. Generate the tracking data.

6. If necessary, modify the tracking data.

7. Apply the tracking data to the appropriate object.

8. Play back the shot and adjust the tracking data or other effect parameters if required to fine-tune your effect.

Use of Tracking

There are several scenarios in which you might use tracking:

■ Often, you will need to replace an area of an image with some material from a different image. For example, you may have a shot of a billboard that you wish to replace with a different image, or you may wish to place a graphic or a painted shape on to the side of a moving truck.

■ You may sometimes need to hide some part of the image. For example, you may need to obscure a car license plate or someone's face. You learned in the lesson on Paint Effects that you can apply mosaic or blur to obscure part of a scene, but if you want to blur a moving image, you will need to track it.

■ You might wish to place a title so that it appears to "stick" to the background, or even just apply some motion to the title such as a bit of random jitter. Both these effects involve tracking.

■ A shot may have been filmed with motion tracking in mind. For example, you may have noticed that the green screen material used in Lesson 6, "Keying," has lots of little white crosses; these allow you to use tracking to match the movement of the foreground with that of the background. Although this would be done in conjunction with sophisticated 3D tracking applications, you can achieve reasonable results with tracking in Media Composer. Later, you see an example of a TV screen with small dots placed on it to let you track the motion so you can easily replace the image.

■ You will often need to stabilize wobbly shots. In this case, the Stabilizer tool is used to apply the *inverse* of the tracking information gathered from the movement of an object in the shot so that it remains motionless. However, you may have a shot that is panning but also shaking at the same time. In that case, you need to preserve the panning but remove the shake; that is where the SteadyGlide tool comes in.

Effects That Use Tracking Data

Tracking can be enabled in most of the segment effects that move over time, including PIP, 3D Warp, Paint Effects, titles, and any effect that can be promoted to 3D. Within these effects, you will find either a Tracking parameter or trackers that are subsets of other parameters. An example of the former is in the Paint Effects, such as Paint and AniMatte, which have their own Tracking parameter group that enables you to apply up to four trackers to objects that you draw, as shown in Figure 7.2.

Figure 7.2
The trackers in the Paint tool.

Examples of parameters that have Tracking subsets are Scale, Rotation, Position, and Corner Pin. Any effects that have one or more of these parameter groups (such as the PIP and 3D Warp, shown in Figure 7.3) will have trackers associated with each of these groups.

Note: In the 3D Warp tool, trackers can be active in either the Corner Tracking parameter or in the Scaling, Rotation, and Position parameters, but not both at the same time. You can, however, activate trackers in the Scaling, Rotation, and Position parameters all at the same time so that you can use the size and position of an object and its rotation to generate tracking information.

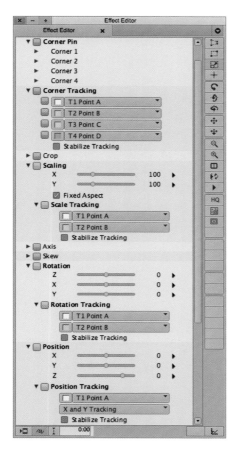

Figure 7.3
The trackers available in the 3D Warp effect.

How Many Trackers?

The Tracking tool allows you to create up to eight trackers, although a maximum of four can be used at any one time. Your choice of how many trackers are used depends on what kind of motion you have in your image. You could be following a shape in the image, or you might be attempting to stabilize it. Every case will have a particular kind of motion.

One Tracker

This is the simplest case, where the motion of the camera or the object you are tracking is in only the XY plane. By that, I mean the object is not rotating or coming toward you. In this case, one tracker will suffice to lock onto an object, and your Position values will update to maintain a good track.

Two Trackers

If your camera is rotating as well as moving in the X and Y planes—or if you are tracking an object that is rotating or moving toward you—then you also need to consider rotation and scale (or both). In this case, two trackers are needed to obtain tracking data for either Scale and/or Rotation parameters as well as Position.

Three Trackers

Occasionally, you will have to deal with cases where the skew of the object changes. This can happen when the camera is not just rotating in the Z plane, but also in the X and Y planes. Technically speaking, this calls for 3D tracking, which Avid doesn't do, but using three trackers is worth a try for difficult cases such as these.

Four Trackers

When you have a TV screen or some kind of object that you wish to replace with a video clip, you will need four trackers, and you will need to use the corner pin tracker to generate tracking data for the four corners of the screen. This is widely used, and there is an example of this later.

Camera Lens Considerations

Another point to bear in mind is the lens angle of the camera. If the camera is using a telephoto or narrow-angle lens, there is much less perspective, and motion tends to be more two dimensional. A wide-angle lens, however, will cause much more distortion in the image when the camera moves. This will create problems for multiple trackers, as the perspective will change. When choosing tracking points, try to keep them in the same plane with respect to the camera. It is not good to choose one point close to the camera and one point far away, especially with a wide-angle lens.

Using the Tracking Tool

Let's use a simple example to introduce the main concepts of tracking. Open the 07 Tracking bin and find the Book Worm sequence. You will see a young man reading a book. We want to obscure his face with a Mosaic effect.

To begin the process of obscuring the man's face:

1. Apply the Mosaic effect (in the Image category) and open the Effect Editor.

2. Before you can open the Tracker tool, you need to draw an object to track. Go to the first frame of the shot and ensure that both keyframes are active (pink).

3. Select the **Oval** tool and draw a small circle around the man's face.

4. Because he is walking toward the camera and his face is getting bigger, you need to use two trackers—for changing the position and scale of the mosaic shape. Open the **Tracking** parameter and enable the top tracker by clicking the **Enable Tracker** button to the left of the tracker.

5. The Tracking window will open. Move it to one side for the moment and add a second tracker. You should now see something like what is shown in Figure 7.4.

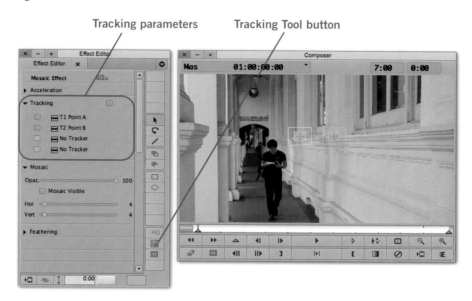

Figure 7.4
Two trackers applied.

You can see two trackers in the effect preview monitor (provided you are parked on the first frame). Before you perform the track, you need to explore the Tracking tool interface. Move the Tracking tool back into view and let's look at the main features. (If you have closed the Tracking tool, you can open it again by clicking the Tracking Tool button, shown in Figure 7.4.)

The Interface

The main features of the Tracking tool, shown in Figure 7.5, are as follows:

■ **Start Tracking button.** Click this to start the tracking.

■ **New Tracker button.** Click this button to create a new tracker.

- **Go to Previous Tracker Region and Go to Next Tracker Region buttons.** Use these for offset tracking. (This will be discussed shortly.)

- **Tracker Engine menu.** Use this to choose the type of tracker you are going to use.

- **Track Background/Track Foreground menu.** This is for choosing which layer to track when you have an effect on top of another layer.

- **Display Tracking Data section.** This is where you can choose how to display tracking data.

- **Modify Tracking Data section.** Switch to Stretch Points mode here.

- **Tracker Timeline.** This is where you manage your trackers and their corresponding data.

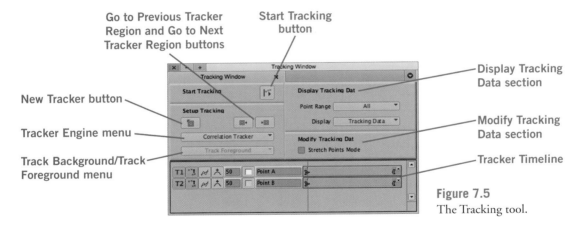

Figure 7.5
The Tracking tool.

Choosing a Good Tracking Point

You have created two trackers; now you need to decide where to place them. Here are some tips to bear in mind when choosing a tracking reference point, also known as a tracking target.

- Look carefully at the shot you want to track for an area of detail that remains reasonably consistent throughout the shot.

- Does anything pass in front of the target area where you want to place the tracker, or does the target leave the screen? If so, is there a substitute point in the image that has the same movement as your preferred point?

- Does the target area remain in sharp contrast to the background throughout the shot?

In this case, you are tracking a man's face. He is approaching the camera, so his face will get bigger. Thus, you have two trackers so the mosaic shape will also get bigger. But the head is also moving from side to side quite a lot, so it might not be the ideal thing to track. Although his glasses might be a good candidate, they are not very clear at the very start of the shot. Perhaps the corner of his collar might be a good place to start.

The exact position of the trackers in relation to the position of the mosaic shape is not critical. You can move the shape once you have your track. The important point is that the tracking points are going to generate the same type of movement that the face would. You could consider using his arms or part of the book as long as they move together with the face. If the position of his arms were to move relative to his face, they would be no good as tracking points.

Now let's look at how the trackers work.

How a Tracker Works

A *tracker* is basically two boxes, one inside the other (see Figure 7.6). The box on the inside—the target area box—is taking a snapshot of the group of pixels it encloses. The box on the outside is the search area. The snapshot is taken on frame one, and the tracker goes to frame two and searches for a similar pattern inside the search area.

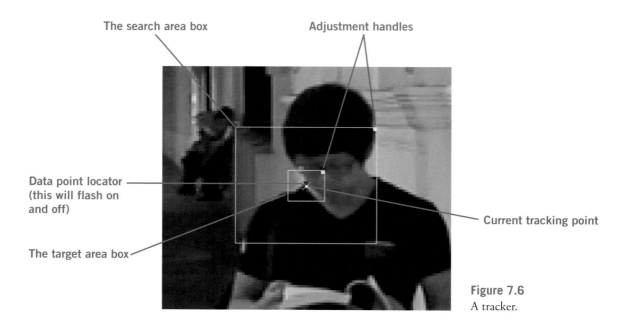

Figure 7.6
A tracker.

Military Technology Put to Good Use

Tracking technology originated in the military arena. The idea was that the gun on a tank should remain pointing at the target, even though the tank was moving over rough terrain. The information derived from the tracker was applied to the position of the gun to keep it locked onto target—a kind of mechanical stabilizer.

Adjusting the Size of the Search Area

Use the adjustment handles on the top right of the search area to change the size of the box. The larger the search area, the longer it will take the tracker to find the same pattern and the more likely it is that it will find another (i.e., wrong) pattern somewhere else that could be a reasonable match. However, if you make it too small, the target may move outside the search area in the next frame. Scroll through the shot looking at the target and see how quickly it is moving. If it only moves a small amount from frame to frame, then the box can be quite small. If it moves quickly, the box must be bigger.

Adjusting the Size of the Target Area

Here, you need to consider what is happening to the target pixels throughout the duration of the shot. Of course there will be some changes, and the algorithms used to calculate the track will take that into account. As long as the pixels don't change too much, the snapshot will match from frame to frame. If the pixels change by more than a certain threshold, the tracker will stop.

Think about the things that make the pixels change. If you are tracking something on the edge of your target (as in this case, on the man's shoulder) is there a possibility that the background could change significantly and interfere with the snapshot? Generally, the box should be quite small so as not to include data that could change from frame to frame.

Tip: The tracker is looking for areas of contrast. If your chosen target is not sufficiently distinguished in tonal range—or color—from the background, then you might consider putting a Color effect on the shot to increase the contrast or change the color so that the target stands out better. Once you have obtained the tracking data, you can delete the effect.

Let's continue with this example by moving the two trackers so there's one on each shoulder. Click anywhere inside the outer box and drag; both boxes will move together. You can try other places as well to see what kind of results you get. You can even name your trackers so you don't get confused about which is which. It is also a good idea to enlarge your image a couple of times to get a better idea of where to place your trackers. You should now have something like Figure 7.7.

Figure 7.7
Trackers in position.

It doesn't matter if the outside boxes overlap. What is important is that the inside boxes are looking at distinctly different patterns of pixels. They will independently search for the same pattern (or similar) in the outside box on the next frame. If it finds a good match, a new tracking data point will be created, the position and shape of the target will be updated, and the next frame will be searched.

Performing a Track

Okay, let's go! Performing a track is as simple as clicking the Start Tracking button and watching the tracking process to make sure the trackers don't drift. If the trackers *do* drift or if for any reason you want to stop tracking, press the space bar. In the unlikely event a tracker loses its target, you will need to reposition the tracker. See the next section, "What to Do When a Tracker Goes Astray," for help. If all went well, you should see something like Figure 7.8, which is also showing an enlarged view.

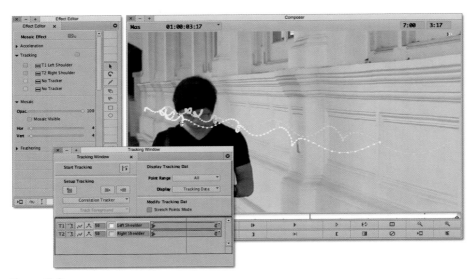

Figure 7.8
Completed tracks.

Notice that the tracks have been applied to the shape you drew. If you look at the Tracking section of the Effect Editor, you will see that your two trackers are now being used to move the Mosaic object. Because there are two of them, the object will get bigger as the tracks get farther apart. At the moment, you can't see your object because you are viewing the tracking data. So you need to set the Display drop-down list in the Tracking window to Effect Results, as shown in Figure 7.9.

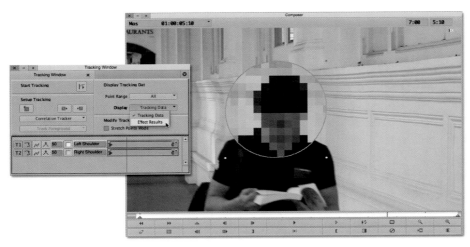

Figure 7.9
Showing the effect results.

Another thing to notice is that the Tracker Timelines have changed slightly. Before you started the track, the Tracker Timeline showed a red line along the bottom to signify that the tracking data was missing or incomplete. After the track, you can see the red line has disappeared, signifying that you have tracking data.

What to Do When a Tracker Goes Astray

It isn't always a perfect world. Trackers can go adrift for all sorts of reasons. The shape of the target pixels may change, or something may pass in front of them that causes the tracker to track a different shape. It may be that the target leaves the frame, and you wish to apply your track to a different target. If this happens, you can easily stop the track and reposition your tracker.

If your tracker starts to drift:

1. Press the **SPACE BAR** to stop. The display will show the tracking data points analyzed so far. Note also that the Timeline of the tracker is showing a partially completed set of tracking data, as shown in Figure 7.10.

Figure 7.10
Tracker Timeline with partial tracking data.

2. Scroll back to see where the point started to drift. If it is not clear what is going on, you can zoom by clicking the **ENLARGE** button.

3. By default, you see all the tracking data, but you change that. Open the **POINT RANGE** menu and choose **CURRENT**, as shown in Figure 7.11, to see just the one point for that frame.

Figure 7.11
View the current point.

Note: You can also mark an **IN** point and an **OUT** point on either the effect Timeline or the tracker Timeline and select In to Out in the Point Range menu. This will display a range of points between the marks.

4. You need a new tracker box, so right-click the tracker Timeline and choose **ADD NEW TRACKER REGION** from the drop-down menu, as shown in Figure 7.12.

Figure 7.12
Choose Add New Tracker Region.

5. A new tracker appears. You can reposition it or adjust the size of the search area or target area boxes.

6. Continue the track until the end or until it drifts again.

Applying the Tracking Data

Once you have your tracking data, it is time to apply it to the shape. Assuming the Mosaic shape you originally drew is still selected, you can now attach the tracking data to the shape.

To apply the tracking data:

1. In the Tracking tool, right-click the **Display** drop-down menu, which is currently set to Tracking Data.

2. Choose **Effect Results**. You should see your mosaic shape perfectly tracked to the young man's face.

Changing Nontracking Parameters

There are still some adjustments, however. In this case, the tracking data you have generated is applied to the *position* of the shape. There are two trackers, so the shape should automatically get bigger as the trackers get farther apart. However, there are other parameters that you can adjust that don't use the tracking data. An obvious case is Feathering, which is one of the parameters in the Paint Effect.

To adjust the Feathering parameter:

1. Close the Tracking window.

2. Make sure your Mosaic object is selected. Also make sure both keyframes (at the start and end of the animation) are selected (pink).

3. Click the triangle to reveal the **Feathering** parameters and adjust the **Feathering** sliders so you get a nice soft edge to your shape.

You can animate the position and size of the shape with either the tracking information *or* the keyframes. In Lesson 5, "Paint Effects," you looked at how to use keyframes to move shapes around, but using the tracker takes a lot of the laborious work out of the procedure. However, you can also use keyframes in conjunction with the trackers. This is a separate type of animation.

For example, you could use keyframes to readjust the position of the mosaic if it should drift. This might happen, for example, if you were tracking someone's nose and the person's head turned. The track would move with the nose, but you might need to adjust the position of the mosaic to compensate. You can do this by adding a keyframe at the point before the drift, adding a keyframe after the drift, and manually repositioning the mosaic to cover the head. Just as you learned in Lesson 5, you can also use keyframes to adjust the size of the shape—or even the *shape* of the shape. The tracker info is still used, but you can fine-tune the animation manually if you need to.

Advanced Tracking Features

Most of the time, you will be doing fairly simple tracking, and the tools you have looked at already will cover all but the most difficult cases. Occasionally, however, you'll need to use some of the more advanced tracking features.

Tracking Engines

When you set up your tracker, you can choose between different tracking engines. The default for the trackers you will use in most of the effects is the Correlation Tracker engine. If you apply the Stabilize effect, however, you will use the Fluid Stabilizer engine by default (more on that later). In addition to these two, there is another tracking engine: the FluidTracker engine (see Figure 7.13).

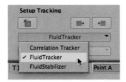

Figure 7.13
Choosing the FluidTracker engine.

The FluidTracker engine works differently from the others. Rather than looking for a particular snapshot, it has algorithms that perform motion analysis of every pixel in the target area. The same motion analysis methods are used when performing a FluidMotion Timewarp.

Note: For more information on correcting FluidMotion artifacts, see Appendix A, "Working with FluidMotion and Photoshop."

The FluidTracker engine takes longer to generate tracking data, but it can be more accurate. It is particularly useful if the search area is large because a large search area will slow down the correlation tracker as it is scanning a larger section of the frame each time.

Offset Tracking

In some circumstances, the object you are tracking may leave the frame or disappear behind a tree. You can still generate tracking data by choosing another reference point, but the shape you are applying the data to will stay fixed to the original point. This is called *offset tracking*.

To perform offset tracking:

1. Make sure **OFFSET TRACKING** is enabled. (It is on by default.) As shown in Figure 7.14, you turn on Offset Tracking in the tracker Timeline. Offset Tracking can be enabled on a per-tracker basis.

Figure 7.14
Offset Tracking enabled.

2. Start your tracker in the normal way on the first frame of the shot.

3. When the target area leaves frame or disappears from view, press the **SPACE BAR** to stop the track.

4. Step back a few frames to see where the last good tracking point was. If necessary, set the **POINT RANGE** to **CURRENT** and zoom in to the area of interest.

5. Right-click the tracker Timeline and choose **ADD NEW TRACKER REGION**. A small vertical bar will appear on the tracker Timeline to indicate a new tracker region has been created, and you will see a new tracking box.

6. Move the tracking box to a new location that is moving with the same speed and direction as the one that has disappeared. For example, if you are tracking a man on a bike and his head goes behind a tree, you can still use another part of the bike to carry on the track until his head reappears. This is an exercise for later!

Note: When you restart the track from a new region, Media Composer will step backward one frame before it starts tracking. This is normal behavior to ensure that the tracking data is correct.

7. Repeat these steps as necessary to select additional target areas until the original target has reentered the frame or the entire object has left the frame.

Again, when choosing an alternative tracking target, always bear in mind the way the camera is moving and the relationship between the camera and the object. Try to choose an offset target that is the same distance from the camera and is moving in the same direction. If you are on a wide-angle lens, some distortion may arise—particularly if you choose an alternative target that is too far from the original.

Video Layers and Tracking

Sometimes, the object you want to track is on a different layer from the one to which you are applying the tracking effect. For example, suppose you have a PIP or a 3D Warp on an image on track V2, but you want to attach it to the motion of an object underneath, on track V1. In the Tracker tool's Setup Tracking area, you can switch between tracking the foreground and tracking the background by choosing from the drop-down menu shown in Figure 7.5. By default, when you are in a two-layer effect and you have applied a track to the top layer, you will be set to tracking background. If you are in a single-layer track—such as a Paint Effect—you can only track the foreground, and the menu is grayed out.

There may be occasions when the material you want to track is on the top layer and the material that receives the effect is on the bottom layer. In that case, you would choose Track Foreground. An example of this is the man with the gun chroma key clip used in Lesson 6. In this shot, the man was moving, but the camera was also moving. The background (in this case, the tiled floor) needs to move as well so that when the man is keyed on top, the floor moves with the camera. You could apply a 3D Warp to the man and perform a position track using one of the crosses on the green screen, but in that case, you would need to track the foreground, not the background, as the tracker points are on the green screen and not on the background floor clip. When you have obtained your tracking data, you can apply it to the floor shot underneath so it moves with the camera. You will look at this workflow in Lesson 8, "Refining the Composite."

Viewing Tracking Data

Sometimes, the tracker just won't be able to track your target, no matter how hard you try. But all is not lost! You can edit existing tracking data or create your own data manually. Before you can do that, however, you must know how to view existing data.

After you perform a track, you can see tracking data in two places:

- **The Effect Editor Preview monitor.** The Preview monitor, shown in Figure 7.15, shows the tracking data points. As mentioned, you can select to view all the points, the current point, or a range of points between the IN and

OUT marks. You can also select points—either by clicking on a single point or lassoing a group of points. When they are selected, they will have a little circle round them. The current point (where your blue position indicator is parked) is always flashing on and off.

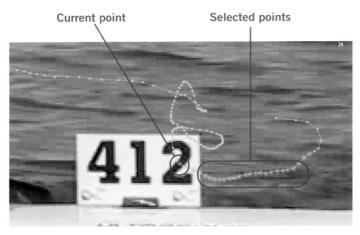

Figure 7.15
Tracking data points. Some have been selected.

■ **The tracker Timeline.** This shows you the status of your tracking data for the duration of the effect. As shown in Figure 7.16, there are various buttons that enable certain features. In addition, you can see which of your data points are selected for further editing.

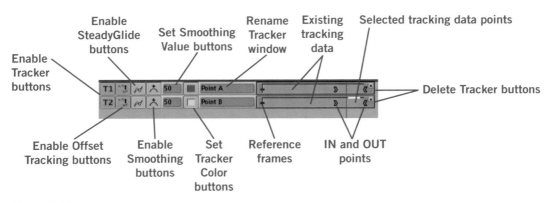

Figure 7.16
The tracker Timeline.

The Enable Tracker button is useful because you may wish to try tracking more than one point to see which one works best. Once you have created a tracker, you can keep it, but deselecting the enable button turns it off so it doesn't interfere with other trackers and doesn't show in the Preview monitor.

Tip: You can toggle all the trackers on or off at once by Option-clicking (Mac) or Alt-clicking (Windows) the Tracker Enable button.

Tip: The trackers don't show up well on certain backgrounds. Fortunately, to improve visibility, you can change the color of a tracker with the Set Tracker Color button, which opens up a color swatch window. You can also rename a tracker in the Set Tracker Name box so you can keep tabs on what you've done.

When you are viewing the tracking data, you have various options for applying, editing, or adjusting the data, as you will see in the next section.

Manually Adjusting Tracking Data

If all else fails, you can manually edit your tracking information. There are various reasons why you might do this. For example, you may find that your tracker just can't stick to the target because it loses focus or other objects get in the way. In that case, you can zoom into the display and move the points yourself. There are many ways to do this:

- You can move individual points.
- You can move groups of points, either moving them together or stretching them as if they were on a piece of elastic. (More on this later.)
- You can delete points and make your own path.

Moving Individual Points

To move individual points, simply select a point and drag it to a new destination. You can isolate the point by opening the Point Range drop-down list and choosing Current. Then, when you step along the Timeline, you can simply move the points to exactly where you want them to be.

Moving a Group of Points

Moving a group of points is particularly useful when you have a tracker that has drifted slightly from the original target, but still represents the motion fairly well. You can move a group of points from the place where it started to drift instead of having to move them one by one.

To move a group of points:

1. Set your view to either **ALL** or **IN TO OUT**.

2. Select or deselect **STRETCH POINTS MODE**. With Stretch Points mode off, all the points you select to move will move together. With Stretch Points mode on, they will move as if on an elastic string. (See Figure 7.17.)

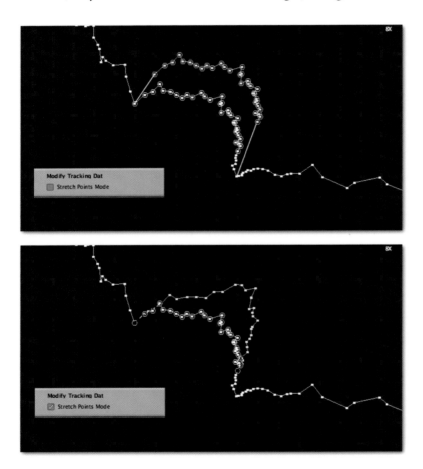

Figure 7.17
Moving points with Stretch Points mode off and on.

3. Using the lasso, select the range of points you want to move.

4. Drag all of the points to a new location.

Deleting Points

You have one more option: Instead of moving selected points, you can delete them. When you delete existing points, Media Composer will create a series of brand-new points. These new points will appear in a nice, orderly line, all equally spaced and they predict the movement between the last two good reference points. (See Figure 7.18.) This is very useful if your target should, for example, move behind a lamp post or leave the frame. In the latter case, you could move the very last data point outside the boundary of the frame, placing it so that it follows the direction of the existing good tracking points. (You will need to zoom out to do this.) Then, delete all the points between the last good point and the point outside the frame. The points you have deleted will now lie on a straight line. You can readjust the last point to get the spacing between the points to match the good data.

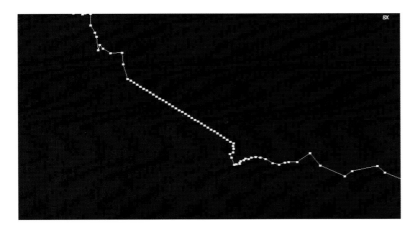

Figure 7.18
Deleted points.

Tip: This method also works for objects coming into the screen. Track any point you like until your desired point has entered the screen. Then track the correct target. When the tracking is done, delete the invalid points and place the very first point outside the screen.

Tip: You can also use offset tracking to find another point that moves relative to your target that has not left the frame yet. For example, if you are tracking two points on a car and the front point leaves the frame, you can offset the track to another point on the car.

Setting a Reference Frame

Media Composer uses a reference frame to establish the relationship between your tracking data and the object you are tracking. A *reference frame* is a frame at which no change is applied to the object you are tracking. By default, this is the first frame of video in a clip, and is signified by a small red diamond that lurks at the beginning of the tracking Timeline.

Using a reference frame is the closest the tracker comes to being able to track backward. Once you have established some tracking data, you can move your position indicator anywhere in the shot and set the reference frame. At this point, your object—perhaps a PIP or a Paint object—is set to its default position. At any point before the reference frame, it is going to move backward in relation to the tracking data; at any point after the reference frame, it will move forward.

For example, you might want to pin a PIP to a TV screen that moves on screen from a point outside. You can create tracking data using the various methods in the last section, but your object can't be placed outside the frame using corner pinning because there is nothing to attach it to before the TV screen enters the picture. However, all you have to do is move to the middle of the clip, where the TV screen is fully on screen, adjust your corner pin so that the PIP is attached correctly and set your reference frame there. The object will now track forward and backward.

To set the reference frame:

1. Move to the frame that you want to serve as the reference frame—in other words, where you would like your object to be at its default position.

2. Right-click on the tracker Timeline and select SET REFERENCE FRAME, as shown in Figure 7.19. This frame will now be the *null frame*, where your effect is applied to the tracker without any adjustment, as indicated by the little red diamond.

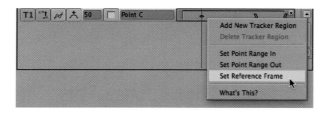

Figure 7.19
Setting the reference frame.

Note: A reference frame is applied to all trackers at the same point in time. You can't position it individually for each tracker.

Trimming Segments with Tracking Data

Unlike keyframes, which are by default elastic (refer to Lesson 2, "Animating with Keyframes"), tracking data is attached to a frame and therefore fixed. When you trim a clip that has an effect with tracking information, the data is preserved for the existing frames. If you trim the edge of a clip to reduce the length, the tracking will remain correct for the remaining segment. If you trim out, you will need to track over the range of new frames to generate new data. If you trim in and then back out again, the data is still available within the tracker.

Making Use of Tracking Data

Tracking data can be recycled. That is, after you have generated data for one clip, you can use it somewhere else. An example would if you tracked a TV screen with dots on the corners of the screen so that you could replace the screen with a different picture, and you then used the same tracking data to remove the dots with a Paint Effect. (See Figure 7.20.) After you have obtained the tracking information, you can simply copy and paste the tracker Timeline.

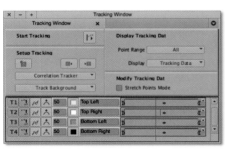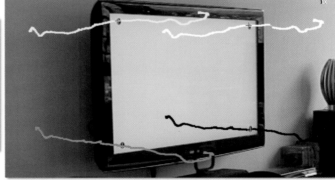

Figure 7.20
Tracking data for the TV dots.

To copy and paste tracking information:

1. Make sure the tracker Timeline is active—i.e., the **ENABLE TRACKER** button is on. (This works for multiple trackers.)

2. Press **COMMAND+C** (Mac) or **CTRL+C** (Windows).

3. Open a Tracker window in any other effect.

4. There has to be at least one tracker enabled. If no trackers are in the Tracker window, you need to create a "dummy" tracker. It does not have to track anything; it just needs to be there.

5. Press **COMMAND+V** (Mac) or **CTRL+V** (Windows). The duplicated tracker or trackers appear in the new window. If you want, you can change the name or the color of the trackers to distinguish them.

Tip: **If you are planning to edit your tracking information by manually repositioning the points, you may wish to duplicate the tracker Timeline first so you have the original data still available.**

Just because the trackers are there doesn't mean they are attached to anything. If you want to use the tracker, you need to associate it with a parameter (in the case of the 3D Warp effect) or an object (in the case of the Paint Effect).

To associate a tracker with a different parameter or object:

1. Choose a parameter with a tracking subset or select an object in a Paint Effect.

2. Select a tracker from the **TRACKER SELECTOR** pull-down menu (see Figure 7.21) or, in the case of a Paint Effect, the tracker selector **FAST** menu. Note that there may be more than one tracker to choose from.

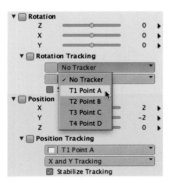

Figure 7.21
Choosing a tracker.

Tip: **Here is one fun thing you can do by reusing tracking data. Have you ever tried tracking a flame? Or water ripples? Or time-lapse clouds? You'll generate some nice random jitter that can be copied somewhere else and used—for example, to make titles jump around the page. Just apply the jitter to the X Y position tracker of a title effect, as shown in Figure 7.22. In this case, the tracker was used to track some cloud time-lapse footage and was renamed "Jitter."**

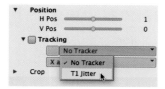

Figure 7.22
Applying jitter.

Tracking Examples

Let's step through a few specific examples that will cover some of the advanced features of the Tracking tool.

Tracking Two Faces with Mosaic

You have seen how easy it is to apply a Mosaic effect to one face and track it, but what if you need to track two faces? Or three or four? You can do this all in the same effect. (For more than four, you would need to nest the layers—just composite one Mosaic effect on top of another.)

1. Load the **MAN AND BOY** sequence in the **LESSON 07 TRACKING** bin. Two faces means two trackers. They also walk out of shot, so you'll have to deal with that, too....

2. Add a **MOSAIC** effect to the clip and enter Effect mode.

3. Park on the first frame and draw two circles around the two faces. Adjust the size and position if necessary. Make sure you apply some feathering as well.

4. Open the **TRACKING** parameter and turn on two trackers.

5. Adjust the size and position of the target area and search area boxes. The target area should just cover the face. It should not include the street behind, or it will interfere with the track.

Tip: **Keep the boxes small—a nose is always a good point to try to track.**

6. Start the tracking and watch to see that the trackers don't drift. (You may need to stop from time to time and readjust, especially when the bus goes by.) If they do, stop the track, add a new tracker region, and reposition the boxes.

7. When you get to the end, the faces leave the screen, meaning the trackers will try to track something else in the picture. Let them do that for now. You'll fix it in a moment.

Now you need to get rid of the tracking points that couldn't follow the faces off screen. This can be a little difficult because you have a jumble of points, all on top of each other, and it is rather hard to tell what is going on. (See Figure 7.23.) Fortunately, there is a neat way of doing this.

Figure 7.23
Points that failed to find a target.

To get rid of the tracking points that couldn't follow the faces off screen:

1. Go to the very last frame and select CURRENT from the POINT RANGE drop-down menu so you just see the last tracking point.

2. Drag this last tracking point off screen.

Tip: You don't actually have to zoom out to do this. You can drag the points to an imaginary place off to the left of the Composer window and the points will go there, even though you can't see it. If you don't believe me, zoom out and you'll see what I mean.

Now you need to delete the points in between. Let's start with the man as he leaves the screen.

To delete the points:

1. Scroll back to the last good tracking point that is still attached to the man's nose.

2. With the Tracking window selected, click the MARK IN button to mark an IN point. You'll see a new IN point icon on the tracker Timeline.

3. Change your **Point Range** setting to **View In to Out**.

4. Now you are seeing just the bad points that were created when the man left the screen. The final point is off the screen because you just moved it; you don't need to delete that one. Select the points on the man's track (you may need to zoom in a bit), as shown in Figure 7.24, and press the **Delete** key. Because you still have one remaining point off the screen, you have a nice neat line of points that lead from here to the last point.

Figure 7.24
Select the bad points.

5. Repeat the procedure with the boy's track. He leaves the screen later, so you'll need to go to the last good point for him and mark an IN point. There should only be a few points to delete. Figure 7.25 shows the tracking data points leaving the screen.

Tracking data points
leaving the screen

The white line shows the region
where data points have been deleted

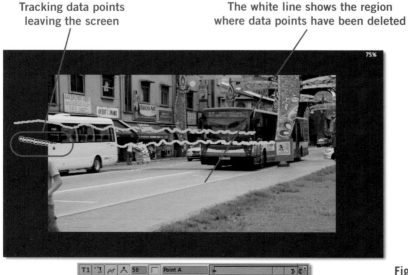

Figure 7.25
The trackers leave the screen.

Note: You could turn on **Stretch Points** mode and try to "bend" the new predicted curves to match the existing points, but all you really need to do in this case is have the mosaic leave the screen so you don't need to worry about exactly how it moves.

6. Click the **Display** drop-down list in the Tracking window and choose **Effect Results**. (Refer to Figure 7.9.) The mosaics should leave the screen.

Note: If the tracking information does not update and the mosaic shapes don't leave the screen correctly, simply copy and paste the two trackers and apply the shapes to the duplicated trackers.

Once you have your trackers working, you need to make one last adjustment. The size of the shapes don't change over the shot, but the characters are moving toward you. It is much easier to animate the size of the mosaics by using keyframes than to create two trackers for each face.

To animate the size of the mosaics:

1. Go to the last frame of the effect. (You will need to zoom out for this because the shapes are off screen.)

2. Adjust the size of both of the shapes with the corner handles so they are big enough to cover the faces. Of course, you can't see the faces, but you can now scroll back a bit to check that the shapes are okay.

3. Make more adjustments if necessary—for example, resizing the shapes or moving them slightly so that the mosaics are covering the faces.

Creating a Corner Pin Track

Another common type of tracking example is the corner pin. Normally, a PIP is a rectangular shape that floats on top of the video layer below. But suppose, for example, you want to put a PIP into a TV screen or onto the side of a building or a moving van. In these situations, the PIP will need to be adjusted so that its corners match the exact shape of the surface to which it is attached. For this we use corner pinning.

1. Load the **TV Track** sequence. In this example, you have a TV screen that has four tracking points on it. You can use these to create a corner pin track and then superimpose a new picture.

2. Add a new video track and edit in any picture you like. In the example here, I used the flower shot.

3. Add a **3D WARP** effect to the top track and enter Effect mode.

4. You need to fix the picture to the TV screen. For this, you use corner pinning. Enable the **CORNER PIN** button in the top-right corner of the Effect Editor.

5. Make sure you are on the first frame.

6. You need to drag the four corners of the picture to the corners of the TV screen. But now you have a problem! How can you see where to put the picture when it is covering the TV screen? The trick here is to turn off the video monitoring on track 2 and switch to track 1. That way, you see the corner handles, but you also see the picture underneath! When you do finally drag the four corners of the picture to the corners of the TV screen, don't put them on the dots, or even on the exact corners of the screen. Instead, put them somewhere on the black edge of the TV, as shown in Figure 7.26.

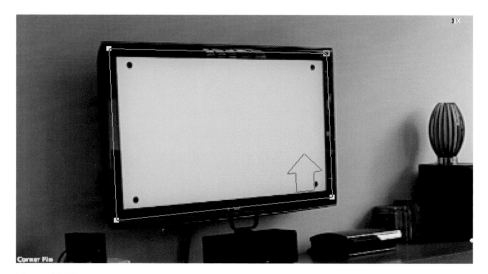

Figure 7.26
The corner pin, just outside the edge of the TV frame.

7. In the Effect Editor, open the **CORNER PIN** parameters and then open the **CORNER TRACKING** group.

8. Enable all four of the **ENABLE TRACKER** buttons to create four trackers.

Tip: **It is a good idea to name your trackers so you can keep them straight. In this example, I have also changed the color to make them stand out better against the green screen as shown in Figure 7.27.**

Figure 7.27
Assign the trackers.

9. Position your trackers over each of the four dots on the screen. You can reduce the size of both the target and the search boxes as shown in Figure 7.28.

 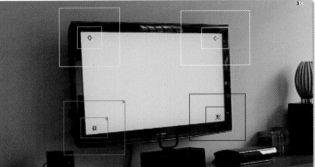

Figure 7.28
Four trackers, named and ready to go!

10. Are you ready? Let's go. Start your tracking and keep an eye on the four points to make sure they don't drift. If they do, stop, add a new tracker region, and reposition as needed.

11. When you are finished, you will have four trackers, and they should be assigned to the four corners of your shape.

12. Make sure you are displaying the PIP and not the trackers by setting the drop-down list in the Tracking window to **EFFECT RESULTS**. *Voilà!* You have a new picture in your TV screen!

Scroll through and make sure the screen is covered all the way along the clip. A minor drift in the track can cause a major shift in the corner position. If you should find a bit where you can see the green of the screen underneath, you may need to make some small adjustments.

To make final adjustments:

1. If necessary, park on a frame that needs adjustment. If it is a small correction, just adjust the corners to cover the screen.

Note: **Each time you make an adjustment to the position of the corner pins, you will create a new keyframe.**

2. If more drastic correction is required, you can set a new reference frame somewhere in the middle of the clip. This will set your corner pinning to the default position at the new frame.

Note: **If you have created some keyframes, you will need to remove all keyframes before changing the reference frame. Essentially, setting a new reference frame is like starting afresh, only on a different frame of reference.**

3. After you set a reference frame the corner pins will need to be readjusted. Drag the corners again to just overlap the edge of the screen. This will create a new, redundant, keyframe; to remove it, right-click in the Effect Editor window and choose REMOVE REDUNDANT KEYFRAMES.

4. Check the results by scrolling back and forth along the Timeline in the Effect Editor. Again, don't worry about the exact position of the edges of the picture. The main aim is to get a picture that exactly follows the motion of the original TV.

Although you now have a picture on the TV screen, the edges are not exactly correct. However, the TV screen was not only providing the tracking points, it was also providing a key signal. You can use that to make an even better composite. For that, you will need to read Lesson 8.

Apply Tracking Data to a Static Background

In Lesson 6, you saw an example of a chroma key shot that had a man filmed against a moving background. Let's see if you can improve this shot.

1. Load the MAN WITH GUN sequence. It has the key you applied in Lesson 6, but the floor looks wrong because the man is moving whereas the floor is static.

2. Go into Effect mode and click the PROMOTE button in the bottom-right corner of the Effect Editor to promote the SpectraMatte effect to a 3D Warp.

3. Close off all the parameters except the **POSITION** parameter and display the **POSITION TRACKING** group. Click the **ENABLE POSITION TRACKING** button. This opens the Tracker window.

4. You are not tracking the floor because that is static. You are tracking the key shot, so switch the tracker to **TRACK FOREGROUND**. You will now see the green-screen shot without the floor. Note that lots of tracking points —little white blobs—have been placed on the green-screen background.

Note: **The original shot for this was slightly longer. To make it work, you would need to do some rather complex offset tracking. Although you should be well able to do this by now, I will use a shortened version of the clip to make life a little easier. You can try the full version as an exercise if you like. It's called Man with Gun_Long and is in the Exercise bin for this lesson.**

5. Because there is not only camera panning, but also some zooming, you'll need two trackers, so click the **CREATE NEW TRACKER** button to add a second one.

6. You'll need to scroll around a bit to see where the points are and whether the man's arm or the gun passes in front. There is one point that remains in shot throughout on the right, but you'll need some offset tracking for the point on the left. I have chosen the two points shown in Figure 7.29.

Figure 7.29
Select two points.

7. Start the tracker and watch for drifting or points leaving the screen. If you see the latter, stop, add a new tracker region, and reposition. (The one on the left will need a few updated tracker regions because the points keep leaving the screen!)

8. You don't actually need to track this layer; you need to track the floor. But you are generating your tracking data. You have seen already that you can copy and paste the data, but there is another simple trick: Just apply the entire effect to the bottom video layer! Drag the effect icon from the Effect Editor to the **TILED FLOOR** clip.

9. While still in Effect mode, select the effect on the top video layer and turn off **POSITION TRACKING**. This will lock your shot off.

10. Select the bottom layer. You don't need the keyer on this, so go to the **FOREGROUND** parameter and switch back to full key. (It actually makes no difference, but I'm just being neat and tidy here!)

11. Now for the magic! Make sure **POSITION TRACKING** is switched on; then go to **SCALING** and turn on **SCALE TRACKING**. Lo and behold, your floor is now moving with the camera!

12. Actually, the floor is not quite filling the screen. The idea is that it just needs to remain in shot throughout, so you can scale it up a bit. Make sure **FIXED ASPECT** is on and zoom out so you can see the wireframe of where the floor will go as you scroll along. (See Figure 7.30.)

Figure 7.30
Adjusting the floor scale and position.

Note: It doesn't really matter if the floor drifts inside the shot on the right side of the image because that half of the screen is always hidden by the man.

When you're finished, you should have a fairly realistic effect where the man appears to be correctly attached to the floor.

Stabilizing

Stabilizing is a special case of tracking in which tracking data is used to eliminate the motion of the object you have tracked. The result is that a part of the image will be locked in space, but the edges will appear to move around. That means you always need to enlarge the image after stabilizing to compensate.

There are two ways to stabilize a shot:

■ Using the Stabilize effect

■ Using 3D Warp's Position, Rotation, and/or Scale parameters

The Stabilize effect is by far the easiest way of stabilizing a shot, so we'll discuss that here.

Note: The sharp eyed among you may have noticed a third option: the Region Stabilize effect, in the Image category. This was the best option before the super-duper Stabilize effect came along. Now, however, it is old and weary and best left well alone! What's more, it is not real time—so even less reason to use it.

The Stabilize Effect

The Stabilize effect does such a good job, you should always try it first when faced with jittery video. Not only that, but it displays a lovely "fairy dust" effect that can keep you entertained for a few minutes while you take a short break.

To use the Stabilize effect:

1. Load the TEMPLE STABILIZE sequence.

2. Drag the STABILIZE effect from the IMAGE category onto the clip in the Timeline.

3. Sit back and enjoy the show. It is fully automatic. You will enter Effect mode, and lots of fairy dust will twinkle all over your picture.

The fairy dust is there because this effect uses the FluidStabilize engine, which places little trackers all over the place that somehow figure out what is going on.

What is really amazing is that it will even track things like water ripples, which are constantly moving. Not only that, it then calculates how much the picture needs to be enlarged to hide the black edges that will always appear when something is stabilized.

By default the FluidStabilize engine applies SteadyGlide (discussed momentarily) when it does its job. In the example here, there was quite a lot of movement in the original shot. SteadyGlide has smoothed out some of that movement, but when you play the effect you'll see that there is still some movement (particularly at the start). Try turning it off and play the effect again (refer to Figure 7.16 to locate the Enable SteadyGlide button). This time, you will see that the picture is now absolutely steady (though somewhat enlarged).

Using Correlation Trackers to Stabilize

Very occasionally, the FluidStabilize engine doesn't do the job well enough—meaning you may need to try another approach. You can track with correlation trackers when you use the 3D Warp effect, or you can simply switch to the Correlation Tracker engine from within the Stabilize effect. You then perform the tracking manually by choosing your own tracking point as discussed earlier. In most cases, one tracker will do the job, but occasionally you'll need two.

Using SteadyGlide

One simple and rather elegant feature of the Stabilize effect is SteadyGlide. Imagine you have a camera man with the shakes (it's practically a requirement for the job these days). He has done a nice pan along the side of a building, but it is very wobbly. If you tried to stabilize this shot, you would certainly be able to lock the shot down—but as the pan started off, your shot would go flying off screen. That's where SteadyGlide comes in!

To use SteadyGlide:

1. Open the **Canoe Race SteadyGlide** sequence in the **Lesson 07 Tracking** bin. The Stabilize effect has been applied to this sequence, but no trackers have been created.

2. Play the clip and observe the wobbly camera work.

3. Open the Effect Editor and display the **Tracking** section.

4. Click the first two of the four **ENABLE TRACKER** buttons in the tracking pane of the Effect Editor. This opens the Tracker window with two new trackers.

5. Apply the trackers to the building in the background. Remember, they need to be in the same plane, so using the pillar on the left and the building would not be as good. They should look like Figure 7.31.

Figure 7.31
Position the trackers.

6. Click the **START TRACKER** button to start the trackers; then wait for the data to appear.

7. Click the **PLAY LOOP** button and watch the effect. It is perfectly stable at first, but then it all goes horribly wrong! That is because as the camera moves, you are locking the object down, which means the black edges drift in from the right.

8. Click the **ENABLE STEADYGLIDE** buttons for both trackers (refer to Figure 7.16). All is well again!

SteadyGlide filters out small changes in the tracking data, but keeps the big changes. Thus, a pan will stay as a pan, but the small wobbles will go. SteadyGlide can be enabled after the event—meaning you can try the clip with and without to see the difference.

Figure 7.32 shows before and after SteadyGlide shots. In the before shot, the pan went to the left, causing the shot to lock off and leave the screen. With SteadyGlide enabled, the pan is retained but the jitter is removed. If you turn the tracking data back on again, there is actually a small display in the center of the screen that shows what has been filtered out, as shown in Figure 7.33.

Figure 7.32
Before and after SteadyGlide.

The amount of smoothing is determined by the value set in the Smoothing Value field (refer to Figure 7.16). The default is 50, but you can change this by typing in a new value. The larger the value, the more smoothing is performed. Of course, when you smooth out the jitter, you still have to enlarge the image slightly to keep the image in frame throughout. A scaling value of 105 is usually sufficient, but if you increase the smoothing, you'll need to increase the scaling to compensate.

Figure 7.33
Enlarged view of the data that has been filtered out by SteadyGlide.

Smoothing Options

Smoothing is a similar operation to SteadyGlide. Instead of filtering out jitter, however, it simply plots a curve of best fit around your tracking data points. Again, the Smoothing Value field sets the amount of smoothing of the curve. (See Figure 7.34.)

Figure 7.34
The data points without Smoothing, with the Smoothing Value set to 20, and with the Smoothing Value field set to 80.

Note: **SteadyGlide and Smoothing are mutually exclusive. You can use one or the other but not both.**

Review/Discussion Questions

1. How many trackers do you need if your shot is wobbling and there is rotation in the wobble?

    a. One

    b. Two

    c. Three

2. Name three types of tracker engines.

3. Which of the following statements is true?

    a. The smaller of the two tracking boxes is the search area, and the larger is the tracker region.

    b. The smaller of the two tracking boxes is the target area, and the larger is the tracker region.

    c. The smaller of the two tracking boxes is the target area, and the larger is the search area.

4. Your tracker has started to drift. What do you do?

   1. Press the _____ _____ to stop the track.

   2. Right-click the _____ _____ and choose _____
      _____ _____ _____.

   3. Adjust the _____ and _____ of the new tracking boxes.

5. You are attempting to stabilize a shot that has some sideways panning. You
   can track it, but when you view the effect the picture starts to drift off
   screen. To remedy this, you do which of the following?

   a. Turn on Offset Tracking.

   b. Animate the shot with keyframes to reposition it.

   c. Turn on SteadyGlide.

6. How do you transfer tracking data from one effect to another?

7. True or false: The reference frame is the frame at which the tracking data
   makes no change to the appearance of the effect.

8. The object you are tracking temporarily disappears behind a pole. Which
   of the following remedies would you *not* use?

   a. Turn on Offset Tracking.

   b. Turn on SteadyGlide.

   c. Delete the points for which no correct data exists.

9. Your tracker target moves off screen. You have performed the track to the
   very end, but the last few data points are not correct. What do you do?

   1. Move to the last frame and change the _____ _____
      setting to Current.

   2. Move the _____ _____ outside the screen in the same
      direction as the previous motion.

   3. Mark an _____ _____ and an _____ _____
      for the incorrect data points.

4. Change the Point Range setting to _____ _____ _____.

5. Select the points and _____ them.

10. Which of the following parameters does not have a tracker associated with it?

    a. Corner Pin

    b. Scaling

    c. Position

    d. Target

    e. Rotation

Lesson 7 Keyboard Shortcuts

Key	Shortcut
Command+C (Mac)/Ctrl+C (Windows)	Copy tracking data
Command+V (Mac)/Ctrl+V (Windows)	Paste tracking data

Tracking

Betty Blooper is back with some more challenges for you! She has a few shots that need some kind of treatment for her latest project.

Media Used:

Open the bin 07 Exercises to find your material

Duration:

45 minutes

GOAL

- Experiment with tracking and stabilizing

Stabilizing the Big Boat Shot

You'll start with an easy one. Load the 01 Big Boat sequence. It is a nice time lapse of a boat in the container port, but there is a bit of jitter. Betty thinks this can be improved. Apply the Stabilize effect and see what happens!

Tracking a "Knock Back" Effect

This time, instead of hiding a part of a shot, you are going to *emphasize* something. Load the 02 Little Boat sequence. Betty wants to highlight the man in the boat with a circle—but outside the circle, the scene needs to be knocked back, perhaps by reducing the luminance—so that you focus on the boat. (See Figure 7.35.) The boat can be tracked as well. What effect will you use for this?

Figure 7.35
What Betty wants.

Let's try a Paint Effect:

1. Open the Effect Editor and create a rectangle shape that covers the entire picture. Next, use the Color Adjust mode to color-correct the shape so that it is darker and has less contrast.

2. Create a circle shape and apply an Erase effect to it. This is what will be tracked.

3. To apply a simple track, deselect the color-corrected shape and select the erase shape. Then, open the **TRACKING** pane and turn on a tracker. The Tracking tool will open, enabling you to perform the track.

4. Perform the track. Your erase shape will follow the boat.

5. Add the finishing touches—a bit of feathering would look nice.

Creating a Dancing Girl

Word is spreading about your skills. The famous Kiwi director Jack Peterson is impressed with what Betty has been telling him, and he wants you to help him select a couple of shots for his latest three-part blockbuster movie, *Agent Zero*, set for release in 2025. His team at Wota Digital is working on the background plates, but he wants to get an idea of which shot works best. He has given you two possibilities, and they need to be keyed against the floor provided. The problem is that the camera is moving, so you'll need to track the shot and apply the data to the background. This was discussed in the lesson; here is another example.

1. Load the **03 DANCING GIRL** sequence. There are two shots on track V2 and a tiled floor on V1. Your mission—should you choose to accept it—is to use a tracker to make the girl dance on the floor.

2. The girl has already been keyed out and composited on the floor below. It was also a very "dirty" key so an AniMatte effect has been applied over the SpectraMatte to help clean up the floor. Step in to the effect so you can see the key layer, not the layer with the AniMatte effect. Now enter Effect mode.

3. Promote the SpectraMatte key to a 3D Warp so you can use the Tracking tool.

4. Open the **SCALING** parameters and click the **ENABLE TRACKER** button to give you two trackers.

5. In the Tracking window, set the trackers to **TRACK FOREGROUND**.

6. Fix the two trackers to two of the tracking points in the green-screen background and let the trackers do their stuff! You may need to offset the trackers if your chosen tracking reference points leave the screen or are obscured by the girl's movement.

7. When you are happy, save the 3D Warp effect into the bin and step back out so you can see the tiled floor layer below. Add the saved 3D Warp to this layer.

8. The girl layer doesn't need to be tracked so in the Effect Editor for the (promoted) 3D Warp, turn off the **SCALING** enable button.

9. Now in the Effect Editor for the Floor layer, switch the foreground from SpectraMatte to Full key.

10. Now you need to fix your trackers to the Position and the Scale parameters. Open the **POSITION** parameters and turn on **POSITION TRACKING**.

11. Click the disclosure triangle to expand the group and make sure one of the trackers is selected.

12. Go to the **SCALING** parameters and make sure **SCALE TRACKING** is also turned on. This time, you'll need to check that both of your trackers have been applied. Now increase the scaling of the floor so that you don't see the black edges. (Remember to turn on the **FIXED ASPECT** option.)

13. Stand back and admire your work! If you have time, try the other shot.

Tracking the Man on the Bike

If time permits, have a go with this one. You need to put a mosaic (or a blur) on the man's face so we obscure his identity. It is quite a difficult track but very good practice. This time you are on your own! The sequence is called "Man on bike." Play it through, and you'll see the challenge that faces you when the man passes behind the tree!

Here are a few points to help you out:

■ Create a mosaic shape, and the open the Tracker window. You will see one tracker in the window. Don't try to attach the tracker to the shape at this point.

■ You won't be able to find two points on his face to track, so just use the one tracker and use the keyframes later to animate the size of the mosaic shape.

■ When starting out, set your tracking target area to be as small as possible so that the background doesn't interfere.

Tip: At first, the man's face is very small. Try tracking the V of his shirt until the face becomes clearer.

■ Your next problem will be when he passes behind the tree. Let the track go astray until he reappears, and then fix it back to his ear. When the track is done, you will need to remove the erroneous tracking points by marking an IN point just before the tracks go wrong and an OUT point just after. Then display the points from IN to OUT to select and delete them.

■ Show the effect results and select the shape. In the Tracking section, you can now attach the tracker to the mosaic shape. You will need to animate the size of the shape with keyframes because you only have one tracking point.

When you are finished, you will have a mosaic that passes in front of the tree. What might you do to have the mosaic only affect the man and not the tree? You will deal with this in the next lesson.

Refining the Composite

This is where you combine all that you have learned to make more complex composites that use many effects—some nested and some on different layers.

Media Used: The media for this lesson is in the MC205 Pro Effects Project. Open the bin called Lesson 08 Refining the Comp.

Duration: 45 minutes

GOALS

- Master the workflow for convincing composites
- Explore advanced nesting
- Save a Submaster effect with source
- Work with multilayer effects templates
- Explore third-party plug-ins

Exploring the Workflow for Convincing Composites

So far, this book has covered many Avid effects, such as 3D Warp, keying, and the Intraframe effects. You have learned how to animate effects and apply tracking. But often, you need to combine all these concepts in one overall effect—and that is why it is good to know some tricks for compositing. Let's look at some examples from previous lessons.

Using AniMatte: Man on Bike

In the exercise in Lesson 7, "Tracking and Stabilizing," you tracked a mosaic on the face of a man on the bike. The track had to be adjusted when the man went behind the tree, but of course the mosaic stayed in front. In this case, the tree was quite blurred, so you might not notice the mosaic. But in many similar cases, you wouldn't get away with it. So how can you remove the mosaic when it passes over the tree?

Think about the elements you can use. You have a layer with the mosaic on top of everything, including the tree, and you have the original clip. You can use the original clip as a "clean" layer and use the AniMatte effect to reveal the "mosaic" layer underneath. Let's try it out.

To use the AniMatte effect to reveal the mosaic layer:

1. Open the **Lesson 08 Refining the Comp** bin and load the **Man on Bike** sequence. This has the track already done from the previous lesson. To make this a bit more obvious, the mosaic has been replaced by a red blob.

2. First, you need to key out the section of the effect when he passes behind the tree. To start, move to the point just before the mosaic shape hits the tree.

3. Press **Command+Y** (Mac) or **Ctrl+Y** (Windows) to create another video track.

4. Match frame the shot at this point. Although the Match Frame button is an essential button, there is an even quicker way to match frame a shot: Place the blue position indicator just prior to where the blob hits the tree, right-click the video track selector, and choose **Match Frame Track**, as shown in Figure 8.1. The original shot will load in the Source monitor and will be marked at the same place.

5. Move along in the Source monitor until the man emerges from behind the tree and mark an OUT point.

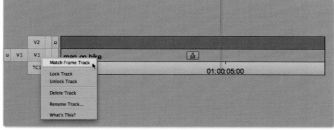

Figure 8.1
Match frame at the IN point.

6. Edit this same shot into track 2. You will now see the original shot (without the red blob) between the IN and the OUT points. To make this effect more convincing, you need to isolate the tree so that it composites above the shot with the red blob underneath. That way, that the red blob will appear to go *behind* the tree.

7. Apply an **AniMatte** effect to the section of the clip on **V2** and open the Effect Editor.

8. Go to the first frame—the man's head should be just about to go behind the tree—and use the **Polygon** tool to draw a shape around the part of the tree that will cover the man, as shown in Figure 8.2.

Figure 8.2
Draw a polygon around the part of the tree that will cover the man.

9. The polygon will mask out the tree and reveal the shot below—the man with the red blob on his face! Apply a small amount of feathering to soften the edge.

10. Now you need to animate shape to follow the tree. Think about how you might do this. You could apply another tracker, but the tree is blurred and rather difficult to track. However, you are only covering a few frames, so it is quite easy to do this manually using keyframes instead of a tracker. Remember your technique of going by halves. Position the shape correctly at the first keyframe and then select just the last keyframe. Make sure the first keyframe is gray (deselected).

11. Move the shape to cover the tree. Then move about halfway between the two keyframes and adjust the shape again. If necessary, move halfway between the new keyframes and readjust until you are happy. Now you have a clean tree as the mosaic (or red blob in this example) appears to go behind it! (See Figure 8.3.)

Figure 8.3
The blob goes behind the tree.

Note: As you do this, you will realize that the exact position of the shape is not critical. You are looking to cover the right side of the tree as the man approaches and the left side of the tree as the man emerges. The other edges of the shape can be anywhere.

Using SpectraMatte: TV Screen

In the previous lesson, you did a corner pin track for a TV screen. Although the image was following the edge of the screen, your TV screen did not look terribly convincing. You have generated a good track, but you need to make the edges work better. Fortunately, you can use a SpectraMatte to improve the screen. The original clip was a green screen, so you can use that to make a good composite.

To improve the TV screen with a SpectraMatte:

1. Load the **TV CORNER PIN** sequence.

2. Create a new video track. You need to put the original TV picture on this track, on top of everything else.

3. Make sure the **V1** track selector is highlighted and the others are off.

4. Go to the first frame and use **MATCH FRAME** to load up the original clip. Edit this onto the top track of the sequence. All your hard work gone! Not really—it is just hiding underneath. You can reveal it again by applying a key.

5. Drop a **SPECTRAMATTE** onto the top track and key out the green screen. Make adjustments as necessary to get a nice key. (See Figure 8.4.)

Figure 8.4
The keyed-out screen.

6. It looks pretty good, but you can still see the dots. You can get rid of these with a Paint Effect. But you already have the tracking information, so use those to make your life easy! Click the **STEP IN** button to step into the nest for the top track and add a **PAINT EFFECT** to the **TRACKING TV 1** clip. (You are stepping in rather than expanding because you want to see the original unaffected clip, not the result of your composite.)

7. Enlarge the image so you can see the TV screen and make sure you are on the first frame. Then open the Effect Editor for the Paint tool and, using the Oval tool, draw four small circles to cover the dots. Leave them as the default red for now—it makes it easier to see them. You can change the color later. Resize and reposition as necessary. See Figure 8.5.

Figure 8.5
Draw the dots.

8. While still in Effect mode, step back out of the top layer and select the **3D WARP** effect on **V2** (the flower track).

9. Click the **TRACKER TOOL** button to open the Tracking window. You should see your four trackers.

10. Press **COMMAND+C** (Mac) **OR CTRL+C** (Windows) to copy the trackers; then click the top track and step in again so that you are back on the segment with the Paint Effect.

11. Your Tracking window should still be open, but this time it is empty. If you try to paste your trackers in here, nothing will happen because you haven't activated the tracker yet. To do this, select one of the shapes (it doesn't matter which one) and open the **TRACKING** parameters. Click the first tracker to create a new tracker—and thus enable the Tracking window.

12. Paste in your trackers from the 3D Warp. (You will have one extra tracker, but you can delete this.)

13. Now you need to assign your trackers to your shapes. Select the top-left shape. If you have carefully labeled your trackers, it is now easy to choose which tracker to link to each shape. See Figure 8.6. Now select each of the remaining shapes and link to the appropriate tracker.

Figure 8.6
Assign the trackers.

Note: Each of the four buttons in the tracking pane has a fast menu. It doesn't matter which fast menu you use to assign a tracker. When you select a shape, you are assigning a tracker from the menu, but which menu you choose out of the four is not important.

14. Set the color of the blobs. To do so, select the first red blob and Shift-select the rest.

15. Use the eyedropper to choose the green color from the screen. All the blobs will turn green. Because they are now tracked, they will follow the original black dots and replace them with green from the screen. Your dots will have disappeared.

16. Step back out and admire your handiwork!

Note: Depending on the power of your system, you may need to render this effect. Remember, though, that you have three layers of HD, a 3D Warp with a tracker, a Paint Effect with a tracker, and a key, so older systems might struggle a little bit to play this!

Advanced Nesting

As well as compositing effects using different tracks, sometimes it is necessary to make use of some advanced nesting techniques. For example, you may wish to put an entire sequence with multiple effects inside another effect. In cases like this, it is good to understand some of the more powerful features of nesting.

Adding Effects Inside a Nest

Let's go back to your TV composite. You have put a picture on the screen, but what if you want to go further? What about having several pictures? What about replacing a picture with an entire sequence that you have previously built? The flower picture was used as a placeholder, but you can replace it with anything you like. In the bin there is a sequence called Dancing Girl. Let's put this on the TV.

To put the Dancing Girl sequence on the TV:

1. Load the **Dancing Girl** sequence. Note that it is a two-layer sequence, whereas the Flower clip was just one layer. How do you get a two-layer sequence into a one-layer placeholder? There are two ways to do this (as is so often the case with Media Composer), but you'll go the most obvious route for now: collapsing the Dancing Girl sequence into one layer. The second method involves creating two layers in the nest itself, which is discussed in the next section, "Nesting Within a Nest."

2. Click the SEGMENT MODE SELECTION tool and Shift-select both of the layers in the DANCING GIRL sequence. Then click the COLLAPSE button to merge them down to one layer.

3. Select the track V2 and press the DELETE key to delete the top track. You won't be needing this anymore.

4. Load the TV CORNER PIN sequence again and drag the DANCING GIRL sequence into the Source monitor.

5. Expand the middle layer (the FLOWER layer) and patch the V1 of the source side to the 1.2 layer of the sequence, as shown in Figure 8.7.

Figure 8.7
Patch the tracks.

6. Press T to mark the entire segment it the Timeline and overwrite the dancing girl. She is now in your TV screen.

You can of course put any clip (or clips) you like in this layer to make them appear on the TV screen.

Note: You saw earlier that some effects (notably the DVE) create two tracks when you expand them. The bottom track is labeled 1.1 and is always left empty. The top track is labeled 1.2 and is the source track for the DVE. You can't do anything with the 1.1 track—it must always be left blank for the DVE to work correctly.

Nesting Within a Nest

Not only can you add new pictures to your TV DVE, you can also add new layers inside the nest. For example, suppose you wanted to have your dancing girl in the TV screen, but you also wanted to add a graphic—perhaps one of the lower third straps you imported in Lesson 4, " Importing Graphics and Mattes." Or perhaps you want to edit in a two-layer sequence as you had in the previous section before you collapsed it.

To nest within a nest:

1. If your **TV Corner Pin** sequence is still in the Timeline, expand it so that the dancing girl layer (**V2**) is revealed.

2. Now here's the trick: Remember that pressing Command+Y (Mac) or Ctrl+Y (Windows) creates a new video track? Well, you can create a new video track *inside* a nest, too. It all depends on which segment is selected. Click with the **Segment Selection** tool to select the track *inside* the nest (**V2**, **1.2**) and press **Command+Y** (Mac) or **Ctrl+Y** (Windows). Lo and behold, you have created a new track inside the nest! See Figure 8.8.

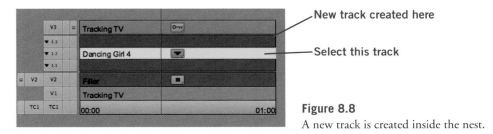

New track created here

Select this track

Figure 8.8
A new track is created inside the nest.

3. Add anything you like to this layer. For this example, try adding the animated lower third you created in Lesson 4. This now appears in your final composite, as shown in Figure 8.9.

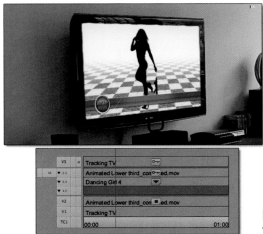

Figure 8.9
The lower third added.

The bottom line? There is no limit to what you can add to a layer or inside a nest. You can keep adding tracks. If you reach your allocated limit of 24 video tracks, just collapse them down and keep adding more.

Adding Finishing Touches

This book has talked about a lot about advanced nesting techniques that will help you to understand how Media Composer composites images, but let's continue this lesson by talking about aesthetics. You need to make your compositions look convincing, and for that let's turn to some third-party plug-ins. In this lesson, you will see two sets of effects that enhance your Avid capabilities: BCC from Boris and Sapphire from GenArts (although many other third-party developers make excellent plug-ins). The next lessons go into much more detail about how these work and the possibilities they open up for you; for now, let's look at one example from GenArts, the Edge Flash, that will help make a key look much more realistic.

Note: This section requires you to have installed Sapphire plug-ins onto your system. If you are in an Avid class, this will have been done for you. If you are working on your own system, you can install a trial version of Sapphire by going to their Web site at www.genarts.com/software/sapphire/avid.

The Sapphire plug-ins from GenArts are widely used to make glows, light rays, and lens flares. They also include some useful effects that can help you perfect a chroma key. One problem with keys is that the background and foreground often have different lighting, so when you combine them, it can look very much like you have two different layers. One way around this problem is to use a technique called *edge flashing*, in which you create a kind of halo around the foreground that looks like the light from the background is reflecting on the foreground. To do this, you must separate the key so that Sapphire can treat it as a matte.

To use an Edge Flash effect:

1. Open the Chroma Key–Edge Flash sequence in the Lesson 08–Refining the Comp bin. As you can see, you have a key with a SpectraMatte applied. For the plug-in to work, you need to separate out the key as a matte.

2. Open the Effect Editor and, in the Matte Analysis controls, select the Show Alpha option. This will output the key as a matte.

3. Notice that there is some garbage. Previously, you removed garbage with an AniMatte effect. This time, however, AniMatte won't work because you don't want to reveal the track underneath. Instead, you want to mask the garbage with a black shape. That means you need the Paint Effect. If you want to apply your own Paint Effect, go ahead by all means. Alternatively, if you are feeling lazy at the end of a long day, you can use the one I have prepared for you in the bin. Just Option-drag (Mac) or Alt-drag (Windows) the Paint Effect (mask the Edge Flash) to the key layer to apply the garbage removal.

4. Now you have a black-and-white alpha. But to make a three-layer key, you need the original chroma key clip on track V2 and the matte on track V3. Go to the start of the clip and match frame the **V2** track to load the original clip into the Source monitor.

5. Create a new track 3 and drag the existing clip with the Paint Effect from track 2 to track 3.

6. Edit in the original clip on track 2. As shown in Figure 8.10, you now have a three-layer effect: a matte on track 3, the foreground on track 2, and the background on track 1.

Figure 8.10
Three-layer effect.

7. At this point you could just drag a Matte Key effect to track 3 and you'd have a perfectly good key. But instead of using the Avid Matte Key effect, you are going to use the Sapphire equivalent. It is called the S_MakeRGBA effect, and it is found in the Sapphire Composite group in the Effect Palette (see Figure 8.11). Option-drag (Mac) or Alt-drag (Windows) this effect on top of your matte on track 3 and open the Effect Editor.

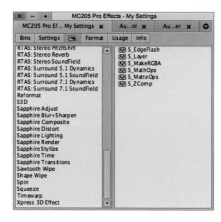

Figure 8.11
The Sapphire S_MakeRGBA effect.

Note: Also in this group of Sapphire Composite effects is S_MatteOps, which enables you to blur, shrink, or grow the matte and apply a post blur. You also have S_MathOps and S_Layer, which give you most of the blending modes you would find in Photoshop, such as Multiply, Screen, Overlay, Xor, and so on.

8. As you can see in Figure 8.12, this effect has lots of controls. But the only setting you need to change is **INVERT MATTE**, which needs to be deselected.

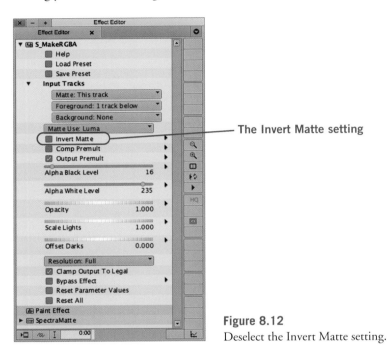

The Invert Matte setting

Figure 8.12
Deselect the Invert Matte setting.

9. Now, Option-drag (Mac) or Alt-drag (Windows) the S_EdgeFlash effect on top of everything else.

10. Here you need to change one thing: in the **INPUT TRACKS** section, choose **BACKGROUND: 2 TRACKS BELOW** from the first drop-down list. This will use whatever you have on the bottom track as the source for the edge reflection.

11. You can tweak various controls to refine your composite. The three main parameters to adjust are **FG FLASH AMP(LITUDE)**, **BG FLASH AMP(LITUDE)**, and **FLASH WIDTH**. (See Figure 8.13.) Figure 8.14 shows the result.

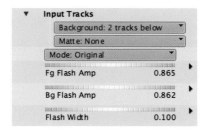

Figure 8.13
Adjusting the Edge Flash effect.

Figure 8.14
The result.

Note: There are two modes for this effect accessible from the drop-down menu shown in Figure 8.13. Original is the default and more subtle mode while LightWrap mode is more like a glow around the edge of the keyed figure.

As you can see, this makes the composite work much better because it makes the images look as if they were really shot together. It is a very subtle effect, and you'll find that you don't need to use very high values for the width of the flash. Of course, you'll need to render this to play it. Most third-party plug-ins are non-real time, which means you'll see a small blue dot instead of a green dot in the corner of the icon. As processing speeds improve, however, I suspect that even these effects will be real-time one day! Even so, you can get a reasonable preview of the effect in not-quite-real time by clicking the Play button (or pressing the space bar) while you are in Effect mode. This is just the beginning! In the next lesson, we will go into much more detail....

Saving Complex Effect Templates

Sometimes, you will spend a lot of time building an effect with multiple video layers, and you may want to use it again without having to repeat everything. For example, in Lesson 3, "Using the 3D Warp Effect," you created a flash pan effect that animated between two shots. How can you use the same effect with different shots?

Recycling the Flash Pan

Load the Flash Pan sequence in the Lesson 08 Refining the Comp bin. As you can see, it is an effect with four video layers. You could save the effect from each layer and apply it to another transition, but that would be a bit tedious. Instead, you can save it as one effect.

To save the flash pan effect as one effect:

1. Collapse the effect. To do so, select all the layers and click the **Collapse** button. This creates a Submaster effect on top of the other four effects.

2. Select the segment with the Submaster effect and enter Effect mode. You will now see the Effect Editor for the Submaster effect.

3. The Submaster effect has no controls; after all, it's just a container that has other effects inside. You can change the effects contained by the Submaster effect, but you can't change anything about the Submaster effect itself. You can, however, save it. You save it not by dragging the Submaster icon into a bin; that will save only the empty "container." Instead, you need to save the contents. To do that, you Option-drag (Mac) or Alt-drag (Windows) the Submaster icon into a bin—for example, the bin in which you have saved all your other effects.

4. A Submaster effect called Submaster (with Src) appears in the bin. Rename it to something you'll recognize—say, **Flash Pan (with Src)**.

This can now be loaded into the Source monitor and used like any clip. When you apply the effect, however, you'll need to change the contents.

To change the contents of the effect:

1. Load the **Flash Pan New** sequence. It contains three clips from around Singapore Marina; notice that the last one has a Color Correction effect.

2. Load the **Flash Pan (with Src)** effect into the Source monitor and overwrite onto the area where the first two clips in the sequence transition. Then repeat this step for the second transition.

Note: For the purposes of this walk-though, it doesn't matter exactly where you overwrite the Submaster effect as long as it covers the transition.

3. Double-click the first transition to expand it. You will see four layers inside the nest. You need to replace the bottom two. This is done with some careful match framing.

4. First, the outgoing clip (Marina Bay Sands). Park your position indicator on the last frame before the effect and match frame the clip.

Tip: Remember the quick way to line up your position indicator on the last frame of a clip is to press the Option+Command (Mac) or Alt+Ctrl (Windows) keys as you navigate the Timeline.

5. In the Source monitor, step forward one frame and add a new IN point.

6. Double-click the bottom track in the nest to expand the nest further.

7. Mark the clip and replace the Singapore Harbour shot in the original effect with the Marina Bay Sands shot, which is now lined up nicely in the Source monitor. See Figure 8.15.

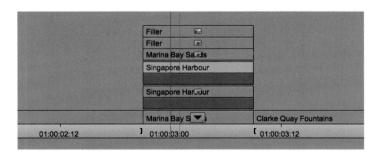

Figure 8.15
The bottom track expanded and marked ready for replacing.

8. Now for the incoming clip (Clarke Quay Fountains). Go to the first frame of the incoming shot in the sequence (make sure **V1** is selected) and use **MATCH FRAME** to load the same clip into the Source monitor.

9. This time, step back one frame. This represents the *outgoing* frame of the clip in the transition effect.

10. Mark a new OUT point. Then press **D** to delete the IN point.

11. Expand the second clip from the bottom and mark it. (In the original Submaster effect, this clip was the Marina Bay Sands shot.)

12. Overwrite the **CLARKE QUAY FOUNTAINS** clip in the Source monitor using the OUT point as your edit reference. You now have your flash pan effect with two new clips.

13. Repeat steps 3 through 12 for the second transition. Once you get the hang of it, you should be able to do this quite quickly.

14. The final clip (Esplanade) has a Color Correction effect applied. Remember to apply that same correction to the segment inside the transition effect, or there will be a jump in video levels. When you are in Effect mode, you can easily drag the Color Correction icon into a bin to save it for reuse.

Note: **It doesn't matter if you delete the media for original clips. The Submaster effect will still work. Just replace the offline clips inside the effect.**

Using Plug-ins

Although it is relatively easy to save effects like this as templates, you may wish to shortcut the process even further by using a plug-in. Both Sapphire and Boris Continuum have a similar flash pan effect already built for you as a one-stop effect, as well as many other transition effects that do similar things with glows, shapes, rays, and so on. You just add a single, pre-built effect to the transition. For example, Sapphire S_SwishPan does the same, but you can also choose whether the effect goes from left or right or even up or down. The equivalent effect from Boris is the BCC Swish Pan, which has additional controls for the kind of blur you want. The next few lessons, found in PDF form on the DVD accompanying this book, cover plug-ins.

Recycling the Video Wall

Often, you have a situation in which you have built a title sequence with a series of shots that appear in some composite. But suppose that each week, you need to create a *new* title sequence, only with different shots. In that case, you can recycle the existing sequence but add the new shots. You can use the video wall you created in Lesson 1, "Effect Design and Techniques," as an example of how to do this.

To recycle the video wall:

1. Load up the VIDEO WALL sequence. Notice that it already has a Submaster effect because you collapsed it down so that you could add a fade at the start and end. Although this is a very simple effect, the same principle applies with much more complex animations.

2. Enter Effect mode and Option-drag (Mac) or Alt-drag (Windows) the SUBMASTER icon to the bin that you use to save your effects to create an effect with source. Rename it VIDEO WALL (WITH SRC).

3. This time, you didn't include the background clip in the nest. Create a new sequence with a background of your choice.

4. Add one more video layer and load the **Video Wall** Submaster effect to the Source monitor.

5. Edit the Submaster effect into the sequence and double-click it to expand it.

6. Choose four new clips from the **Beauty Shots** bin and replace each layer by expanding and patching the source to the **V2.2** track on the appropriate layer. In the example shown in Figure 8.16, I have replaced the flower shot with the Marina Bay Hotel shot.

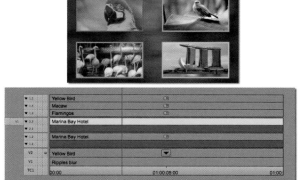

Figure 8.16
The flower shot replaced by the hotel shot inside the video wall.

7. Optionally, alter the background clip by adding a color effect or perhaps a blur.

Saving Title Templates

Titles can also be saved into a bin. There are two ways to save titles. First, select the title and enter Effect mode. Then, do one of the following:

■ Drag the title icon into the bin to save the title with source.

■ Option-drag (Mac) or Alt-drag (Windows) the title into the bin to save the title effect only—i.e., without source.

In other words this is the exact opposite of how normal effects are saved.

Suppose you want to save a title with source. That is, you have a title you want to reuse many times in a sequence. If you apply a fade up and down or any kind of animation by promoting to 3D Warp, the effects are saved along with the actual title. You can load this into the Source monitor to use just like a normal clip.

But what if you want to save just the title *effect*—in other words, the way the title animates? For example, suppose your show has a series of titles, each with a particular effect. Maybe each title grows slowly over time and fades out at the end. Or maybe you have a more sophisticated title transition, such as a blur in or out. You can easily promote a title to 3D to achieve this, but you don't want to have to animate 30 titles. Wouldn't it be nice if you could apply the same animation to all the titles in your Timeline in one shot? Well, you can. When you Option-drag (Mac) or Alt-drag (Windows) the title icon into the bin, you save a title effect *without* source. Saving it without source saves just the animation, not the title itself. This can now be applied to any other title in the Timeline without affecting the existing title text—just how it animates.

To save a title template:

1. Create a title and promote it to 3D.

2. Apply some kind of animation to the title—resize, fade, or whatever.

3. Option-drag (Mac) or Alt-drag (Windows) the TITLE EFFECT icon into a bin. You will now see a title effect icon with the suffix "without src." Saving without source enables you to apply the same animation to a *different* title.

4. Drag the TITLE EFFECT (WITHOUT SRC) icon onto another title in the Timeline. (See Figure 8.17.) You don't need to Option-drag (Mac) or Alt-drag (Windows); just drop it onto the title in the Timeline. The new title will acquire the same animation, but will preserve the original text and style.

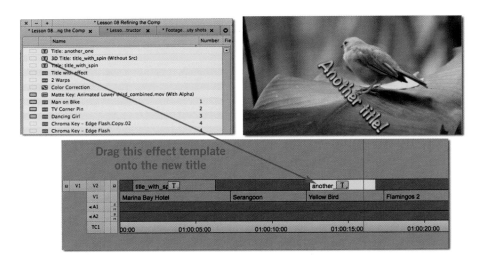

Figure 8.17
Drag the saved effect from the bin to any new title in the Timeline.

Adding Other Title Effects

Again, third-party plug-ins let you do much more with your titles. You can add rays, glows, and distortions simply by adding a premade effect to your title in the Timeline. This is discussed later in this book.

Understanding the Limitations of the 3D Warp Effect

Lesson 3 introduced the 3D Warp effect. Although this effect has many uses, you saw that you can't change the order in which parameters such as rotation are applied.

I used an example where you have a picture that animates from left to right, but also has a rotation applied (see Figure 8.18). Because the position is applied *after* the rotation, you will simply move the rotated clip across the screen. However, what you really want to do is to have the image move back into the screen in the direction of the rotation. You will see later that this is possible with Avid FX because it is easy to change the order you apply transformations, but you may want to try it using the 3D Warp just for fun. For example, suppose you tried to get around the problem by trying *two* 3D Warps—one with a move from side to side and then on top of that apply a rotation?

Figure 8.18
A rotated image.

Try this with the prepared sequence called 2 Warps. This has a PIP with a position animation applied in the first 3D Warp. Option-drag (Mac) or Alt-drag (Windows) a new 3D Warp on top of this one and adjust the Y rotation to 45 degrees. Oh dear… you will see that there is one big problem. When you apply a second 3D Warp on top of the first, your PIP clip animates correctly, but both the clip *and* the background are rotated (see Figure 8.19), which means that the clouds are affected too. Not good.

Figure 8.19
Two 3D Warp effects applied.

You might want to give up at this point and wait till you get to Avid FX, but there is a way around this problem: using your old friend the matte key. The idea is that you need to remove the clouds somehow, and to do that, you need to turn this entire effect into a matte. For this, you need to copy the two nested effects that you have just created and put them on to a new video track.

To convert the effect into a matte:

1. Mark the effect. Then press **OPTION+C** (Mac) or **ALT+C** (Windows) to copy it to the Source monitor.

2. Now edit the same double 3D Warp onto the **V2** track above. There are now two 3D Warps nested together and duplicated on two tracks. This will look a bit strange at first because you have doubled the problem, but hold on, you are nearly there!

3. Select the top track and enter the Effect Editor. Here, you can see the two 3D Warp effects. The one on bottom has the PIP scaled down and the position animated, and the one on top has the rotation applied.

4. Expand the controls for the lower 3D Warp and, in the **Foreground** parameters, select **Show Alpha**. This will make a matte out of your rotated image.

5. To hide the clouds on this matte, switch to the top 3D Warp effect and turn on the **Background Color** setting. Make sure it is set to black. See Figure 8.20.

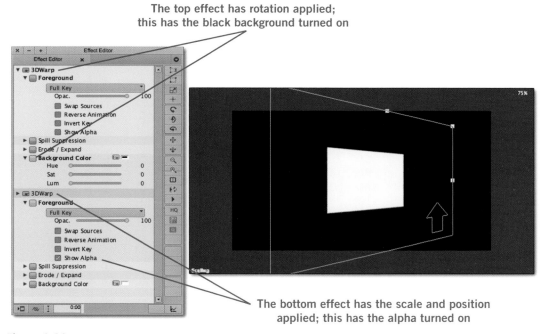

Figure 8.20
The matte is created.

6. Step out, and you'll see you have created a nice mask. All you have to do now is to Option-drag (Mac) or Alt-drag (Windows) a matte key on top of this mask and invert it. The result is a rotated shape that animates into the distance.

There are other ways of dealing with this kind of animation. For example, you might want to move your PIP off screen to off screen. You can do this by adjusting the position animation in the original effect so that it is off screen at the start and end, and then apply the rotation on the next level. You may need to use the Perspective and Target parameters to adjust the overall position of the effect.

Using the Alpha Output

Although this technique may seem a little contrived for overcoming a problem like this, you will often need to generate an alpha from ether the 3D Warp or the SpectraMatte key. Alpha channels can be used as a source for applying further effects—for example, you saw earlier in the section "Adding Finishing Touches" that Sapphire plug-ins can make use of this alpha for applying an effect to just part of a picture. Thus, it is good to have an understanding of how an alpha works and how to generate one from your existing effects.

Review/Discussion Questions

1. You are tracking someone with a mosaic effect, but he disappears behind a tree. What steps would you take to fix this?

    1. Mark the clip for the _____ of the person's disappearance.

    2. _____ _____ the original clip and edit this on to a track above.

    3. Apply an _____ effect to the segment of the original clip on this track.

    4. Create a shape to _____ _____ the tree and animate this to move over the section.

2. You have copied some tracking data from one Tracking window and you want to paste it into another empty tracker. What must you do first?

3. A Submaster effect is which of the following?

    a. A kind of container

    b. An effect that has no parameters

    c. The result of collapsing tracks

    d. All of the above

4. True or false: You can apply an effect to a Submaster effect.

5. What steps do you take to create a Submaster effect with source?

   1. Double-click the Submaster effect to load it to the _____
      _____.

   2. Edit the Submaster effect into the _____ at the point where you
      wish to use it.

   3. _____ _____ to the Submaster effect.

   4. Load a new clip in to the _____ _____.

   5. Replace the clips _____ _____ _____ _____
      by patching the tracks and reediting.

6. How do you create a new layer inside a nest?

   a. Press Option+Y (Mac) or Alt+Y (Windows).

   b. Click the top track and press Command+Y (Mac) or Ctrl+Y (Windows).

   c. Click the nested track and press Command+Y (Mac) or Ctrl+Y
      (Windows).

7. What are two limitations of the 3D Warp effect?

8. Which effect allows you to reorder the way a rotation is applied?

9. What Sapphire plug-in would you use to create an edge around a keyed
   element to blend it into the background?

Lesson 8 Keyboard Shortcuts

Key	Shortcut
Q	Go to mark IN
W	Go to mark OUT
E	Mark IN
R	Mark OUT
D	Clear mark IN
F	Clear mark OUT
T	Mark IN and OUT
G	Clear both IN and OUT marks

Compositing and Beyond!

Betty is back for more! This time, she has a mad plan, and it's *your* job to humor her. She wants one more stab at a composite for the Singapore Tourist Board. She has a shot of the Merlion, which is Singapore's mascot. She wants it to be looking at a series of shots as if they were on a big screen in the harbor. But she also wants a circle in the bottom corner that animates on and off. Her graphics department has an animated circle shape that you can put on top of everything. Are you feeling up to it?

Media Used:
Open the bin 08 Exercises to find your material

Duration:
45 minutes

GOAL

- Create a composition that uses many of the compositing techniques discussed in the lesson

Take a look at the effect (there is a "finished" version called Betty's Grand Plan in the bin). How many layers will you need? There are three different components: the background, the screen and its contents, and the circle and its contents. But there are also other considerations. The background has a look that makes it blue, and the water jet is also partly covering the screen. What effect would you use to achieve that? Finally, the screen and the circle have images inside that are animating; this adds more layers to your composite.

The shots inside the PIP are easy; you made your slide show earlier in the lesson using your flash pan effect. You just need to plug that in somehow.

Here are some of the steps you'll need for this effect:

1. Load the **MERLION COMP** sequence in the **08 EXERCISES** bin. The background shot is the Merlion.

2. Start by adding a Paint Effect to knock back the image a bit. Draw a shape to cover the entire image and use the Colorize mode to give a color wash. Choose any color you like, but experiment with the saturation and luminosity levels. Remember, subtlety is always good!

3. Experiment with the opacity. In the finished example, I used about 50 percent, which colors the image but leaves the clouds white.

4. The next layer is the 3D Warp. Earlier in the lesson, you created a sequence with some transitions called **FLASH PAN NEW SEQUENCE**. You'll find a version of this in the bin. Drag the sequence into the Source monitor and edit it onto track 2.

5. Now apply a 3D Warp to the entire layer. (Remember how to do that? You simply select all the segments on V2 and option-double-click (Mac) or Alt-double-click (Windows) the effect to Autonest it.)

6. Set up the 3D Warp to look as though the Merlion is looking at a screen somewhere. It needs to look roughly like Figure 8.21, with the 3D Warp covering the big building in the background. The water spout needs to coincide with the bottom edge of the image.

7. Animate the picture so it comes in from the left during the first second and out to the right for the last second.

8. Next, make the water spout appear to come in front of the 3D Warp. You'll need an AniMatte to do this. Option-drag (Mac) or Alt-drag (Windows) this on top of your 3D Warp.

Figure 8.21
3D Warp set up to create a screen.

9. Draw a shape that covers the arc of the water spout. Remember: The picture is going to animate off to the right; it would be a nice touch to have it disappear behind the Merlion, so draw along the edge of the Merlion as well.

10. Apply some feathering and lower the opacity so that the picture appears as if it is behind the water, as shown in Figure 8.22.

Figure 8.22
The AniMatte shape.

11. You have keyed the bottom corner of the 3D Warp to reduce the opacity, but what about the rest of it—which has now disappeared? You can bring it back with another AniMatte shape, also covering the arc—but this time covering the top part of the 3D Warp. This one needs to be at 100 percent opacity. (See Figure 8.23.) Remember, you can copy and paste the first shape to "reuse" it; just rearrange the points so that it covers the top-left side.

Figure 8.23
The second AniMatte shape.

12. The next stage has two layers. You have been provided with an animating circle shape (**Durian Ring.mov**); you can use this as a guide for what goes inside. Create a couple more video tracks and put this on track 4.

13. Put an image inside this ring. How? An easy trick is to use a circle wipe—only instead of using it as a wipe, you put it on the entire segment. Add a picture of your choice from the **Beauty Shots** bin; then drop a circle wipe on top of it. (A circle wipe can be found in the **Shape Wipe** category of your Effect Palette.)

14. Position the circle wipe so that the image inside the circle appears exactly underneath the ring. A scaling of 80 percent should do the trick for the size. You might like to temporarily set the opacity of the top layer to 50 percent so you can see how they line up. Don't worry about the position and size of the picture inside the circle; you'll fix that in a minute.

15. You need to match the animation of the ring so that the wipe appears at the start and moves off screen at the end. Add keyframes one second in and one second before the end. Then animate the scale from zero at the start and the position to off screen left at the end. You will need to set the animation type to **Linear** to follow the ring properly.

Tip: It is not easy to animate the position of the wipe on the last keyframe. You can't see the final position of the ring because it is off screen. A good trick is to select the last keyframe but move back a few frames where the ring is visible. Next, adjust the Horizontal Position parameter until the ring is in the right place. It should now follow nicely off screen.

16. Remember to bring the ring's opacity up to 100 percent when you are happy.

17. Finally, you have a wipe pattern that matches the ring graphic, but you need to place the picture you have chosen so that it appears inside the ring correctly. For this, expand the nest inside the circle wipe and add a 3D Warp. Set the scale to 80 percent and position it inside the ring as shown in Figure 8.24.

Figure 8.24
Position the 3D Warp.

18. As a final flourish, animate the scaling (and position) of the 3D Warp to match the ring graphic as it appears on screen during the first second and the roll off at the end during the last second. You'll need keyframes for the scale and position at the start, as it won't quite match the position of the ring. The outgoing roll off is exactly one turn (−360 degrees), and you animate the position off screen at the same time.

19. If you have time, edit in some other pictures to the contents of the ring. In the finished example I used a plasma wipe to animate between various images.

There you have it! Pure cheese, but Betty loves it. And after all, she *is* paying your bills.

Working with FluidMotion and Photoshop

To finish, here are some topics for help when you are working with FluidMotion Timewarp effects and some extra guides for preparing and importing graphics with Photoshop.

Media Used: The media for this lesson is in the MC205 Pro Effects project. Open the Lesson 13 Appendix bin. There is also a file for importing in the Graphics for Lesson Appendix folder on the DVD.

Duration: 60 minutes

GOALS

- Use the Paint tools to correct FluidMotion
- Use Photoshop to prepare graphics for import to Media Composer
- Prepare graphics and lower thirds with alpha for importing

Correcting FluidMotion Artifacts

Media Composer has a Timewarp effect for achieving different types of motion adjustment. You can use it to create slow motion, speed bumps, and time-lapse effects. For outputting the result, there are different rendering options, which produce results of varying quality.

Basic use of the Timewarp effect is covered in *Media Composer 6: Part 2–Effects Essentials*. This section covers one more advanced aspect of the Timewarp effect: the use of FluidMotion, and how to correct some of the artifacts that can occur when you use this as a rendering option.

Suppose you are working in a 24-frame project, like the one that accompanies this book. Whatever Motion effect you apply, you will always need to output 24 frames per second. If you want to apply a 50% slowdown of your footage, you will need to use 12 of your source frames to cover one second of output. In other words, you will need to somehow create an extra 12 frames to fill in the gaps between your original source frames. If you were to apply a 25% slowdown, you would use six source frames for each second, and you'd need to find an extra 18 frames to fill in the gaps—and so on.

The various rendering options define how these extra frames are created. For example, you could simply duplicate your source frame and hold it for an extra three frames to achieve your slowdown. However, the result would look very jerky if you were attempting a 25% slowdown.

Another option is to attempt a blend between existing frames, which means you create frames with a dissolve between two of the original source frames. (In the Timewarp, this render type is known as "Blended Interpolated.") This produces a much smoother motion, but the filler frames have a much softer output. This is illustrated in Figure A.1, which shows a simple example of a ball moving across the screen. The top line is the source frames, the second line shows duplicated frames, and the third line shows blended frames. In the third line, the intermediate frames have a kind of weighted blend of the original source frames.

There is another option called FluidMotion, which uses a special kind of interpolation algorithm that creates intermediate frames by analyzing the motion vectors of all the pixels in the image. The resulting frames are generated by predicting where the pixels would be in the interim. This can give very sharp results and exceptionally smooth motion. In the case of the ball, the system predicts exactly where it would be in the frames between the original source frames; no blending is necessary. (See Figure A.2.)

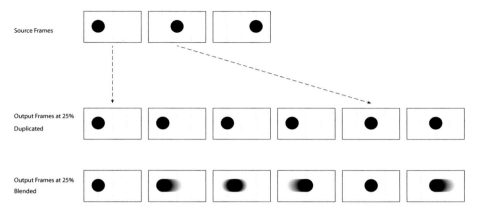

Figure A.1
Duplicated and blended options.

Motion Effects and Fields

Slowing down progressive footage is fairly simple: You create intermediate frames using some form of interpolation, such as blending the frames together. Things get a little more complicated when you use interlaced footage, such as PAL, NTSC, or 1080i. In this case, each frame of footage has two fields. These can be put to good use when slowing down your material because the lines of video in the two different fields will be different if the object is moving. Thus, each field can be used to create new intermediate frames to give a smoother output. With interlaced footage, you can use the Interpolated Field or VTR options available in the Timewarp effect's Render options; both use slightly different algorithms for calculating the missing frames. In the project you are using for the book, the footage is all progressive; because there are no fields, the Interpolated Field and VTR options don't apply.

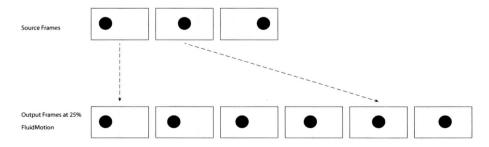

Figure A.2
FluidMotion.

Of course, the real world is not as straightforward as a ball passing across a white background. Typically, you are slowing down action such as someone walking or a car zooming past. These cases can be a little more complex for the system to figure out.

If you are only slowing down the action by 50%, the blending option is usually sufficient to create fairly smooth slow-motion footage. However, for speeds as low as 25% or 20%, blending is not a good option because the intermediate frames can be very soft, as you've seen. FluidMotion is a good option for very slow speeds. That being said, there are drawbacks:

- Rendering times are much longer.

- The algorithms are sometimes fooled by instances where one moving object is moving in front of another. As a result, you will occasionally see artifacts. These artifacts—seen, for example, when someone's legs cross in front of each other—make it appear as if the pixels are being smeared across the screen in areas close to the moving object.

Fortunately, help is at hand. FluidMotion has some correction tools that use a special form of the Paint tool to mask these artifacts. Basically, you define a region around the artifact and modify how FluidMotion creates new material from the source within that region. Any pixels created by FluidMotion outside the region you draw are not altered.

Applying a FluidMotion Effect

Let's walk through an example so you can see how this works.

To view a FluidMotion artifact:

1. Open the the **Appendix** bin and load the **Timewarp** sequence in the Timeline. This clip already has a Timewarp applied, and the speed is set to 20%. There are two examples of different interpolation methods in the Timeline, plus a third clip that is a repeat of the second. The first is where the interpolation method is Blended Interpolated. You can see that as the woman walks over the bridge, the motion is smooth, but the parts that are moving—for example, her legs—are rather blurred.

Note: Although the icon for the effect may have a green dot on it to signify it is real time, Blended Interpolated is not actually a real-time effect. When you play an unrendered Blended Interpolated Motion effect, you'll actually play it as a duplicated field, which is the lowest quality render method. So you should always render this effect if you want to see it play as it should.

2. The second is the same speed, but the interpolation method is set to FluidMotion. In this case, you can see that the motion is much smoother, and sharper. However, if you look closely—especially at her legs and feet— you will see a few frames where the foot appears to shift down a little and the background greenery is "pulled" along by the legs. This is highlighted with a few markers (formerly known as *locators*).

3. There is a repeat of this clip in the Timeline for you to play with. To begin, choose this final clip and enter Effect mode to view the Motion Effect Editor, shown in Figure A.3. Note that the Type option is set to FluidMotion.

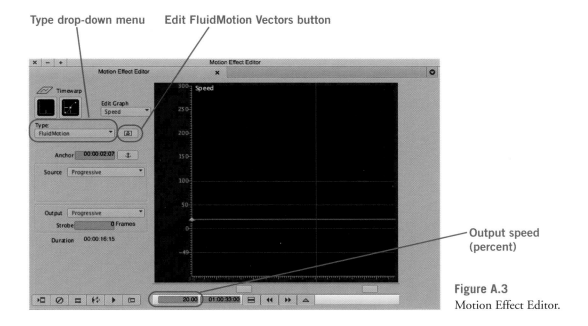

Figure A.3
Motion Effect Editor.

4. Zoom in to the image in the Composer window so you can see the feet more clearly.

5. Move to the first of the three markers to see the artifact that appears on the foot, as shown in Figure A.4.

6. If you step forward and backward one frame at a time, you'll also see some artifacts in the ground below her feet and the greenery in the background behind her leg. These are what you will attempt to remove. To do this, you need to open the FluidMotion Edit interface.

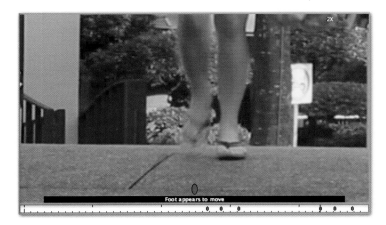

Figure A.4
A FluidMotion artifact.

Opening the FluidMotion Edit Interface

Click the Edit FluidMotion Vectors button shown in Figure A.3 to open the FluidMotion Edit interface. This resembles the Paint effect interface, although it has a couple of extra settings that enable you to remove artifacts. First, let's look at your viewing options. When you are in Effect mode, you don't see all the resulting frames; you see just the input frames (plus one intermediate frame, if you choose). In other words, when the effect is rendered, you have a series of frames: a source frame (that is not changed from the original), which is followed by some in-between frames that are derived from this original frame and the following good frame in the original clip. The source frames from which the in-between frames are derived are known as *bracketing images*.

In this case, where the speed is reduced to 20%, you will have four intermediate frames inside the bracketing images. You can only see the bracketing frames, although you can also choose to see the middle of the intermediate frames as well. The position indicator in the Composer window is green to reflect that you are not seeing all the possible frames. Figure A.5 shows the Effect Editor for the FluidMotion Edit interface and the different viewing options.

Note: Fluid Motion will only display the different viewing options when your Video Quality menu in the bottom-left part of the Timeline is set to Full Quality (green/green) or Full Quality 10 Bit. You will need to change this for the following section.

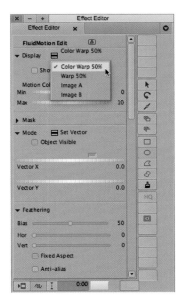

Figure A.5
FluidMotion Edit interface.

Displaying Vectors in the FluidMotion Edit Interface

You can display the following in the Composer window:

■ **Image A.** This is the start source frame.

■ **Image B.** This is the end source frame.

■ **Warp 50%.** This is the predicted frame that lies midway between the two bracketing images above. (See Figure A.6.)

Figure A.6
Warp 50%: the midway frame showing artifacts on the foot.

- **Color Warp 50%.** With this, you see the midpoint frame in black and white, but superimposed are some colored blobs. The colors represent *motion vectors*, which show you how FluidMotion perceives the pixels to be moving between the two bracketing frames. The more saturated the color, the more motion is occurring. The direction of the motion dictates the hue of the blobs, which is in turn derived from the colors of a vectorscope diagram. If you imagine the standard color wheel that you get with a vectorscope, a red blob translates as movement in the direction of 11 o'clock, green is the direction of 7 o'clock, and so on. (See Figure A.7.)

Figure A.7
Color Warp 50%, with a vectorscope display superimposed.

- **Vectors.** Click the Show Vectors button, shown in Figure A.8, to superimpose little red lines that show the amount and direction of motion between the bracketing frames.

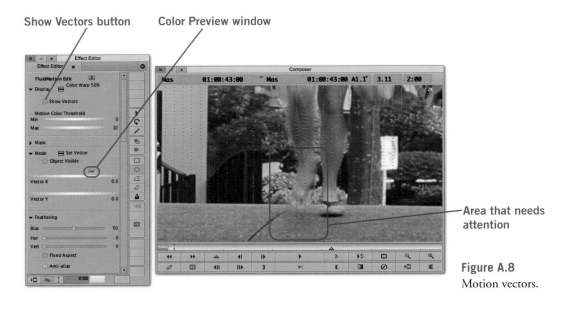

Figure A.8
Motion vectors.

If the application has analyzed the image correctly, in the regions where there is no motion (in this case, the background, because this is a locked-off shot) the image should be gray and the red lines reduced to dots. Where there is motion—for example, the legs—different colors are superimposed. These colors represent the different directions the legs (and the parts of the legs) are moving. But it doesn't always go so smoothly, and sometimes it gets things wrong.

Colors where they shouldn't be, or the wrong colors, indicate where artifacts are occurring. If you look at the ground underneath the foot (the one on the left, or her right foot), you can see it is also yellow/green, signifying horizontal movement—which of course should not be the case. The foot itself is also not displaying correctly, so these are the areas that you need to correct. You will do this by drawing a shape that isolates the area from the FluidMotion analysis.

Defining a Region Around an Artifact

Drawing a shape around areas where artifacts occur replaces the FluidMotion calculations with a simple blend between the two bracketing images. All the vectors inside the shape are reduced to zero; you will simply see a region of the image that will look exactly as if you had rendered the effect as Blended Interpolated.

In many cases, this is all you need to do. In this example, drawing a shape around the ground under her foot will set the vectors back to a gray image, signifying no motion and thus removing the artifacts. However, it is possible to refine the motion analysis by applying your own guess to the direction of the motion to a region that you draw. The shapes you draw are neutral by default—in other words, no motion vectors are applied. But as you'll see shortly, you can copy the color from one part of the image where the motion is going in the direction you want to the region you have drawn.

When you draw a region, you use the same Paint tools that you learned about in Lesson 5, "Paint Effects." You can draw an oval or rectangle, or you can draw an irregular shape with the Polygon, Freehand, or Brush tools. The only difference is that the shapes don't animate. They exist only for the frames between the bracketing images. When you draw a shape, you will see a keyframe that shows you a shape exists at that point, but if you move down the Timeline, you will see the next midpoint frame, which will not have a shape applied yet.

FluidMotion Workflow

Each time you draw a shape, you will need to rerender the frames that were covered by the shape. The rest of the clip is not affected. With this in mind, let's look at the workflow for correcting FluidMotion artifacts such as those seen in the example of the woman walking.

To correct artifacts that occasionally occur with FluidMotion:

1. Apply the **TIMEWARP** effect and set the speed to the desired amount. (You may find it easier to do this using the Blended Interpolated setting first, to get the Timeline graph curves working the way you want.)

2. Click the **TYPE** drop-down menu and choose **FLUIDMOTION**. Then render the effect.

3. Scroll through the effect and note the areas where you see artifacts.

4. Park on a frame with an artifact and draw a shape around the "infected" area.

5. Apply a new motion vector if necessary.

6. Render the effect and play it again to see the results.

In the case of the woman, you would begin by drawing a shape around the area underneath her foot. (You might also include the foot, as there was some problem there, too.) This will remove all motion vectors from the enclosed area, as shown in Figure A.9. This might look okay; the background is now defined as not moving and will have no artifacts. However, the foot is included in this selection and thus defined for the moment as not moving. But you know it really is moving, so you can try to correct that, too.

Figure A.9
Shape to clear vectors.

To correct the foot:

1. Draw another shape around the foot. This time, it should more exactly follow the shape of the foot, as shown in Figure A.10.

Figure A.10
Drawing a shape
around the foot.

2. The foot should be moving in the same direction as the ankle. (Otherwise, the woman would find walking rather difficult!) To achieve this, you will copy the color from the ankle to the shape around the foot. With the shape around the foot still selected, move your mouse pointer to the **COLOR PREVIEW** window (refer to Figure A.8); the pointer will become an eye-dropper.

3. Click and drag the eyedropper to the area on the image just above the ankle, where the vector color is red.

4. Release the mouse button; the red color is applied to the shape, as shown in Figure A.11. The new shape inherits the same direction vector as the rest of the ankle and cuts a hole through the neutral shape underneath that has removed the artifacts from the ground.

Figure A.11
Corrected shape
around the foot.

5. Move to the next available frame in the Timeline—the 50% image between the next bracketing images in the sequence.

6. Draw a shape around the green area on the ground under the foot. This will remove the artifacts from the ground. The foot on this frame appears to be correctly moving, as shown in Figure A.12.

Figure A.12
The shape under the foot.

7. Continue stepping through the Timeline and drawing shapes around any areas of the ground that appear to have motion vectors applied.

8. When you are satisfied, rerender the effect and play back the result.

9. If you see any more artifacts, go back and draw some more isolating shapes until you are happy.

You may not be able to correct every single artifact, but using the correction tools you can usually improve the results when using FluidMotion and you'll certainly achieve significantly better results than you would with a Blended Interpolated mode render for very slow speeds.

Preparing Images in Photoshop

In Lesson 4, "Importing Graphics and Mattes," you saw that aspect ratios are very important when importing images into Media Composer. Whatever television standard you are working in, the output will be either 4:3 or 16:9. Working in high definition is much easier, as all the high-def televisions sets around the world are 16:9 and square pixels. In standard definition, however, there are complications due to the fact that the pixels on the TV screen are not truly square. Thus, what you are seeing on a computer screen in square pixels may not match exactly what you will get on a TV.

Nowadays, most images are obtained from digital cameras; these will have square pixels, but will most likely have completely different aspect ratios. Thus, you will usually have to do some kind of preparation before you import to Media Composer. You can either crop the image first to match the output aspect or import it and preserve the aspect of the picture but pad it out with black at the sides or top. The advantage of cropping to match is that you will fill the screen with the image and preserve the maximum amount of resolution available from the original image.

In this section, you'll see that you can use Photoshop to get the most out of your image before attempting to import it to Media Composer. (This section covers using Adobe Photoshop CS5, but it also works for CS4 and CS3.) Using Photoshop, you can easily prepare images and crop them correctly for importing into Media Composer. If you are working in standard definition, you can actually make an image template that matches the format of your project and then reuse it for all your graphics. Even though you have to deal with those pesky nonsquare pixels, Photoshop makes it very easy for you. Let's walk through some examples— first in standard definition and then in high definition.

Preparing an Image for NTSC 4:3

First, let's create a template for preparing your images. When you create a new file in Photoshop, you have various options for the size and aspect of the file, as shown in Figure A.13.

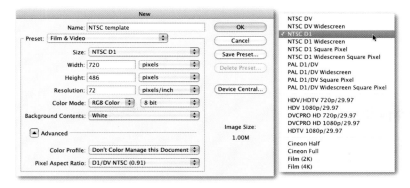

Figure A.13
Image size options in Photoshop.

At the top of the dialog box is the Preset drop-down menu, which includes many basic options for the kind of image you want. Because you are working in the world of TV, you choose the Film & Video preset. Within that preset, the Size menu has many options for TV output; the one you need is NTSC D1. This automatically creates a blank document with the correct pixel aspect 720×486. (DV would be 720×480.) Although the image has been created with the correct aspect, it is displayed in nonsquare pixels, which is how you would see it if viewing it on a TV. If you take a look at the Pixel Aspect Ratio drop-down menu at the bottom of the dialog box, you will see that it is displayed at D1/DV NTSC (0.91), which is the ratio that has been applied to the pixels to squeeze them down. Thus, Photoshop is making your life easier because the image is in the right proportions, but you will view it adjusted for TV.

The image is also created with guides for safe title and safe picture. These may not be turned on by default, however. If you can't see them, you can turn them on by choosing View > Show > Guides or pressing Command+; (Mac) or Ctrl+; (Windows). You can also display the rulers by choosing View > Rulers or pressing Command+R (Mac) or Ctrl+R (Windows). By default, the rulers are in inches, which is not much use in the world of TV. To change this, right-click a ruler and choose Pixels, as shown in Figure A.14. What you have now is a blank document with the safe picture and safe title guides, correctly displayed as a 4:3 image, exactly as it would appear on TV! To illustrate this, Figure A.14 shows an NTSC template with a blue circle drawn on it to show the aspect ratio is being displayed correctly.

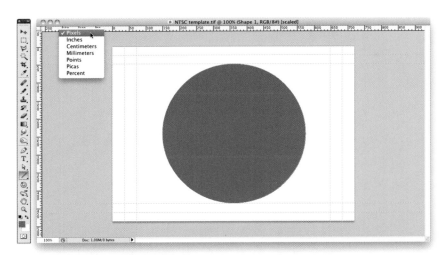

Figure A.14
Image scaled correctly.

The secret is in the name bar at the top of the window, where it says "Scaled." This means Photoshop is forcing the pixels to stretch so they look 4:3, even though the picture would look elongated if you were viewing in square pixels. You can easily toggle between the two views in the View menu. Go to View > Pixel Aspect Ratio Correction, which can be toggled on or off. The result, when toggled off, is shown in Figure A.15.

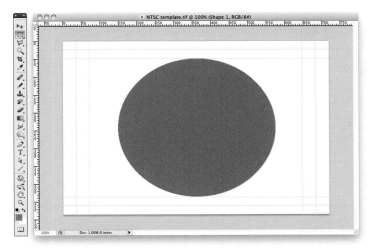

Figure A.15
Image seen as square pixels.

Although you can view the image in square pixels, it is not going to give you a correct result, and it will not end up like this when imported to Media Composer. So leave it with the Pixel Aspect Ratio Correction selected in the View menu from now on. Now you have a template that has the correct aspect, so let's use this to import an image from your camera. Figure A.16 shows a typical file that has an aspect of 1,134×816 pixels, which is not a ratio that scales exactly to 4:3.

Image size

Figure A.16
Image from camera.

Tip: When working in Photoshop, you can quickly see the dimensions of the image by clicking the image size at the bottom-left of the window, shown in Figure A.16. This opens a small window that gives you the aspect of the image, as shown in Figure A.17.

Figure A.17
Image aspect.

Now you need to crop the image to match the correct TV aspect. You can do this easily using the Transform tool.

Using the Transform Tool

You are going to copy your square pixel image from the original photo and paste it into your (nonsquare) template. Photoshop will do the conversion for you and display your image with the correct aspect.

To copy and paste the image:

1. Press **COMMAND+A** (Mac) or **CTRL+A** (Windows) to select the photo.

2. Press **COMMAND+C** (Mac) or **CTRL+C** (Windows) to copy the photo.

3. Select the template you created and press **COMMAND+V** (Mac) or **CTRL+V** (Windows) to paste your photo as a new layer in the template. It will most likely be bigger than the template frame, but that is okay because you can rescale it.

4. In the template, press **COMMAND+T** (Mac) or **CTRL+T** (Windows) to apply a Free Transform. This will give you a box that shows you your full picture.

5. If your photo is significantly bigger than the template, you can press **COMMAND+0** (Mac) or **CTRL+0** (Windows) (that is zero, not the letter O) to zoom out the image to fit the screen, as shown in Figure A.18.

6. To rescale the photo, Shift-click one of the corner handles and, with the Shift key still pressed (to preserve the aspect), drag inward (or outward if you need to make the image bigger). (See Figure A.19.) You can move the image around and scale it so the area of interest is inside the picture safe guides. Note that although you are viewing this image in nonsquare pixels mode, Photoshop still gives you the correct aspect for the original picture. This is because it is doing all the work of converting the aspect for you; you are seeing what you will eventually see on the TV screen.

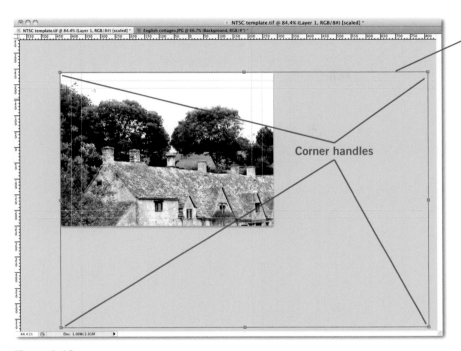

Figure A.18
Free Transform.

Figure A.19
Scaling with Free Transform.

7. When you are happy, either double-click the image, press **Return/Enter**, or select the **Commit Transform** button in the toolbar below the Photoshop menu bar (see Figure A.20) to save your changes.

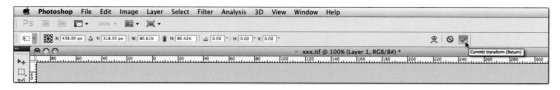

Figure A.20
Committing your transformation changes.

If you wish, you can open a series of files and copy and paste them into your template, each on a different layer. You can then use the Free Transform command to rescale them. (Be sure to use the guidelines to ensure that the area of interest is inside the safe action box.) What you have now is a collection of images as different layers in one Photoshop file. You can save this and import everything into the Media Composer—and choose the layers you need for the edit in your bin.

An alternative workflow is to save each layer as a separate TIFF file. The editor can then choose which file to import. To do this, you can choose Save As rather than just Save. If you have lots of layers to export, it is a good idea to select the Save As a Copy option (see Figure A.21) so the original template stays open. Then you can deselect the Layers option to create a file with just the top visible layer in a folder somewhere on your system. (If the Layers option is selected, all the layers are saved in one file; when it is deselected, just one layer—the top one—is saved as a new file.) After you have saved the top layer, you simply turn off the eye icon for that layer, and the next time you save a copy you'll save the next layer down as a new file.

After you've done this, you can import your files to Media Composer in the usual way. Remember, you can select multiple images by Command-clicking (Mac) or Ctrl-clicking (Windows) the ones you want to import. Because it was created in an aspect that wasn't 4:3 but was simply being *displayed* as 4:3 in Photoshop, it will be stretched on import so that it will look correct in the Composer window.

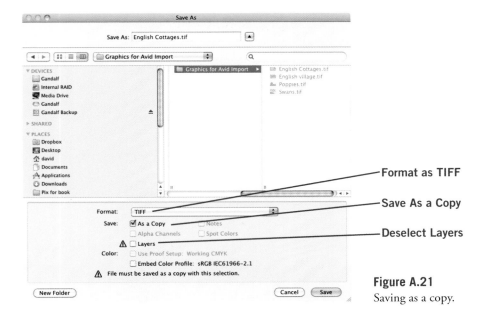

Format as TIFF

Save As a Copy

Deselect Layers

Figure A.21
Saving as a copy.

Preparing an Image for NTSC 16:9

Working in standard definition 16:9 is just as easy. Because the standard definition picture is always 720×486 pixels, regardless of what aspect you are using, you have to squeeze the pixels down to see the image in a widescreen format. It would be almost impossible to work in square pixels because you would see a very distorted view of your image, but again, Photoshop makes it easy for you by compensating on screen so that you see the image as you will on TV. (See Figure A.22.) Again, you will see a blank template with the guides showing safe title and safe action.

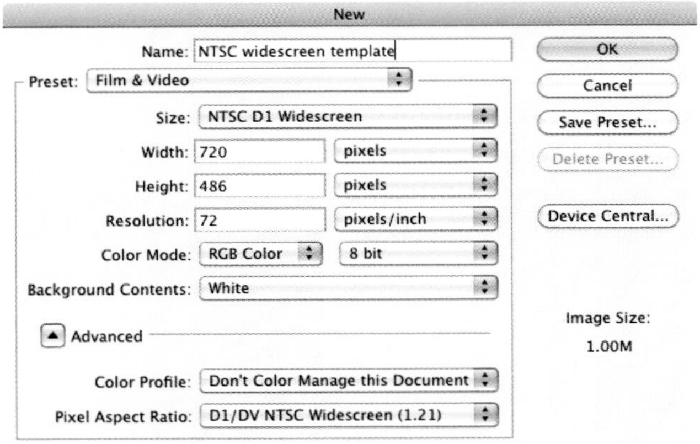

Figure A.22
NTSC 16:9 template settings.

To prepare your image for widescreen viewing:

1. Go back to the original photograph and copy and paste it into the template. This time you'll see the same image, only viewed in widescreen.

2. Press **COMMAND+T** (Mac) or **CTRL+T** (Windows) to select the Free Transform tool; then resize and move the image so it appears correctly in the template, as shown in Figure A.23. (Remember to hold down the Shift key as you do move and resize the image to preserve the aspect of the original photograph.)

Figure A.23
Image rescaled to 16:9.

3. When you are happy, double-click to apply the transform.

In the same way as before, you can import multiple images to the template, each one as a separate layer, and then export each individual layer as a copy so that you have a series of images for importing to Media Composer.

Preparing an Image for PAL 4:3 and 16:9

In a similar way, you can create a template, again using the Film & Video presets, but this time choosing PAL options—either PAL D1/DV or PAL D1/DV Widescreen.

In both cases, your image is created at 720×576 pixels, but Photoshop very kindly stretches it out so you don't have to worry about those pesky nonsquare pixels. For 4:3, the Pixel Aspect Ratio setting is 1.09; for 16:9, it is 1.46. (See Figure A.24.)

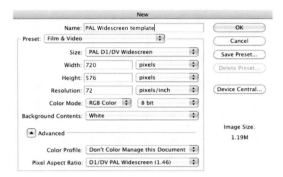

Figure A.24
PAL templates.

To prepare your image, again open the image you want to import and copy and paste it as a new layer into your template. Then use the Free Transform tool to crop your image to fit the template.

Preparing Images for HD Projects

As you might imagine, the procedure is much simpler for HD. You are back in the world of square pixels, and no compensation is necessary. However, there are still some oddities. There are various flavors of HD, too. Some cameras work in 720P instead of 1080. There are also issues when working in HDV, which has an aspect of 1,440×1,080 instead of 1,920×1,080. DVCPRO HD is 1,280×1,080. So again, you may need to stretch pixels to see the image correctly. However, although you may be using HDV or DVCPRO HD footage in your project, it is more than likely that you will be outputting at full raster 1,920×1,080, in which case your graphics will always remain at full HD.

The general rule here is to create a template with the HDTV 1080p 29.97 option. Don't worry about the fact that it is called 1080p; this template works for projects that are progressive or interlaced. And don't worry about the frame rate, either. Photoshop doesn't work in frames, so if you are working in the PAL world, this option works fine for 25 fps or 24 fps.

The image I used in my standard definition examples is of course too small for an HD frame; it would have to be scaled up rather than down. But the majority of cameras these days create images in sizes well beyond the 8 megapixel range, and all these will be much larger than an HD frame.

Creating Lower Thirds in Photoshop

Photoshop is widely used in graphics departments for creating captions and lower thirds as well as many other types of graphics. In these cases, you will need to key the graphic over an existing video image. For that, you'll need to create an alpha channel. Media Composer will recognize an alpha created in Photoshop, provided it is created using the correct procedure. This section will guide you through creating an alpha in Photoshop and introduce you to an easy way of exporting a series of lower thirds using an automated batch operation that comes with the Photoshop Actions, or macros.

Alpha Channels: Photoshop Versus Media Composer

For a graphic to key over a video layer in Media Composer, it must have an associated alpha channel. As you saw in Lesson 4, Media Composer recognizes embedded alpha channels, but only straight alpha and not premultiplied alpha. Photoshop, however uses premultiplied alpha, so you need to do a bit of work before importing into Media Composer.

Perhaps the best way to illustrate this complex and often confusing subject is with a couple of examples. Let's look at your red blob and try to add a soft edge. Figure A.25 shows a red foreground graphic with a soft edge alpha compositing (in Media Composer, so black is opaque) onto first a white and then a black background. The image on the right represents what you would see in Media Composer if you key the graphic with its alpha over the background track.

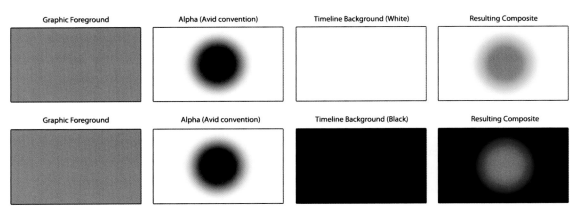

Figure A.25
Red blob (straight) on white and black backgrounds.

Premultiplication

Normally, an image is described by three channels: red, green, and blue channels, known as RGB. When keying an object over a background, you use an extra channel that contains information about the transparency (or opacity, if you like) of the image. An image with alpha is thus described by the RGBA channels. The alpha is a grayscale image where white normally represents fully opaque (by which I mean the RGB image is opaque and thus seen composited over the background track) and black represents fully transparent (which means you don't see the RGB image; you see the background track). Media Composer reverses this convention, but that is not the issue here, as it is a simple matter to invert an alpha channel on import. The real issue is when you wish to have some degree of transparency—for example, a soft shadow. For this, the alpha is gray and the amount (or darkness) of the gray will determine the amount of transparency.

So what is premultiplication? Well, you have seen the terms *premultiplied alpha* and *straight alpha*, but technically the alpha is the same in either case. What is different is how the RGB channels are treated. A straight alpha is when the RGB channels contain only the foreground information and no background information. How it is composited is determined by the alpha only. Premultiplication is when the transparency information is included in the foreground by multiplying the background color with the alpha and including this information in the RGB channel. Thus, for premultiplication to work, you need to know what the background color is at the time you create the graphic. If you are working with a program that recognizes premultiplication (for example, Avid DS or Adobe After Effects), then all is well because you can display these correctly. However, Media Composer needs a straight alpha to make the key work correctly.

The bottom line: Straight is much more *straight*forward and premultiplication is a *pain*! If you import a premultiplied image to Media Composer, the tell-tale sign will be a halo wherever you have soft edges because you are applying a level of transparency to an image that is fading to black (or white) already.

In this case, the graphic foreground is entirely red, although the actual shape of the foreground doesn't really matter as long as it completely covers the soft edge alpha. If you create titles using Media Composer's Title tool, you will see a similar effect: The edges of the titles are very jagged and always spread over the shape of the alpha. That doesn't matter, however, because the alpha is the cookie cutter through which you see the composited graphic.

Now let's look at the same thing, only using a premultiplied graphic. In this case, the red blob with the soft edge is created on a white background in the original graphic application. If you look at Figure A.26, you can see that if the graphic is composited on a white background it looks fine. But if you composite it on a black (or any other colored) background, you will get the halo that shows you something is wrong.

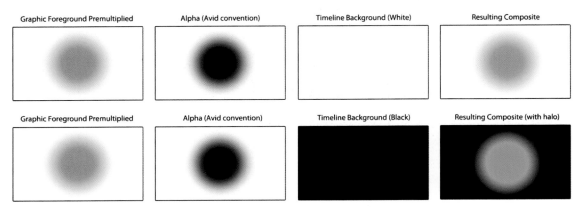

Figure A.26
Red blob (premultiplied) on white and black backgrounds.

If the original graphic had been composited on a black background and you had tried to import it to Media Composer and then applied it on any other background than black, you would also see a halo—this time a black halo.

Tricking Photoshop into Producing Straight Alpha!

When you use Photoshop, you use the standard layer masks to composite the various layers. All is well until you try to export the layers; Media Composer can't recognize the way Photoshop premultiplies the RGB channels. All is not lost, however. You can create perfectly good straight alpha channels that will work beautifully with Media Composer. You just need a little know-how.

First I will show you how to do it manually so you understand what is going on. Then I will show you the easy way! Let's try a title with a soft shadow. The following steps are done with Photoshop CS5, but CS3 and CS4 work in the same way. This is not really meant to be an in-depth Photoshop tutorial; I am assuming you have some basic knowledge of Photoshop.

To produce straight alpha channels manually:

1. Create a new Photoshop document using the Film & Video presets and size, as described earlier in this appendix. In this example, I am using an HD 1080p preset. The default background is white, which works fine for creating titles.

2. Using the Horizontal Type tool, shown in Figure A.27, create a nice, big, juicy title.

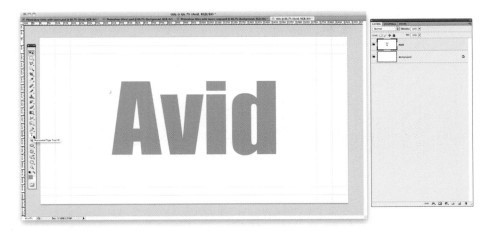

Figure A.27
Title in Photoshop.

3. Press the **F7** key to display the Layers window. You will see that the title is on a separate layer, composited above the white background. Now let's add some layer effects.

4. Choose **LAYER > LAYER STYLE > DROP SHADOW**. Alternatively, click the **ADD LAYER EFFECTS** button in the Layers window. (Look ahead to Figure A.29.) The Layer Style dialog box opens, where you can create several effects. In this case, I have added a shadow, a fill, a stroke, and a bevel emboss effect. (See Figure A.28.)

Figure A.28
Title effects.

5. Any effects you create on a layer in Photoshop are not recognized in Media Composer. To export these successfully, you need to rasterize the layer to make a bitmap. To start, click the **CREATE NEW LAYER** button, shown in Figure A.29.

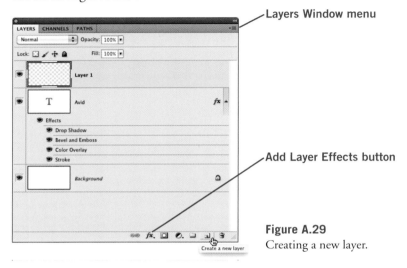

Layers Window menu

Add Layer Effects button

Figure A.29
Creating a new layer.

6. Drag the empty **LAYER** thumbnail in the Layers window down below the **TITLE** layer.

7. Select the **TITLE** layer. Then open the **LAYERS WINDOW** menu (refer to Figure A.29) and choose **MERGE DOWN**, as shown in Figure A.30, or press **COMMAND+E** (Mac) or **CTRL+E** (Windows). You have now created a rasterized Title layer.

8. Next you need to create an alpha channel. To begin, Command-click (Mac) or Ctrl-click (Windows) the **TITLE LAYER** thumbnail. This automatically creates a selection based on the Title layer, including the soft edge. You will see a series of animated dashes around the title, known as *crawling ants*; this indicates you have made a selection. You need to convert this into an alpha channel.

9. Choose **WINDOWS > CHANNELS** or click the **CHANNELS** tab to display the Channels window.

10. Click the **SAVE SELECTION AS CHANNEL** button, shown in Figure A.31. This creates an alpha channel in the image that Media Composer will recognize, based on the text layer and its transparency.

11. Press **COMMAND+D** (Mac) or **CTRL+D** (Windows) to deselect the crawling ants.

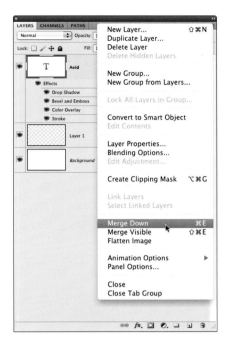

Figure A.30
Merge down the layer.

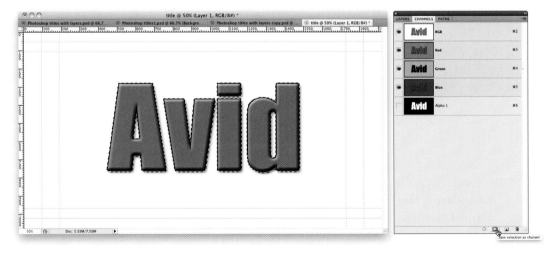

Figure A.31
Make an alpha from selection.

12. Save the title as a Photoshop (.psd) file. Make sure the **ALPHA CHANNELS** and **LAYERS** options are selected.

13. Import the file into Media Composer. Import either the Title layer or the whole file as a sequence of layers.

14. Edit the title matte key on to a video background. The title will composite correctly with the soft shadow on any background, as shown in Figure A.32.

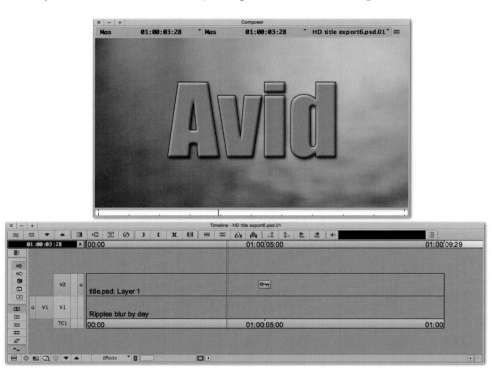

Figure A.32
Title composited in Media Composer.

Although this method works for any titles you might wish to create (with the various effects available in Photoshop), you can also use it to create any kind of graphic you like—for example, a selection from an image with a soft shadow or a strap for your titles with a graduated transparency. Here is a quick example of a strap that might be used as a background for a series of titles. Suppose you have created a basic shape (of any kind) with a texture that you want to use as a semi-transparent object in Media Composer. In this example, I have created a strap and used the standard Photoshop layer effects to create a colored texture fill and a bevel/emboss. (See Figure A.33.)

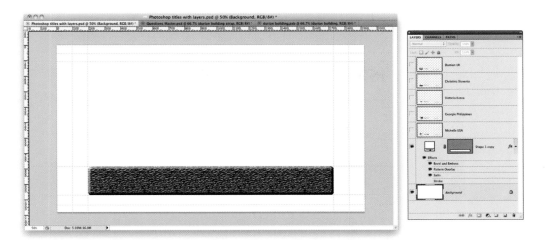

Figure A.33
Textured strap.

To prepare a strap for importing into Media Composer:

1. The first thing you need to do is rasterize the image, as in the previous example. To begin, create a new layer and move it below the Strap layer.

2. Press **COMMAND+E** (Mac) or **CTRL+E** (Windows) to merge the two layers. This creates a rasterized layer with just the strap.

3. Click the **ADD LAYER MASK** button, shown in Figure A.34. This creates a layer mask for the strap, which is indicated by a second thumbnail next to the strap. This layer (which is white by default) is used to composite the Strap layer over the layer below.

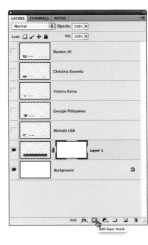

Figure A.34
Creating a layer mask.

4. Now you are going to create a gradient transparency on the mask layer using the Gradient tool. To begin, select the **LAYER MASK** thumbnail. (You will see a small box around the Layer Mask thumbnail instead of the thumbnail for the strap.)

5. Click the **GRADIENT TOOL** button (look ahead to Figure A.35) or press **G** to select the Gradient tool.

6. In the toolbar above, click the triangle next to the gradient swatch to reveal the Gradient palette. Then select the default white-to-black gradient and make sure you have a horizontal gradient type selected, as shown in Figure A.35.

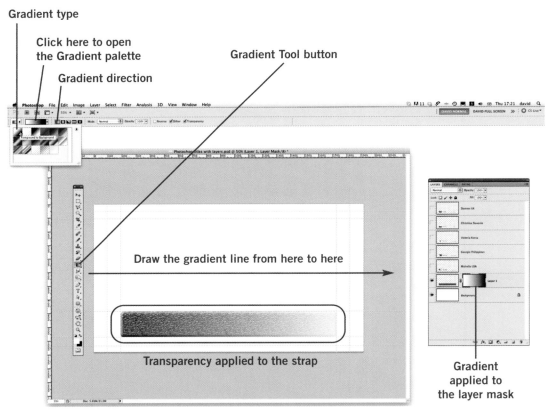

Figure A.35
Drawing a gradient.

7. While holding down the **SHIFT** key to constrain the gradient to a horizontal direction, click and drag to draw a line across the screen from left to right, starting before the left side of the strap and ending beyond the right edge of the strap. You have now drawn a gradient on your layer mask. This will turn your strap into a semi-transparent shape that becomes more transparent in the direction of the gradient.

8. Again, Media Composer doesn't recognize layer masks, so you need to apply this—a kind of rasterization that includes the transparency. To do so, right-click the layer mask and choose **APPLY LAYER MASK** from the menu that appears. The layer is now a combined strap with transparency.

9. Command-click (Mac) or Ctrl-click (Windows) the strap thumbnail to create a selection for the layer.

10. Choose **WINDOWS > CHANNELS** or click the **CHANNELS** tab to display the Channels window. Then click the **SAVE SELECTION AS CHANNEL** button to save the selection as a channel. (See Figure A.36.)

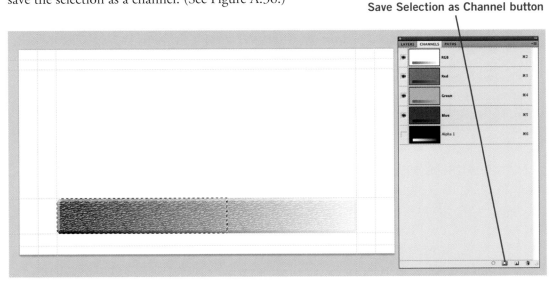

Figure A.36
Saving the selection as a channel.

In this example, I have also created a series of titles. These can be rasterized and saved with an alpha channel using the same technique. For each Title layer, you would Command-click (Mac) or Ctrl-click (Windows) the Title thumbnail to create a mask, and then save the selection as a channel in the channel window. What you would have is a series of RGB layers with either a transparency or a soft shadow and an associated alpha channel, as shown in Figure A.37.

Figure A.37
Saving series of titles.

Somehow, Photoshop magically seems to know which alpha is associated with which layer. (I have tried swapping the order of the channels and it still works!) When you import this file into Media Composer, you will see a series of titles in a sequence in your bin, along with the strap and its transparency. All of these will key beautifully on to any background you like in the Media Composer Timeline. There is an example of this file for you to try in the Graphics for Lesson Appendix folder.

Creating Alphas the Easy Way

Well, that wasn't too difficult. Besides, I wanted to show you the theory behind what you need to do to make the alpha work for you when using Photoshop. But if you have to do lots of this kind of work, then you'll be glad to know that you can use a macro (in Photoshop, these are known as *actions*) that will automate the process for you.

Suppose you have a series of titles and a background strap, as you had in the last example. You can use an action that will automatically create an alpha channel for you from the layers that you select. To see the actions available, open the Actions window by choosing Window > Actions or pressing Option+F9 (Mac) or Alt+F9 (Windows). In this window, you can use some prebuilt actions or create your own. If you click the Actions Window menu and choose Video Actions (see Figure A.38), you'll see a new folder full of actions (see Figure A.39).

Figure A.38
Video Actions.

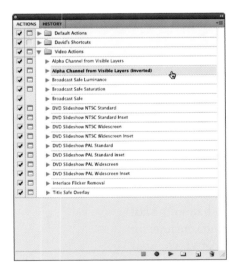

Figure A.39
Creating an alpha from visible layers.

The top two actions are the ones you need. Adobe has provided an inverted version of the macro just for us Avid folk, which is the one highlighted in Figure A.38. However, if your Import Settings are set to Invert on Import, you can use the same action as everyone else—i.e., the noninverted option—and let Media Composer invert it for you.

As you might use this action quite a lot, I am going to make one more refinement: adding a shortcut key so you don't even have to click the Play button. If you select the action and double-click anywhere except on the name of the action, you'll open a dialog box like the one shown in Figure A.40. In my case, I've assigned the F7 key as a shortcut for the action. These function keys are program specific, so F7 will only run the action when you are using Photoshop.

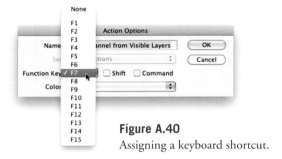

Figure A.40
Assigning a keyboard shortcut.

Okay, you're ready to use your shortcut. In this example, I have a series of lower thirds, with a background strap that has some transparency, a person's name and nationality, and a flag. All are created with various effects—shadow, stroke, etc. Now I have to export a series of lower thirds. The original document had around 30 different lower thirds that required various combinations of names and countries, but in this example I have made just two and organized them into two groups, as shown in Figure A.41.

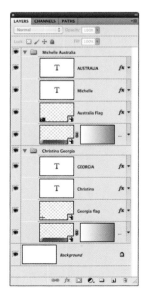

Figure A.41
Lower thirds organized in groups.

Because these layers are using effects that Media Composer won't recognize, you will need to rasterize them again—but this is easy when you group your layers. All you have to do is to choose Layer > Merge Group or press Command+E (Mac) or Ctrl+E (Windows) to merge the group and all its contents into one layer with the correct transparency and effects that can be seen by Media Composer. The resulting layers from the two groups are shown in Figure A.42. In practice, you could have as many layers as you like, as long as they are all rasterized.

Figure A.42
Merge each group into a separate layer.

Now for the action. You need to make an alpha channel for each layer. The macro works by selecting a visible layer and saving the alpha for that layer. So before you start, you must hide the other layers or they will be included in the alpha. In this case, I have clicked the eye icon to hide the Background layer and one of the other layers, leaving just one layer visible. Then I pressed my shortcut key—F7—to activate the macro. A warning message will come up to remind me that all the other layers must be turned off, as shown in Figure A.43.

Figure A.43
Creating an alpha channel from visible layers.

The alpha is automatically created and appears as a new channel in the Channels window. You can now repeat this for all the other layers (in this case, there are just two). The background is a simple white layer with no alpha required, as there is no masking here. (See Figure A.44.)

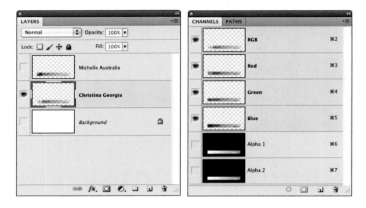

Figure A.44
Alpha channels created from visible layers.

Now you have a file that can contain all your lower thirds as separate layers, each with its own alpha. This can be easily imported into Media Composer as a series of layers, and each will key over the video background. If you have labeled the layers in Photoshop, they will import with the titles so you can easily see which layer is which. (See Figure A.45.) If you would like to try this, there is an example called Photoshop Titles in the Graphics folder for the Appendix on the DVD.

Figure A.45
Titles edited in the Media Composer Timeline.

An alternative method would be to export the strap just once as a separate document and edit that onto V2 in the Media Composer Timeline. Then, each of the names could be combined into one document with multiple layers, which is then imported and the different titles edited onto V3 of the Timeline.

Answers to Review/Discussion Questions

Lesson 1 Answers

1. b

2. Command-click (Mac) or Ctrl-click (Windows) on the Track Monitor icon.

3. Create a bin called Quick Transitions and drop your custom effects into that bin.

4. Hold down the Command+Option (Mac) or Ctrl+Alt (Windows) keys and click and drag the image to pan.

5. c

6. Double-click on a nested segment or use the Step In and Step Out buttons. The first shows all the effects as different layers in an expanded nest, and the second shows just one effect at a time.

7. Select the segments and click the Collapse button.

8. It is when you create a new media file from an effect with multiple components. You can reedit it into the sequence and apply new effects such as fade ins, fade outs, or Timewarps.

9. False

10. 1: Step into; 2: double-clicking; 3: the Timeline track above

Lesson 2 Answers

1. Use the right-click menu to choose from the various options.

2. a

3. 1: keyframe graph; 2: Reverse Keyframes

4. These are fixed keyframes. They don't move in time when you trim the segment.

5. Shelf, linear, spline, and Bézier. Shelf keyframes keep the value of the last keyframe until the next keyframe. Linear keyframes interpolate the value in a straight line. Spline keyframes interpolate the value in a smooth curve. Bézier keyframes interpolate the value using curves with Bézier handles.

6. b

7. Set the Rotation Z parameter to Linear Extrapolate and make a continuous slope between two keyframes.

8. c

9. Use the Trim buttons, press the M key, press the comma (,) key, press the period (.) key, or press the forward slash (/) key.

10. If a keyframe is added on a graph curve that has the same value as the curve would have had at that point, the keyframe is redundant. It does not affect the overall shape of the curve. To remove a redundant keyframe, right-click the graph, the keyframe track, or the effect track, and choose Remove Redundant Keyframes.

Lesson 3 Answers

1. Option-click (Mac) or Alt-click (Windows) the enable button.

2. False

3. Move the axis first, then apply the rotation.

4. a

5. It is like adjusting the camera lens angle. It applies to the entire animation after all the other parameters have been applied.

6. 1: Highlight; 2: Shape, Reverse Manual Highlight; 3: enable button; 4: Highlight; 5: Lowlight Color

7. Go to Foreground and enable Swap Sources.

8. Use FG Only in Defocus.

9. First, promote the title to 3D. Then choose Defocus > Foreground and Key. Finally, use keyframes to animate the blurred title.

10. b

Lesson 4 Answers

1. True

2. c

3. d

4. It has been imported with the wrong field ordering. Change the field ordering in the Import dialog box and reimport.

5. c

6. Use the Reformat column in the bin and choose either Pillarbox or Center Crop from the menu.

7. 1: Two; 2: track V2, track V3; 3: Matte Key, track V3

8. Use Batch Import and choose Set File Location from the dialog box to navigate to the new location.

9. NTSC D1 is 720×486 and DV is 720×480. There are six fewer lines. Change the import setting to Crop Pad for DV Scan Line Difference.

10. Everyone sees standard definition TV in 4×3, even though NTSC has fewer lines than PAL. The only way to make this work is to adjust the size of the pixels.

Lesson 5 Answers

1. e

2. Use the Outline/Path button to show just the outlines.

3. Option-click (Mac) or Alt-click (Windows) the Bring Forward button.

4. b

5. Select with the Selection tool and use the grab handles, or use the Reshape tool to move the handles.

6. c

7. True

8. 1: Scratch Removal; 2: Rectangle tool; 3: thin line; 4: Gasp (The fourth one is just for fun, at the end of a long day.)

9. Applying a soft edge to a shape

10. Spot Color is for adjusting the color on part of the image; Color changes the entire image.

Lesson 6 Answers

1. Bottom: background; middle: foreground; top: key

2. c

3. c

4. It is an aid for adjusting a chroma key and it displays pixels in the image as a vectorscope display superimposed on a Y, Cr, Cb color wheel.

5. Your chosen color may not be truly representative. Your sample pixel should be in the middle of the crowd.

6. True

7. 1: Spill; 2: Spill Saturation; 3: Spill Angle Offset

8. AniMatte effect

9. a

10. Step inside and apply a DVE.

Lesson 7 Answers

1. b

2. Correlation Tracker, FluidTracker, FluidStabilizer

3. c

4. 1: space bar; 2: tracker Timeline, Add New Tracker Region; 3: size, position

5. c

6. Copy and paste the trackers from one Tracking window to the other.

7. True

8. b

9. 1: Point Range; 2: data point; 3: IN point, OUT point; 4: In to Out;
   5: delete

10. d

Lesson 8 Answers

1. 1: duration; 2: Match frame; 3: AniMatte; 4: key in

2. Create a new tracker first; then remove it when you have pasted in the others.

3. d

4. True. You can Option-drag (Mac) or Alt-drag (Windows) an effect on top
   of a Submaster effect.

5. 1: Source monitor; 2: sequence; 3: step in; 4: Source monitor; 5: inside the
   Submaster effect

6. c

7. You can't change the order of processing parameters, and you can't add one
   on top of another.

8. Avid FX

9. Sapphire S_EdgeFlash

The following lessons are on the DVD located in the back of this book.

Lesson 9 Answers

1. The Avid Marketplace menu

2. b

3. False. It *reduces* the glow as you increase the value.

4. 1: Timeline; 2: S_EdgeRays, Paint Effect; 3: mask, bottom; 4: Track Below

5. c

6. Click the Save Preset button and add a name and details for your effect.

7. True

8. Click the Edit Lens button to open the Sapphire Flare Designer.

9. Drag a Sapphire transition effect to the transition between two clips.

10. True

Lesson 10 Answers

1. Avid FX is an application that allows multiple tracks and effects, whereas BCC plug-ins are individual filters that are applied like any other third-party plug-in.

2. c

3. In the Controls window (by adjusting the slider control, typing a number in the box, or clicking on the value in the box and dragging with your mouse); in the Composite window (by adjusting the OpenGL interactors or the handles on the bounding box); in the Timeline track (by typing a number in the box or clicking on the value in the box and dragging with your mouse); and in the Timeline graph (by dragging a keyframe directly).

4. When active, it will show only parameters in the Timeline that have been changed from the default value.

5. 1: top; 2: Transformations; 3: Controls, Composite; 4: Apply mode

6. Click the Change Track Media button and select an alternative source from the menu that appears.

7. b

8. The Styles palette

9. When applied to the Face track, it affects just that layer in the Timeline. When applied to a track of its own, it affects all the tracks below that are visible.

10. Click the Apply button in the bottom left of the Timeline or the bottom left of the Composite window.

Lesson 11 Answers

1. A Paint Effect is like a bitmap whereas a Spline effect is a vector object that can be edited.

2. c

3. False. You Option-click (Mac) or Alt-click (Windows) between two points.

4. The Roller tool applies a pattern to your image that can be selected from another image or graphic or a collection of patterns in the Styles palette.

5. a

6. 1: Filters, Keys and Matte, Chroma Key; 2: eyedropper; 3: Show Matte; 4: density, balance, lightness

7. Apply an Avid FX transition effect to the transition between two clips.

8. 1: S, Page Turn, M; 2: Page Turn, Flap Face; 3: Flap Face

9. Set the animation to Auto and the track media for the transition filter to show the track underneath.

10. a

Lesson 12 Answers

1. Text page, vector text, and 3D text

2. *Tracking* sets the spacing between all the letters globally, while *kerning* allows you to adjust the spacing between individual letter pairs.

3. 1: top track, Timeline; 2: Controls, Create Texture Track; 3: Texture, Face; 4: Texture

4. False. You would import your text file and place it in a title container, where you can set the animation to roll.

5. You can scale it without losing quality.

6. d

7. Single or multiple faces

8. Place them inside a 3D model container.

9. The Pixel Chooser allows you to apply a filter to certain pixels in your image based on a shape or some property of your image such as the luminance.

10. 1: Appearance, Custom Color; 2: Custom Start Color, Custom Midpoint Color, Custom End Color; 3: Start Size, End Size

INDEX

Note: Page references preceded by the letter E refer to pages in Lessons 9, 10, 11, and 12, which appear in PDF form on the DVD accompanying this book.

License Agreement/Notice of Limited Warranty

By opening the sealed disc container in this book, you agree to the following terms and conditions. If, upon reading the following license agreement and notice of limited warranty, you cannot agree to the terms and conditions set forth, return the unused book with unopened disc to the place where you purchased it for a refund.

License:

The enclosed software is copyrighted by the copyright holder(s) indicated on the software disc. You are licensed to copy the software onto a single computer for use by a single user and to a backup disc. You may not reproduce, make copies, or distribute copies or rent or lease the software in whole or in part, except with written permission of the copyright holder(s). You may transfer the enclosed disc only together with this license, and only if you destroy all other copies of the software and the transferee agrees to the terms of the license. You may not decompile, reverse assemble, or reverse engineer the software.

Notice of Limited Warranty:

The enclosed disc is warranted by Course Technology to be free of physical defects in materials and workmanship for a period of sixty (60) days from end user's purchase of the book/disc combination. During the sixty-day term of the limited warranty, Course Technology will provide a replacement disc upon the return of a defective disc.

Limited Liability:

THE SOLE REMEDY FOR BREACH OF THIS LIMITED WARRANTY SHALL CONSIST ENTIRELY OF REPLACEMENT OF THE DEFECTIVE DISC. IN NO EVENT SHALL COURSE TECHNOLOGY OR THE AUTHOR BE LIABLE FOR ANY OTHER DAMAGES, INCLUDING LOSS OR CORRUPTION OF DATA, CHANGES IN THE FUNCTIONAL CHARACTERISTICS OF THE HARDWARE OR OPERATING SYSTEM, DELETERIOUS INTERACTION WITH OTHER SOFTWARE, OR ANY OTHER SPECIAL, INCIDENTAL, OR CONSEQUENTIAL DAMAGES THAT MAY ARISE, EVEN IF COURSE TECHNOL-OGY AND/OR THE AUTHOR HAS PREVIOUSLY BEEN NOTIFIED THAT THE POSSIBILITY OF SUCH DAMAGES EXISTS.

Disclaimer of Warranties:

COURSE TECHNOLOGY AND THE AUTHOR SPECIFICALLY DISCLAIM ANY AND ALL OTHER WARRANTIES, EITHER EXPRESS OR IMPLIED, INCLUDING WARRANTIES OF MERCHANTABILITY, SUITABILITY TO A PARTICULAR TASK OR PURPOSE, OR FREEDOM FROM ERRORS. SOME STATES DO NOT ALLOW FOR EXCLUSION OF IMPLIED WARRANTIES OR LIMITATION OF INCIDENTAL OR CONSEQUENTIAL DAMAGES, SO THESE LIMITATIONS MIGHT NOT APPLY TO YOU.

Other:

This Agreement is governed by the laws of the State of Massachusetts without regard to choice of law principles. The United Convention of Contracts for the International Sale of Goods is specifically disclaimed. This Agreement constitutes the entire agreement between you and Course Technology regarding use of the software.